ATOMIC CROSSROADS

Before and After Sizewell

John Valentine

MERLIN PRESS
LONDON

First published by The Merlin Press Ltd
3 Manchester Road,
London E14 9BD

Valentine, John, 1947—
    Atomic crossroads: Before and after Sizewell
    1. Nuclear energy—Great Britain—History
    I. Title
    621.48'0941   TK9057

    ISBN 0-85036-336-5
    ISBN 0-85036-337-3 Pbk

cover design by Louis Mackay

Typesetting by Hems & Co.,
The Old Brewery, Tisbury, Wilts.

Printed in Great Britain by Whitstable Litho Ltd.
Millstrood Road, Whitstable, Kent.

ATOMIC CROSSROADS

'I know that most men—not only those considered clever, but even those who are clever and capable of understanding the most difficult scientific, mathematical, or philosophic problems—can seldom discern even the simplest and most obvious truth if it be such as obliges them to admit the falsity of conclusions they have formed, perhaps with much difficulty—conclusions of which they are proud, which they have taught to others, and on which they have built their lives.'
   —*Leo Tolstoy, 1898 (with thanks to Alice Stewart)*

To Christine Palmer

CONTENTS

PREFACE

Large power stations have design lives of thirty to forty years. The last series of large coal and oil fired stations was begun in the early 1960s, and decisions have to be taken very soon about the types of generating stations that will provide the bulk of our electrical capacity for the first decades of the next century. This is the background to the Atomic Crossroads.

Whichever power stations are chosen, the investment will be huge. The Central Electricity Generating Board would prefer to use a preponderance of pressurised water reactors—it would like to reverse the present 10 : 1 ratio between coal and nuclear capacity in England and Wales. Just to replace time-expired plant (that is, assuming no increase in GDP or electricity consumption), and using only PWRs, the Board would expect to build and commission twenty-six new PWR stations by 2010, at a capital cost of a little more than £1 billion each, at today's prices. The CEGB's central forecasts involve a 1 per cent p.a. increase in GDP to 2000, and a corresponding rise in demand. To meet this would involve building 39 PWR stations by 2010. Even higher projections, requiring up to 52 PWRs by the same date, have been recognised by the Board as unbuildable.

The Sizewell inquiry was of central importance because the plan to meet the bulk of future generating requirements by the PWR depended on getting that type of power reactor accepted for commercial use in Britain. The inquiry dealt with the generic issues of comparative economics and safety as well as the issues specific to the Sizewell site, so that subsequent inquiries could be site-specific only. The application to build the first PWR, and the Sizewell inquiry itself, were the crossroads themselves; the place where people met

i

and talked, for two years and three months.

This book looks at the road behind, and the possible roads ahead. As far as the history is concerned, it quantifies in a new way the appalling economic record of British nuclear power. Perhaps more importantly, and also in a new way, it attempts to identify those factors which have favoured, and which still favour, nuclear technology in the UK. Atomic proficiency, military and civil, has played a large (if largely unstated) part in maintaining our national self-esteem, to the extent that the normal criteria of profitability have been suspended. Great efforts and resources were expended in an attempt to maintain British post-war Great Power status, and the institutional momentum generated by that expenditure is still a powerful political lobby. Britain's self-assessment and self-esteem has a particular relationship with her nuclear capability, and it is still powerful.

This unarticulated pride in British nuclear proficiency is seen at its most direct in Polaris, Chevaline and Trident. Other related historical anomalies linger on, in particular the practice of reprocessing the spent fuel from civilian reactors, which has resulted in the CEGB owning the largest stockpile of separated, unallocated plutonium in the non-communist world. But as far as the roads ahead are concerned, the main problem bequeathed by the nuclear preoccupation is a lack of choice. The gross imbalance between funds allocated to nuclear, and those allocated to everything else, has ensured that no viable alternatives to nuclear and coal will be ready on a commercial scale in time. The consistent bipartisan support for nuclear technology is one of the most interesting features of recent British political history; all governments seem to have assumed that nuclear is automatically in the national interest. The nuclear lobby has never experienced institutional opposition. But the exclusively nuclear policy, if policy it is, seems obviously short-sighted—one serious accident could well render valueless the whole of the 40-year investment in nuclear fission.

Future electricity supply provides a real dilemma for environmentalists. The large-scale coal-fired generation, even if desulphurised, is neither pretty, healthy nor sustainable. There are profound concerns about nuclear, particularly

PWR, safety, about long-term spent fuel management on the scale envisaged, and about our ignorance as to the effects of low-level ionising radiation. The work that should have been done on wind, wave and tidal energy has not been done; they are not available solely because they have been starved of funds. In such a situation, and in the face of a united institutionalised opposition, the environmentalists seem restricted to rearguard actions. Making sure that the reactors are as safe as possible, making sure that 'storage' replaces 'disposal' in the government's vocabulary, above all making sure that the practice of reprocessing, with its wastes and its discharges, stops.

The long-term plan seems to be to have the commercial fast reactor available in time for the next generic decision, in about 2020. The CFRs, which use and breed plutonium, would then provide a self-sustaining electricity generating system, the plutonium economy, the nuclear technician's dream.

We used to joke among ourselves at Sizewell that a Conservative monetarist government offerred the best chance of getting the PWR application thrown out, because its economic base was so risky. In reality, the only way to ensure nuclear power proves to be a temporary phenomenon is to insist on a proper level of support for other technologies so that, next time round at least, there are options. If it is allowed to, the nuclear industry will engineer a Hobson's choice situation. People and government have to be persuaded that a nuclear capability is not a particularly modern or impressive achievement, unnecessary to our present national status, unaffordable by our present national exchequer and unreasonable to impose on future inhabitants of these islands. British nuclear technology, civil and military, has its roots firmly in the strange soil of national status and pride. Nuclear power has survived because it is exempt from the normal financial constraints, but has proved to be counter-productive, in that the status that was supposed to be enhanced has been diminished, both because very large sums of money have been unprofitably invested, and because other profitable investments have not been made.

*   *   *   *   *

I would like to thank the following people for reading, and offering comments on, different parts of the typescript in draft:

Lorna Arnold
Peter Bunyard
William Cannell
James Cutler
Jim Jeffrey
Brian Rowe
Ron Round
Kelvin Spencer

although I am responsible for any inaccuracies that remain, and for all opinion. Thanks are also due to the United Kingdom Atomic Energy Authority for permission to reproduce Appendix 2 and to Rob Edwards and Sheila Durie for the map on which that on page v is based. I should also like to thank the staffs of the inquiry secretariat, and of the CEGB and BNFL teams at the inquiry, for their assistance and courtesy. I am grateful to many people who helped with documents and references, and who answered various questions at different times, and also to Graham Searle who asked many of the right ones at the right times.

It is impossible to entirely avoid the use of technical terms, but I hope that the glossary (page 200) is sufficiently comprehensive to be of help to readers unfamiliar with the subject matter of this book.

PART 1

HISTORY

'It appears that with a smaller initial investment in nuclear power Britain might well haye had the same nuclear expertise, yet have been economically stronger and better able to face up to the challenges of the 1980s.'
— *(Leslie Hannah, Electricity Council historian, speaking of the events of the early 1970s.)*

Nuclear sites in Britain

● Nuclear power stations, operating or under construction
▲ Other key sites in the fuel and weapons cycle

CHAPTER 1

UK ATOMIC HISTORY 1939--63

Wartime

During the late 1930s, discoveries and theories in atomic physics were being made so fast that it is difficult to establish an historical sequence. Research was being conducted in all the great European and American universities, and the results freely published in scientific journals. There was great competition between the laboratories, and great prestige to be won by being the first in print with a new discovery or understanding. Everyone in the small world of theoretical physics knew what everyone else was doing: the 1930s was the last period in which pure science knew no boundaries. Perhaps, in 1938 and 1939, an awareness that this decade of freedom was coming to an end helped to stimulate an extraordinary outpouring of work.

The great theoreticians and experimentalists—Rutherford, Curie, Chadwick and Bohr—had become interested in the phenomenon of radioactivity because it seemed to offer to advance their understanding of the nature of matter. Some of the heaviest elements, particularly uranium, were found to have properties which could not be explained by existing physics; they became the subject of intensive research.

One such property, discovered by Fermi, was that uranium atoms would sometimes fly apart if neutrons were fired at them. The simple explanation—that the big uranium atoms were splitting into two fragments each of about half the weight of the original atoms, and at the same time releasing the energy that had held atoms together—evaded scientists until Hahn and Strassmann in Berlin chemically identified the fragments as being atoms of middle-order elements. Their observations were published in January 1939: the young Austrian physicist Frisch and his aunt Lise Meitner (for many

1

years a colleague of Hahn) received the paper before publication and arrived at a theoretical understanding of the process over Christmas 1938 and called it 'fission'. Frisch confirmed it experimentally and published in February 1939, beating Joliot-Curie by two weeks.

Hahn and Strassmann had noticed that a fissioning uranium atom spat out a spare neutron as well as the two middle-sized fragments and the energy. A team of scientists in Paris, Halban, Joliot-Curie and Kowarski, worked out that uranium fission could produce a self-sustaining chain reaction, because the neutron from one fissioning atom could induce fission in the next.[1] Their results were published in March and April 1939. A few weeks later Bohr and Wheeler in Copenhagen were able to demonstrate that only one rare type, or isotope, of uranium is able to fission.[2] Uranium-235 accounts for less than one per cent of the naturally occurring element: the rest is the non-fissionable uranium-238. Their work was published on 28 August 1939, days before German tanks rolled into Poland and started the Second World War. So it happened that the three discoveries that held the key to the practical application of nuclear physics were made within six months of each other, just before the outbreak of war, and were publicly and internationally available. At least until 1943, Allied scientists were convinced—wrongly—that they were engaged in a race with the Germans to make the atom bomb.

The richest source of uranium ever discovered was in Zaire, then the Belgian Congo. The company that owned it, Union Minière du Haut Katanga of Brussels, extracted and sold the minute quantities of radium that is found in uranium ore. Fabulous prices had been obtained for this substance, but by the late 1930s its use in medicine was less fashionable, the market was dwindling and the mine itself was closed. Processed uranium concentrate was a waste product in the manufacture of radium: thousands of tons of it were piled in waste heaps near the factory at Oolen, Belgium. By the spring of 1939 the British could see that war with Germany was likely; they also knew that German physicists were working in the field of atomic theory. Recognising Belgium's vulnerability, the British tried to buy the uranium concentrate, but when in May 1940 the Germans took Brussels, it was still there, and 1,000 tons were sent back to Berlin.

A further two thousand tons of high grade uranium ore lay at the mine mouth in Zaire, hand-picked by local labour before the mine closed down. The President of Union Minière, M. Sengier, operated from New York after the invasion of Belgium. He was aware of Joliot-Curie's work, and of the British attempt to buy the concentrate. He arranged to have 1,250 tons of the Congo ore barrelled and shipped to Staten Island, New York, where it arrived in September 1940. The material, without which the Hiroshima and Nagasaki bombs could not have been made, then stood on the dockside for two years.[3]

Frisch, an Austrian, escaped to Britain when war broke out and joined his German colleague Peierls who was teaching physics at Birmingham University. In March 1940 they wrote a 3-page memorandum which addressed the problem of making a uranium bomb.[4] It was the first paper to understand the physics of the bomb, and was the direct harbinger of the destruction of Hiroshima. It had an immediate effect; the MAUD Committee was set up in June 1940 within the Ministry of Aircraft Production to report on the feasibility of an atomic bomb. The universities of Birmingham, Liverpool, Bristol and Oxford were immediately involved, as was the research department of ICI. The theoretical work went ahead with remarkable speed, for at this period before Russia and then America entered the war, Britain was without active allies. A sober appraisal of Britain's chances in 1940 (after Dunkirk) or 1941 would not have been optimistic, and a war-winning bomb seemed a very good idea.

By the end of 1940 the MAUD Committee teams had confirmed the possibility of the bomb in great detail. The key problem was the separation of enough pure uranium-235 from the bulk of uranium-238 in the natural metal. The latter, though it later played a key role in the development of atomic weapons, at this stage was understood to act as an impurity in a bomb. Isotope separation is a difficult process because isotopes of the same element have identical chemical properties, but Professor Simon at Oxford (another refugee from Nazi Germany) designed a plant to separate 1kg a day of U-235, and it began to look as though a bomb was possible.

By early 1941 the MAUD Committee's work was finished and its final report was written in July.[5] It concluded that a uranium bomb was possible and could be decisive, and that it could be built in two and a half years. Fifteen months of intensive research had solved many of the theoretical problems, and suggested methods of manufacture and firing. At Birmingham University pure uranium metal was being cast and at Oxford a separation plant had been designed. This had been achieved by teams led by, and largely composed of, non-UK nationals who were all subject to curfew, had to obtain permission to use maps, cars, even bicycles, and were in real danger of being interned in the summer of 1940. Churchill approved the MAUD final report, and the Committee was disbanded. British research and development work continued under the cover name of Tube Alloys.

Work in America, meanwhile, was proceeding at a more leisurely pace—after all, the country was not at war. Attention concentrated on the possibilities of the slow chain reaction for industrial applications, and Fermi, at Chicago, was building a pile using natural uranium oxide with graphite as the moderator. But it was already known that atomic piles would have a military application, because of their production of the man-made element plutonium by the irradiation of uranium-238. (Plutonium had been predicted and christened by the Cambridge team at the end of 1940. Coincidentally, the US team under Seaborg which made the first trace quantities in March 1941, also christened it plutonium.) Lawrence at Berkeley demonstrated the properties of the new element, and had come to the conclusion that a plutonium bomb might be quicker and easier to make than a uranium bomb. Fermi's work began to interest the military establishment.

Copies of MAUD's final report astounded the American scientific and military establishment, and were responsible for a new urgency. America was not aware that the British had got so far in the resolution of the practical problems involved in making an atomic bomb, and it was clear that the intense research of the MAUD period had put Britain into an early lead. Despite Lawrence and Seaborg's work with plutonium, the Report of the National Academy of Sciences of November 1941, which was the first American report to examine the possibilities of a bomb, referred exclusively to the uranium route to the fission bomb.

The MAUD report was decisive in changing the nature of American atomic research from academic to practical. The Americans would certainly have made plutonium, Nagasaki-type bombs without the MAUD report; they almost certainly would have made the Hiroshima uranium bomb as well. MAUD accelerated the time scale by convincing the military of the applicability of atomic research; perhaps without the stimulus that MAUD provided, and the subsequent UK/US collaboration the bombs would not have been ready for use in the war. The MAUD report and the early British research work that it recorded, was, perhaps, midwife to the bomb.[6]

It nearly didn't get to America at all. An atomic information exchange agreement was signed in September 1940 and copies of all the MAUD papers were sent to America. But little of any value came back, to the annoyance of the scientists in Britain; later it transpired that the Washington recipient of the research papers had kept them all, including the final report, locked in his safe, unread and uncirculated, because they were marked 'Most Secret'.[7] It was unauthorised copies of drafts of the final report which made such an impact.

President Roosevelt ordered an 'all-out effort', and, recognising that at the end of 1941 the British work was more advanced than the American, proposed a fully co-ordinated joint project. The British, although happy to retain and improve the information exchange agreement, refused the offer of full collaboration. The reasons for this refusal would continue to dominate the key British atomic decisions for the next two decades, for although they had not actually made one, the British regarded the uranium bomb as virtually their invention, and intended to retain control over it. Associated with this was a complete and consistent mis-estimation of how difficult and costly the transformation from theory to production would be, and underneath it all was British pride: the refusal to recognise the decline in British international power and in particular a refusal to

5

recognise the reversal of the power relationship that was taking place between Britain and the United States.

In December 1941 the Japanese bombed Pearl Harbor and American atomic research was transformed. The Manhattan Project was placed under military control, and the weapons research establishment was set up in the New Mexico desert at Los Alamos, and given a bottomless budget. The key production problem was seen to be the manufacture of fissile material, and the Americans pursued four different methods. Three of these were different techniques of U-235 separation, the fourth was the fabrication of plutonium, firstly at Chicago and later on a large scale at Hanford.[8] In a few months the Americans had forged ahead, but in Britain the problems of isotope separation on an industrial scale were becoming apparent. The Prime Minister finally consented to the joint project in July 1942.

But Churchill's change of heart came too late. By then the Americans neither needed nor particularly wanted the British-based scientists. Military security had taken over in America and, between January and July 1943, the flow of information virtually stopped. Hopes of an integrated atomic programme, even of full communication, were at an end; the Americans suspected the British of over-estimating the contribution that they could make, and of being too interested in peace time commercial benefits deriving from American-funded research. British demands for co-operation, and appeals for a joint project, went unanswered for six months.

Indeed, thoughts of post-war politics played an important role in the two countries' differing estimation of themselves and of each other. America, seeing Britain's present and future status perhaps more clearly than Britain herself could, doubted whether Britain should have (or be allowed to have) atomic weapons after the war, and could not understand the depth of her interest in them. Britain, still in her own eyes a Great Power, considered that the maintenance of that status depended on ownership of the new weapon, and her vision was that the two countries together would police the post-war world, and keep the secret to themselves. There were, during this period, great misunderstandings between America and Britain, a reflection of the shifting balance of

6

power between them. Neither was completely honest with the other: the British, attempting to persuade the Americans to change their mind, overstated their success in isotope separation, and the Americans could never bring themselves simply and firmly to dismiss the British. The British considered that the MAUD report should buy them full knowledge of developments during and after the war: they demanded everything, and seemed to have no conception of their own high-handedness, or of the strength of American feeling that the results of great effort and expenditure should not be handed on a plate to Britain. One has the impression that the Americans, working at top speed, were intensely irritated and distracted by a Britain constantly nagging for co-operation, information and materials, a Britain which had no idea of the urgency and complexity of the American project.

Britain re-examined the possibility of going it alone, and concluded that the price was unaffordable. She—or specifically Churchill—knew that the only way to have her own atomic weapons after the war was to get in on the ground floor in the Manhattan Project. The British determination to have a bomb was already, in 1943, firmly implanted in the minds of the political and military leadership. Perhaps, in addition to feelings of British greatness and her right to the new weapons, there *was* a recognition of the shifts in international status that were beginning to take place, and the conclusion was made that the only way to prevent Britain sliding down into second or third class power status was by possession of atomic weapons.

Britain hung on, trying to persuade the Americans to change their minds. How close Churchill and the Chiefs of Staff came to renouncing their ambitions is one of the tantalising but unanswerable questions of modern history; certainly our perceptions of ourselves today would have been shaped very differently had they done so. But the Americans, were finally persuaded to allow the British a junior role on the project. Perhaps they felt guilty, perhaps they were worn down by entreaty, perhaps because of the race against time they simply needed all the help they could get. In one regard, at least, Churchill was able to reassure the Americans,

7

because the 1943 Quebec agreement, which formally initiated the British involvement in the Manhattan Project, ruled that decisions about the division of post-war profits from atomic energy would be made by the American President alone. Churchill was aware of peaceful applications, but was more interested in the bomb than a possible atomic energy project, and was happy to trade future profits for present knowledge that could lead to future power.

In all, more than fifty scientists from Britain, including Niels Bohr, a Dane, and several senior non-British scientists, went to the various Manhattan Project locations in North America, to be astounded at the progress that had been made in the six months of silence. The extent and success of their integration was due largely to the personality of Sir James Chadwick, the British director: they had access to every department at Los Alamos, including that concerned with the development of the hydrogen bomb. They received more from the Americans than they gave, although they gave far more than their small numbers would suggest. Estimates of the contribution of the British team vary, from saving two or three months to saving a year on the total project time.[9] It seems that the British were instrumental in completing the bomb in time for its use during the war.

Two billion dollars were spent and three bombs made. The first plutonium bomb was tested over the desert at Almagordo; the uranium and second plutonium bombs were tested in the air over Hiroshima and Nagasaki, and man's perception of his own power changed forever. Once the bombs had been made, few voices spoke against their use. Some, the British Ambassador to the USA among them,[10] suggested that the Japanese be given forty-eight hours' warning. Other suggested that the bomb should be demonstrated but not used against a civilian target. The most influential voice belonged to Bohr, regarded by many as the best theoretical physicist of his time. His work in 1939 had been the first to show that only the uranium-235 isotope was fissionable, and he was a man of enormous mental stature, in whose presence and because of whose constructive criticisms others arrived at profound understandings. His Institute in Copenhagen had been a sanctuary for scientists fleeing

Nazism in the 1930s, and after the German invasion he stayed on to protect them as best he could. Bohr finally escaped to Britain in 1943 and went to Los Alamos with the British team, where he was the first to understand the political implications of the bomb, and the possibility of an arms race between power blocs. He talked to both Roosevelt and Churchill, emphasising that the alternative to international control of the new weapons was a vicious arms race. He urged that public discussions be extended, within Britain and America and internationally. He infuriated the secretive Churchill, who had not even told his deputy, Attlee, about the project, but seems to have made more of an impression on Roosevelt. But not enough—the enormous effort had achieved its own momentum and would not easily be stopped. Bohr was the first of many whose wisdom and vision were to be over-ruled by this momentum.

The British Weapons Programme

The Los Alamos teams built one bomb using uranium-235 and two using plutonium-239. The British MAUD report had persuaded both the British and the Americans that a uranium bomb was feasible, but the greatest problems and largest costs lay in finding a way to separate enough of the 235 isotope from the great mass of the non-fissile 238 isotope in the naturally-occurring uranium. The problems were solved, but it proved to be a long and difficult process. The manufacture of plutonium-239, the man-made element from which the Nagasaki bomb was made, involved quite different techniques. It was (and is) made by irradiating uranium containing the natural proportions of the 235 and 238 isotopes in a reactor, formerly called a pile. The U-235 atoms fission, and split into two fragments, giving off heat and neutrons. Some of the U-238 atoms absorb a neutron and transmute into plutonium-239. When the irradiated fuel is withdrawn from the reactor, the Pu-239 can be chemically separated from the fission products and unused uranium, in a process now known as reprocessing.

American scientists were the first to isolate plutonium, and realising that the method of manufacturing plutonium was easier than the method of separating the isotopes of uranium, the American authorities were persuaded to develop simultaneously both methods of making fission bombs.

Fermi, a refugee scientist from Rome, built the first plutonium pile in a squash court in central Chicago in 1942,[11] and the production reactors that supplied the Los Alamos laboratories were built at Hanford,[12] where some of the water from the Columbia river could be diverted to flow through the reactor cores and disperse the waste heat. By the end of the war it was clear that the plutonium route was preferable to the uranium route, because plutonium is more fissile and a better bomb material; less of it is needed for the same sized bang. In addition, although the costs of both methods were astronomical, it seemed possible that plutonium production might become cheaper, if in future the enormous amounts of waste heat from the reactors could be commercially exploited to off-set some of the costs.

The British team arrived home from Los Alamos convinced of the merits of the plutonium bomb, but without expertise in plutonium production. None of the British, except Chadwick, had been allowed to visit the Hanford reactors, and none had worked in the departments concerned with plutonium metallurgy and manufacture. However, other expertise was available: an Anglo-French team studying reactors and slow neutron physics had spent two and a half years working in Canada and was also on its way back to Europe.

In June 1940 Halban and Kowarski had escaped to England from Paris. Joliot-Curie, the senior French atomic scientist, had decided to stay in France, but his two colleagues went to Cambridge to continue work on the theory of the slow neutron chain-reaction. Although scientists in the Cambridge team were aware of the possibility that a new, super-fissile material would be created by the transmutation of uranium-238, the MAUD Committee regarded the work as urgent, but not of direct relevance to the bomb project. It recommended that the team move to America in 1942, to be nearer slow-neutron research teams there, but because so many of the team were non-UK nationals and seen by America at war as security risks, it went to Montreal instead, led by Halban. Although this team suffered from frustrating delays, and neither of the two reactors it was building there were actually working at the end of the war, much basic research into reactor design and construction, plutonium separation and health physics had been done.

After the war the Canadian scientists who had worked with Halban's Anglo-French team continued to develop heavy-water reactors, which Canada still uses and sells, although she decided not to manufacture atomic weapons. The British came home with experience and data that dovetailed well with that of the scientists who returned from Los Alamos: it would enable the first plutonium piles and extraction plants to be built.

Despite the enormous job of national reconstruction waiting to be done, despite the election of a Labour government committed to extensive reforms, despite the horror of the bombs themselves, the British bomb project was resumed, and given the highest category of priority, as soon as peace was declared. Attlee's Labour administration came to power one week before the detonation of the Hiroshima bomb, but neither Attlee, who had been Churchill's wartime deputy, nor any other member of the Labour party, had been among those few who were involved with the atomic decisions. No member of the new government had any conception of the new weapon, nor of the extent of British involvement in its development; most of them first heard about it on the day it was used.[13] Churchill had given a good start to the tradition of atomic secrecy that was to prove so tenacious in British government, and Attlee continued it.

An inner cabinet, or committee, took decisions and Parliament was informed later, sometimes years later, if at all. At no time was there, and still has not been, a debate in Parliament about the manufacture of nuclear weapons in Britain. From the opposition front bench Churchill said, in November 1945: 'This I take it is already agreed, we should make atomic bombs.'[14] He was right—there was no discussion of, and thus no dissent from or agreement with, that proposition, and the project was restarted in absolute secrecy.

The Atomic Energy Research Laboratory at Harwell was begun by the end of the year, and Cockcroft appointed its first Director. The decision to produce fissile material in quantity was also taken in 1945, and Hinton appointed Director of Production in February 1946. The formal decision to build British bombs was taken by the inner cabinet in January 1947, and Penney, who had observed both the first test at Los Alamos and the Nagasaki explosion, was put in charge. In overall command was Lord Portal as Controller of Atomic Energy, who was answerable to the Minister of Supply but who also had direct access to the Prime Minister. The requirement was the production, as soon as possible, of the British bomb and, though the January 1947 decision was taken in the by now habitual secrecy, the expansion of activity so generated made the secrecy impossible to maintain. For that reason, Parliament was finally told in May 1948 that atomic weapons were being developed.[15]

The establishments were quickly built, as money was poured into the project. At Cockcroft's Harwell, the first experimental reactor GLEEP was running by July 1947—thirty eight years later it is still working. The headquarters of the Production Division under Hinton had been established at Risley, in Cheshire, and work began on the satellite factories, the uranium fabrication plant at Springfields (Lancashire), the plutonium piles and extraction plant at Windscale (Cumbria) and the uranium enrichment plant at Capenhurst, also in Cheshire. The weapons establishment was based at Fort Halstead in Kent until the present site at Aldermaston in Berkshire was taken over in April 1950. The project was consistently given top priority in national resource allocation: the priority was granted on the personal orders of the Prime Minister.[16]

At the end of 1945 Britain was economically exhausted. Her government was faced with a huge reconstruction effort and, further, with a programme of socialist reforms which would fundamentally alter the attitudes and institutions of society. And yet the atomic project was seen as overridingly important, by the people as well as by the government; it was with the tide of public opinion, which did not begin to move against British atomic weapons until the announcement of the decision to manufacture the thermonuclear bomb in 1955. Public approval reflected Britain's estimation of herself as a Great Power, and if there was a new weapon available, her status demanded that she possess it. Britain was the leading country of Europe, with responsibilities to her Empire and Dominions, who had aquitted herself brilliantly in a great war against fascism. She was proud and respected, and a force to be reckoned with. There was also a military perception of the usefulness of the bomb, which was more pragmatic. Many military men were aware that the war had been a very close-run thing; they were aware of national vulnerability in a way that they and their predecessors had not been since the Napoleonic wars. They saw the independent bomb as central to the future security. Among the politicians, there were almost certainly those who were perceptive enough to foresee Britain's inevitable decline in the Great Power league, and who saw the atomic bomb as the only way to mitigate the consequences of that decline. A technical pride was also involved, in that scientists from Britain had done the wartime groundwork that had first demonstrated the feasibility of the bomb. It was almost as if it was a British invention, and Britain certainly intended to have some of them.

The United States, which would have preferred to restrict the spread of knowledge, could not understand Britain's insistence on her own bomb, and took the firm view that her atomic project was a misuse of her straitened resources, not to mention Marshall Plan dollars. But the Labour government was committed to the project, and did not consider America to be necessarily a dependable ally. In any case, Britain's military planners knew that the country's greatness depended not on population and land mass but on trade and technical ingenuity. With no great armies to command it was considered that her defence could best be left to a few of the new bombs: the concept of deterrence was understood early on.

The British bomb was built because of a perception of national prestige and an awareness of national insecurity. Although the Manhattan Project and Montreal teams returned home with a clear idea of principles and practice, virtually no post-war help was obtained from America. The McMahon Act, passed in 1946, gave legislative expression to the new mood of technological insularity in the United States that arose immediately after the war, and atomic co-operation, except in uranium procurement, ceased. Britain built the full range of atomic factories and research facilities from her own resources, and in six years exploded her first atomic bomb. In its own terms, it was a remarkable achievement, made possible by a complete lack of administrative, political and financial constraints and the exceptional abilities of Cockcroft, Hinton and Penney. The first test, of what was basically an improved version of the Nagasaki design, took place in October 1952 at Monte Bello, a small group of islands off the west coast of Australia, and the delivery of production bombs to the RAF began late in 1953. One month after Monte Bello the first hydrogen, or thermonuclear, bomb was exploded by America at Eniwetok, and the arms race got into top gear.

In 1945 it was apparently assumed (but never minuted) that a few simple bombs would be enough to display Britain's status as an atomic power, and to deter any aggressor. But the maintenance of Great Power status in the new world order demanded more than a few simple bombs: it demanded continual increase in both effectiveness and numbers. In 1948 the military demand was for 200 bombs by 1957.[17] and in 1952 that number was urgently revised upwards.[18] By 1949 the Cold War had broken out in earnest, and American airmen arrived in Britain once again. Isolationism was waning, America was willing to talk about technology, and the enormous advances that she had made in both numbers and effectiveness became apparent. The proposed British deterrent, still years away from production, could now be compared with the American and, being small and already obsolete, was obviously irrelevant. The long-held hopes of Britain and America acting as joint world atomic policemen began to wane.

Such hopes were finally shattered when, late in 1949, the Soviet Union exploded its first atomic weapon. Both America and Britain were taken by surprise, as neither had thought that Russia would be capable of the technology until the mid-1950s.[19] Britain had not considered the possibility that she would not be the second atomic power, and the shock was considerable. It was now clear that there was a superpower league, the membership of which was beyond her

14

resources.

Sir Henry Tizard led the rebellion. He had been involved with the project since 1939, when he had tried and failed to bring the Belgian uranium concentrate to Britain. In 1949 he was one of the most senior military scientists in Britain, and perhaps the only man close to the centres of power who was aware that stability in atomic weapons production and development was impossible to achieve. He saw that the maintenance of British prestige in the form of a small and unusable national atomic force was too costly; there was a real danger of it causing severe economic decline and thus defeating its own object. His view was firm but unpalatable:[20]

We persist in regarding ourselves as a Great Power, capable of everything and only temporarily handicapped by economic difficulties. We are not a Great Power and never will be again. We are a great nation, but if we continue to behave like a Great Power we shall soon cease to be a great nation. Let us take warning from the Great Powers of the past and not burst ourselves with pride (see Aesop's fable of the frog).

Tizard argued forcibly that the production of the bomb should be stopped, that atomic knowledge be channelled into power production as had happened in Canada, and that resources be reallocated to other urgent civil and conventional military programmes. It was the last chance for Britain to cancel the programme before the bombs started in production, but already the institutional momentum was too great, and the residual Great Power mentality won the day. As a result of the immense investment of money and labour at the highest priority, the RAF began to take delivery of bombs in 1953. A similar priority had not been allocated to the production of bombers, and the RAF did not possess the means of delivering its new bombs until 1957. This rather touching tale perhaps reveals more about Britain's attitude to her bomb than any other.[21]

Although Tizard's views did not prevail, they did mark the beginning of a significant change of emphasis. Britain's atomic pride was increasingly manifested in terms of her having the first and biggest nuclear electricity programme. The first generation of plutonium-producing reactors (then called piles) at Windscale dispersed their waste heat to the air, but the second generation, at Calder Hall and Chapelcross, used theirs to generate electricity. The civil programme used the fuel cycle factories that had already been built for the weapons programme, and reactor design work already done for plutonium production. Nuclear power would not have been developed so early, if at all, without the military requirements, but the need for reactors to produce both plutonium and power imposed on the electricity industry a compromise design. The Magnox power stations, not surprisingly, turned out to be very good at plutonium manufacture but not so good at electricity production, and the 1963 report of the Select Committee on Nationalised Industries agreed with the CEGB that the Magnox power stations were costing £20 million per annum more to run than equivalent coal stations would have done,[22] or about £125 million per annum at 1984 prices. In 1965 the CEGB estimated that the Magnox programme was adding £25–30 million to costs annually, or £150–170 million a year at 1984 prices.[23]

Behind the new civil nuclear stations of the 1950s and 1960s, the weapons programme continued unabated. Both research and production facilities continued to be shared, and the situation developed whereby neither project could be justified except in terms of the spin-off benefits provided to the other. The electricity supply industry subsidised the production of plutonium in reactors it did not choose and, given the choice, would not have chosen. It became the main contributor to what soon became, and still remains, the largest stockpile of separated plutonium in the non-communist world.[24]

The First Power Programme
In September 1947 work began on the two air-cooled plutonium production piles at Windscale, which operated from 1950 until 1957. They were designed to serve an exclusively military purpose; Hinton, in charge of the production of fissile material, had failed to persuade Lord Portal

16

to allow the generation of electricity from the waste heat. Nevertheless Hinton's team continued design work on a reactor that would produce both power and plutonium, which became known as PIPPA. When, because of the increased military demand more plutonium production facilities were required, the chance to build it arose.

The 1957 Windscale fire, the most serious reactor accident to have occurred in Britain, resulted in the closure of the two air-cooled piles. In the morning of 8 October the operator of Number One pile allowed the core temperature to rise to fuel melting point, unaware that the gauges did not take their readings from the hottest part of the core. There was no sign of trouble for 42 hours, until instruments in the stack filters— housed in the bulges at the top of the discharge chimneys often noticeable in photographs of Sellafield—indicated that radioactivity was being uncontrollably released.

By this time a fire was raging in the core, inflated by the cooling fans. Flames shot out of the core from the discharge face, and at its height eleven tonnes of uranium and the graphite moderator were on fire. Carbon dioxide was used in the first attempt to put out the fire, but it served only to intensify it. Despite the real possibility of a hydrogen explosion, fire hoses were coupled directly into a line of fuel channels and turned on. During the morning of 11 October the fire, out of control for more than twenty-four hours, finally subsided.

The stack filters, which had only been incorporated into the design as an afterthought, probably prevented a major accident from becoming a disaster. Even so, quantities of radioactivity were released, the most hazardous of which was some 20,000 curies of iodine-131.[25] Two million litres of milk, from farms covering an area of 500 square kilo-metres, were poured away, but it is impossible to know what, if any, were the health effects on the local people, because the identities of those near the fire were not recorded.

Both the air-cooled piles were shut down and filled with concrete; they had, in any case, been superceded. The first of the new generation of plutonium factories was Calder Hall 'A'. Building work started in August 1953 on the site adjacent to Windscale, and by 1956 the reactors were producing a modest quantity of low-grade wet steam as a by-product. Calder Hall 'A' is a twin-reactor station, as are all British units, and is fuelled by natural uranium, and each reactor is still capable of providing about 50 MW to the grid. Calder Hall 'A' was closely followed by the 'B' station on the same site (there are thus four reactors at Calder Hall), and the almost identical Chapelcross 'A' and 'B' stations at Dumfriesshire.

In 1954 a Treasury working party under Burke Trend reported on the economic feasibility of a nuclear power programme.[26] The fuel situation in Britain at the time was very poor, and coal as well as oil was being imported; there were very real fears, (in the event not justified), that the National Coal Board would not be able to meet the demands of the electricity industry in the early 1960s. These considerations seem to have been dominant in the working party's thoughts because, since the British Electricity Authority was not invited to participate, the working party had no knowledge of coal generation costs, or of new cost-cutting techniques, or of the industry's electricity demand projections. Although unable to compare coal and nuclear generation costs—the latter were, in any case, almost unguessable—the enthusiasm of the new UKAEA and worries about coal supplies combined to ensure a report favourable to nuclear development. Trend recommended a programme of 1700 MW by 1965, although he recognised that such a programme might not become economic until its later stages, if at all. Only a very large credit for the plutonium produced could make a programme even approximately economic.[27]

Although the BEA was not consulted, Trend also recommended that it, rather than the UKAEA, should build and operate the new stations. The working party's report was accepted and the Calder Hall, or Magnox, design of reactor was imposed on the BEA, despite the fact that it was a compromise that would always be rather better, even when optimised for electricity production, at producing plutonium than electricity. The Magnox power stations still have the dubious distinction of producing more plutonium per megawatt of electricity than any other commercial power reactors.[28]

18

The UKAEA, under its first and influential chairman, Lord Plowden, pressed hard to increase Trend's programme. The Central Electricity Authority (which succeeded the BEA in England and Wales in 1955) was conscious of falling fossil fuel costs and the high capital costs of the Magnox stations, and agreed only reluctantly to a new target of 3,200 MW.[29] Then came Suez, and Leslie Hannah, the Electricity Council's historian, commented:

> The mistakes and dishonesty of Suez. . . led to the partial collapse of rationality within Westminster, the AEA and, to a lesser but still noticeable extent, within Whitehall.

The 1949 Russian atomic explosion had been a clear indication that Britain's days as a Great Power were over, and the 1956 shambles of Suez finally marked the end of her period of international authority. The shock to national pride and to international confidence was severe, as it was realised that Britain was heavily dependent on supplies of imported oil but powerless to protect them.

Although the tenders for the first Magnox stations had indicated that construction costs would be about three and a half times greater than for coal or oil, the CEA's worries about the costs of nuclear electricity were over-ruled in a strategic panic to reduce dependence on imported oil. Macmillan, as Prime Minister, took on direct responsibility for the UKAEA, and the civil nuclear lobby began the period of great political influence which has continued ever since. In early 1957 the nuclear programme was increased to 6,000 MW by 1965,[30] despite the CEA's arguments that this would transform the expected coal shortage into a surplus, and its calculation that the capital investment that such a programme implied would make the electricity industry responsible for 12 per cent of the national investment.

In 1957 the CEGB was constituted and Hinton, who had been in charge of the production of fissile material for the bomb programme since 1946 and, since 1954, of the UKAEA support for the civil programme, was persuaded to become its first Chairman. Of the three men primarily responsible for the successful completion of the atomic bomb project, his job had been the biggest. His team had designed and built the two air-cooled piles at Windscale, the plutonium separation and reprocessing plant on the same site, the fuel fabrication factory at Springfields and the uranium-235 enrichment plant at Capenhurst. His team had also designed the new dual-purpose Magnox stations, and work was proceeding on three more, Calder Hall 'B', and the Chapelcross 'A' and 'B' stations. The UKAEA had decided that that basic design should be used for the first nuclear power programme, and Hinton was the obvious choice to take on the new organisation and the large new nuclear programme. The government and the UKAEA expected that Hinton, having been so closely involved with the shape of the new technology since its birth, would ensure its continued health.

But at the CEGB, Hinton soon adopted and reflected the electricity industry's view that the commitment to 6,000 MW of nuclear power was premature, impractical and expensive. The reactors were incapable of achieving steam conditions and efficiencies comparable to those of the new coal stations, and they were much more expensive to build at a time when interest rates were increasing. The CEGB's opinion, soon shared by Hinton, was that nuclear electricity was not, and was not likely to be, competitive with either coal or oil, and that the plutonium credit, the use of which was the only way in which nuclear could be made to appear competitive, was not economically justified. More importantly, it was becoming clear to CEGB planners that the anticipated supply problems with fossil fuels were not materialising. There was now little danger that the NCB's 1954 forecast of a forthcoming coal shortfall would prove accurate, or that fears of a post-Suez threat to Middle East oil supplies would prove valid.

After three years of intensive lobbying, against determined opposition, Hinton persuaded the government to reduce the target for 1965 from 6,000 to 3,000 MW, and the final target for the first programme to 5,000 MW by 1968.[31] He would have been happy to reduce the programme still further, to a level to maintain the nuclear option against future demonstrated economic viability, but nevertheless his achievement was considerable, and was a significant check on the ambitions of the UKAEA. It is possible that only Hinton could have done it; it is certain that, had he not, electricity prices in the coming decades would have been higher than they proved to be.[32]

Despite the cuts, the Magnox programme grew in size and cost, and it became clear by the 1960s that the generating boards (the CEGB and the South of Scotland Electricity Board) were committed to almost 5,000 MW of uneconomic generating stations. Sources differ slightly as to comparative generation costs during this period: the following 1962 figures are typical:[33]

Bradwell	1.12d per kWh
Berkeley	1.23d per kWh
Ferrybridge 'C'	0.48d per kWh

(Bradwell and Berkeley were the first of the CEGB's Magnox stations: Ferrybridge 'C' was at that time the most recently-built coal-fired station. Units are old pence per kilowatt hour.)

In July 1962, Hinton commented that the cost of a kilowatt of capacity from a Magnox station was £120, but from a modern coal station sited on the coal field, £37.[34] The report of the Select Committee on Nationalised Industries, published in the following year, agreed with Hinton that, as the nuclear programme had been imposed on the CEGB for policy reasons, the taxpayer should bear at least some of the additional costs of electricity so caused.[35]

Leslie Hannah (who, as the sponsored historian, had access to all CEGB papers dated up to 1973) is clear about the relative costs of electricity from Magnox and coal stations during this period:[36]

In 1960 the prognostications even for new Magnox orders were still that they would be a third more expensive overall than conventional power.

Partly the reason was that:[37]

. . . the plutonium credit (which had knocked more than a third off the estimated cost of production in 1955) was by 1958 considered likely to contribute perhaps only a fifteenth or a twelfth of production costs. (By the late

1960s its contribution was in fact to become negative as it became evident that no economic use could be found for the waste plutonium and the reprocessing of used fuel cans was a costly business.)

In addition, real costs were hidden by accounting methods:[38]

. . . the (first) nuclear programme was politically determined and exempted from CEGB rate of return tests. Without that exemption no nuclear power stations would have been ordered between 1958 and 1964.

The first nuclear programme finally comprised nine twin-reactor Magnox stations, eight owned by the CEGB and one by the SSEB. Their design capacity was 4,352 MW net, but in 1970/71 all except Berkeley were down-rated because of corrosion problems. (See Chapter 3.) In 1984 the CEGB's eight Magnox stations had a net capacity of only 3,445 MW, which may be compared to the 43,000 MW of its fossil fuelled stations—about 8 per cent.[39] Magnox reactors are unable to raise enough hot dry steam to achieve the thermal efficiencies of the coal stations—the average Magnox efficiency (see Appendix 1, Glossary) is 25.7 per cent, and that of the large coal stations 35.8 per cent.[40] They are neither cheap, efficient, nor large and, as the CEGB's evidence to the Sizewell inquiry has shown,[41] they have not generated electricity more cheaply than coal.

Britain had built the world's first, and until 1964 the largest,[42] nuclear electricity programme. By the end of 1983 the civil Magnox reactors had produced 35.5 tonnes of plutonium, and that figure specifically excluded the civil plutonium sent to the United States before 1971.[43] No figure has been given for the plutonium produced in the military reactors at Calder Hall and Chapelcross.

The chemical process of extracting plutonium from irradiated (or spent) fuel that has been discharged from a reactor is known as reprocessing. It is the only way in which fissile plutonium can be manufactured, in greater than microgram quantities, and the first reprocessing factory was built at Windscale by 1952. Irradiated fuel was provided by the two air-cooled piles on the same site, until they were closed following the 1957 fire, and from the Calder Hall and Chapelcross reactors from 1956 onwards. When the generating boards began to own and operate Magnox power stations based on the Calder Hall design, their irradiated fuel was, and still is, reprocessed in the same factory as the military irradiated fuel (see Chapter 8). The justifications given, then as now, are two-fold: firstly that unused uranium, which is recovered in the reprocessing operation in addition to the plutonium, can be recycled in the reactors, and secondly that civil plutonium will one day be useful as fuel for commerical fast-breeder reactors (CFRs). The continued low price and easy availability of uranium on the world market has diminished the force of the first justification, and the continued deferral of the expected date of introduction of CFRs has diminished the force of the second (see Chapter 11). The fact that the Americans have never reprocessed civil fuel,[44] and that, since 1976, the reasons have been specifically concerned with worries about nuclear proliferation, as well as with economics, diminishes the force of both.

In 1954 the United Kingdom Atomic Energy Authority (UKAEA, or AEA) took over responsibility for the atomic project from the Ministry of Supply. For fifteen years it grew formidably in size and power as it maintained control over civil and military projects that were both expanding. The first atomic activity that it did not directly control was the building and operation of the civil power stations, but it provided the design, and the fuel and reprocessing services were supplied from the factories and laboratories established to provide the same services for the military reactors. Sir John Hill, who was Chairman of the AEA from 1967–1980, and of British Nuclear Fuels Ltd from its inception in 1971 until 1983, wrote in 1969:[45]

By 1955. . . we had the situation where the entire nuclear defence programme and the embryo civil nuclear power programme lay in the establishments of the newly formed Atomic Energy Authority. . . The facilities required for the manufacture and reprocessing of the nuclear fuel. . .

23

were virtually identical to those required for the defence programme.

The AEA's insistence on the adoption of the Magnox design by the generating boards, and its provision of fuel services to the boards, was rooted in the AEA's and the government's determination to obtain for Britain the biggest possible plutonium stockpile in the shortest possible time. But the largest proportion of this stockpile was derived from the electricity programme, and by the late 1960s it was becoming politically unacceptable to apply this plutonium to the weapons programme. The boards formally assumed ownership of their plutonium in April 1969.

In 1964 the military stockpile (that derived from Calder Hall and Chapelcross) was deemed to be large enough for national defence needs, and those reactors were optimised for electricity production by 1967.[46] However, plutonium from them has continued to be exported to the United States for military purposes, at least until 1984 (see Chapter 8), and the government has reserved the right to re-optimise them for plutonium production, should British, or presumably American, defence perceptions demand it.

In 1971 the first serious attempt was made to untie the knot linking the civil and military projects. The all-powerful AEA was broken up; the Weapons Group based at Aldermaston was transferred to the Ministry of Defence and the hugh Production Group, the empire built by Hinton with establishments at Capenhurst, Risley, Springfields and Windscale, was transferred to the newly-formed British Nuclear Fuels Ltd (BNFL). The AEA was left with its research function and, importantly, its role of providing advice to governments. It was still powerful, but not as massively so as it had been.

The knot was transferred, rather than untied, because BNFL has continued to reprocess both military and civil fuel at Windscale, and the stockpile has continued to grow. The convenience, to the CEGB and the SSEB, of paying BNFL to deal with their spent fuel is perhaps becoming outweighed by the opprobrium caused by it. The transfer of civil plutonium to the United States before 1971, and of military plutonium thereafter (see Chapter 8), has become an embarrassment to both government and boards, as has the radioactive pollution caused by BNFL's mismanagement of the reprocessing plant at Windscale (now called Sellafield) that manufactures the stockpile (see Chapter 9).

That, presumably, was not the intention of the AEA and the government. They intended that the plutonium should be of benefit to Britain, that she should have adequate supplies for her weapons programme. Further the surplus was to provide a bargaining counter in her dealings with the United States, to exchange for American technical knowledge; perhaps, in 1963, to exchange for Polaris missiles. Further still, the manufacture of plutonium was seen as a way of maintaining Britain's status, of retaining her place at the conference tables of the superpowers. As such, it is a familiar theme, consistent with the political thread that has run through the atomic project since its inception. The driving force was a widely-held belief in British greatness, and a conviction that atomic projects are appropriate to Great Powers. It became a determination to use atomic knowledge to maintain Britain's international prestige, or at least to delay its diminution for as long as possible.

Great resources were devoted to the manufacture of the bomb, and yet the project failed in its objective of making Britain the second atomic power, the equal partner of America. To a large extent the failure was because of, rather than in spite of, the allocation of national resources. Because they continued beyond the point at which it had become apparent that the military goal was misconceived and unattainable, the result was the unnecessary limitation of resources (of both money and skills) to other national activities. The bomb project weakened the national economy and lessened the possibility of achieving a parity of status with the United States, just as Sir Henry Tizard had foreseen in 1949.

The new technology was self-reinforcing and self-perpetuating, both because of the size of the financial investment, and because the scientific and technical skills were so

25

specialised as to be untransferable, except to the emerging nuclear power project. This prestigious project was to give Britain the first and biggest nuclear electricity programme in the world, but instead of demonstrating the peaceful uses of the atom it tainted the electricity industry with suspicions of subsidising the weapons programme.

The civil project, like the military, demanded a disproportionate share of the national resources of skill and money. It is a non-essential project in terms of electricity generation but has prevented the emergence of competitors by its monopoly of research resources. The primary motivation behind it was the demonstration and maintenance of status; the primary result has been a reduction in status because of the misallocation of funds and talent, and the missed opportunities for investment in other projects which might have proved useful and profitable. The grand gesture of nuclear technology has cost this country dear.

NOTES AND REFERENCES

Primary sources—apart from White Papers, the Hansard record of Parliamentary debates and the reports of Select Committees—are the official histories.

Those sponsored by the Atomic Energy Authority are by Prof. Margaret Gowing, and are (so far) in three volumes, published by Macmillan:

1. *Britain and Atomic Energy 1939-45* (published 1964)
2. *Independence and Deterrence: Britain and Atomic Energy 1945-1952*
   Vol. 1 Policy Making (published 1974)
3. *Independence and Deterrence: Britain and Atomic Energy 1945-1952*
   Vol. 2 Policy Execution (published 1974).

In the notes that follow, these are referred to as Gowing Book 1, Gowing Book 2 and Gowing Book 3.

The official histories sponsored by the Electricity Council on behalf of the CEGB and the Scottish and area boards are by Prof. Leslie Hannah. The first volume of his work (*Electricity before Nationalisation*, Macmillan, 1979) is not referred to. The second volume, also published by Macmillan, is:

Engineers, Managers and Politicians: the First Fifteen Years of Nationalised Electricity Supply in Britain (published 1982).

This is referenced below by the author's surname.

1. See Appendix 2 (A Technical Note).
2. See Appendix 2 (A Technical Note).
3. Lennard Bickel, *The Deadly Element*, (Macmillan, 1979), p. 178 and pp. 213-214.
4. Gowing Book 1, pp. 389-393, gives the text.
5. *Ibid.*, pp. 394-436. A second report, on the use of uranium for power generation, was included.
6. Gowing Book 2, p. 1.
7. Gowing Book 1, pp. 83-84.
8. Hanford is in Washington State, and occupies a 575 sq. mile site.
9. Gowing Book 1, pp. 266 and 267.
10. *Ibid.*, p. 370.
11. *Ibid.*, p. 370.
12. See note 8.
13. Gowing Book 2, p. 5.
14. Hansard, 7 November 1945, col. 1300.
15. Hansard, 12 May 1948, col. 2117.
16. There were three policy directives from Attlee; February 1947, February 1949 and September 1949.
17. Gowing Book 2, p. 216.
18. *Ibid.*, p. 442.
19. *Ibid.*, pp. 221-222.
20. *Ibid.*, p. 229.
21. *Ibid.*, pp. 234-235.
22. House of Commons Select Committee on Nationalised Industries, Report on the Electricity Supply Industry, May 1963. Paras. 392-395.
23. Hansard, 31 March 1965, cols. 257-258.
24. R.F. Pocock, *Nuclear Power: Its Development in the United Kingdom*, (Unwin, 1977), p. 125.
25. For a description of the Windscale fire, see *Ibid.*, pp. 64-71, and Walter Patterson, *Nuclear Power*, (Penguin, second edition 1983), pp. 123-126. It was not admitted that polonium was also released until 1983, because an earlier admission would have revealed that Britain was manufacturing a type of polonium-triggered hydrogen bomb that was already, by 1957, out of date. By 1983 it was presumably considered that such information was no longer useful to our putative enemies. See *New Scientist*, 29 September 1983, and 'An Assessment of the Radiological Impact of the Windscale

Fire of October 1957', NRPB 1983.

26. His recommendations were embodied in the 1955 White Paper, Cmd. 9389, 'A Programme of Nuclear Power'.
27. Hannah, pp. 172-173. The 1955 White Paper (Cmd. 9389) estimated the cost of nuclear electricity at 0.6d per kWh (old pence per kilowatt-hour), but admitted that costs would be substantially more without the plutonium credit. Reference 22 at para. 373 indicated that the credit was between 0.3d and 0.35d in 1955. Gowing (Book 3, p. 294) quotes the 1955 price of nuclear electricity at a fraction over 1.0d per kWh, and the average price at 0.66d per kWh, which confirms this.
28. Hansard, 27 July 1983 col. 437. (Quoted at Chapter 8, note 7.)
29. This and the following paragraph refer to Hannah, pp. 177-181.
30. White Paper Cmnd. 132, 1957.
31. White Paper Cmnd. 1083, 1960.
32. For a detailed account of the 'nuclear retreat', see Hannah, pp. 228-247.
33. Pocock, *op. cit.*, p. 151. As Hannah notes (p. 243): 'This added financial losses of £20 million (3 per cent of turnover) annually to electricity costs.'
34. *Nuclear Engineering,* vol. 7, 1962, p. 339.
35. Reference 22, para. 395.
36. Hannah, p. 244.
37. *Ibid.,* pp. 230-231.
38. *Ibid.,* p. 317 (at note 4).
39. CEGB Statistical Yearbook 1983/84, table 6.
40. CEGB Statistical Yearbook 1983/84, table 6.
41. *Analysis of Generating Costs,* a CEGB document produced during the inquiry. See day 44, pages 32G-35F for a summary. (Revised 1985.)
42. In capacity terms. In terms of electricity produced, the USA did not overtake until 1973. See *Nucleonics,* February 1965 and *Nucleonics Week,* 24 January 1974.
43. Hansard, 1 April 1982, col. 169.
44. With the exception that Nuclear Fuel Services, at West Valley, reprocessed 1.3 tonnes of civil fuel between 1966-1971, as well as 0.5 tonnes from the Hanford 'N' reactor, then operating as a power station. See *Bulletin of the Atomic Scientists,* January 1978, p. 23.
45. *Nuclear Engineering,* vol. 14, 1969, p. 717, quoted by Pocock, *op. cit.,* p. 40.
46. Hansard, 21 April 1964, col. 1098.

CHAPTER 2

UK ATOMIC HISTORY 1964–84

The first 'ten-year programme'[1] of nuclear power, the first such programme in the world, was announced early in 1955, eighteen months before the first prototype reactor was completed. Two years later, in the aftermath of Suez, the size of the programme was trebled, but it was subsequently contracted in stages, chiefly by the device of extending its target completion date. Even so, it finished three years late, with the commissioning of the last and largest Magnox station at Wylfa in 1971.

In April 1964 a White Paper[2] announced the second nuclear programme, the intention of which was to build some 5,000 MW of capacity (four or five large stations) in England and Wales between 1970 and 1975. Four Advanced Gas-cooled Reactor (AGR) stations were built (each station comprising two reactors, as with the Magnox stations), and a fifth in Scotland, with a total capacity of some 6,000 MW. The programme was again late, only two stations having been commissioned by mid-1985.

During the early 1970s, when confidence in the successful outcome of the AGR programme was still high, both the CEGB and the AEA envisaged that the High Temperature Reactor (HTR) would follow the AGR. It was seen as the next logical step, the natural development of gas-cooled technology. The CEGB commented:[3]

The thermal reactor system which the UKAEA, the two nuclear design and construction companies and the Board think may eventually provide lower cost power is the HTR or Mark III gas-cooled reactor, magnox and AGR being Marks I and II respectively.

In its sales pitch, the AEA was more forthright; at the Istanbul IAEA Symposium on nuclear costs and economic development in October 1969 it said:[4]

Great interest is being shown in the HTR, not only in the UK, where the CEGB have indicated that they are likely to adopt it in their system as the successor to the Mark II AGR, but also by West Germany, the USA and elsewhere. Considerable reductions below Mark II reactors in capital costs and initial fuel costs are expected.

In 1974 the CEGB was still writing of the 'rapid development of the HTR'[5] and the Minister of Energy, Eric Varley MP, spoke of 'gas-cooled reactors. . . with Magnox and AGR so far, and HTR as the next stage of development'.[6] But two months later the same Minister abandoned the British project.[7]

In fact, the AGR was proving so difficult to build that the government decided to abandon both it and its successor, and adopt the fourth British reactor choice, the Steam Generating Heavy Water Reactor (SGHWR). This programme was revoked early in 1978 and two more AGR's ordered to prevent the collapse of the nuclear construction industry. At the same time the door was opened to the possibility of using the American designed Pressurised Water Reactor (PWR), which had been the CEGB's preferred choice since 1973.

In December 1979 the Secretary of State for Energy said firmly that 'the PWR should be the next nuclear power station'. He went on to say:[8]

Looking ahead, the electricity supply industry has advised that even on cautious assumptions it would need to order one new nuclear power station a year in the decade from 1982, or a programme of the order of 15,000 MW over 10 years. The precise level of future ordering will depend on the development of electricity demand and the performance of the industry, but we consider that this is a reasonable prospect against which the nuclear and power plant industries can plan.

This programme seemed destined to be as short-lived as the 1974 SGHWR programme had been, and as embarrassing for the new Conservative administration as the earlier one had been for the then-new Labour one. Within a year of the announcement quoted above it was obvious that the ESI's advice had been optimistic—in 1979/80, 1980/81, 1981/82 and 1982/83 the electricity industry experienced a fall in demand for its product[9] —and by the time that the CEGB published its first tranche of evidence for the Sizewell inquiry, the word 'programme' had been firmly forgotten, although the Board was soon reminded of it.

Thus the PWR is the fifth British reactor choice. The Magnox stations are at least working, though with low efficiencies[10] and at reduced ratings (see Chapter 3). The AGR programme was, by common consent, a 'catastrophe'.[11] The HTR and SGHWR reactors were both non-starters. The CEGB's hopes for the PWR are therefore based more on faith than on precedent.

The Construction Consortia

From the earliest days, civil nuclear activities were structured in such a way that the only part of the work available to private industry was the detailed design and construction of civil power stations. The AEA did the research and built the prototypes, and the nationalised utilities ran the power stations once built. The only private capital at risk was, and to a small extent still is, in the construction business. One theme that runs through the history of UK civil nuclear power is that the construction industry has been consistently led to expect a high level of ordering, and been consistently let down. The aftermath of the 1979 announcement is only the most recent example of the way in which eventual ordering has been well below expectations.

The AEA encouraged the design and construction companies to form themselves into consortia, each able to design and build complete nuclear plants. In 1956 there were five, by 1960 three, and in 1973 the National Nuclear Corporation (NNC) took over the interests of the two remaining consortia (see Chapter 6). Private industry's involvement in British nuclear power has contracted painfully and expensively, from an enthusiastic participation to a minority shareholding in the one remaining construction organisation. The reasons include the inherently small national market for electricity, the consistent over-estimation of the prospects for growth in that market by the electricity industry, an increase in the size of individual power stations and the failure to design cheap, exportable reactor systems. Of the three main participants in civil nuclear power, only the consortia were at the sharp end of industrial survival. The AEA was, and is, funded by Parliamentary Vote, and the CEGB has the security of its monopoly position and the relatively small place that nuclear generation has within its operation. The experience of the consortia has been that building nuclear power stations in the UK has not been profitable.

The Atomic Energy Authority and the AGR decision
For seventeen years the AEA was the centre of the centralised and secretive structure that enveloped both civil and military projects. Set up by the Atomic Energy Act 1954, the AEA is a rather special government department,[12] directly funded but able to take on a more commercial role. It had enormous early prestige, because of the success of the atomic bomb project and because of the esteem accorded to its work, and it soon became massive as well as monopolistic, retaining control over all aspects of the atomic projects until 1971. It decided on the direction of the national nuclear research effort, and did the research itself. (Sir Christopher Hinton, when Chairman of the CEGB, said of the AEA: 'I think that their activities are guided by what they think our requirements ought to be'.[13]) It gave advice to the government on nuclear matters. It employed, at peak, 41,000 people, and ran establishments at Aldermaston, Capenhurst, Dounreay, Harwell, Risley, Springfields, Windscale and Winfrith. It was responsible for the entire nuclear fuel cycle, from the manufacture of uranium fuel to the reprocessing of irradiated fuel and the manufacture of atomic weapons.

The AEA was the result of the British decisions independently to design and build the entire range of military and civil atomic facilities; decisions made, or taken for granted, after the 1946 McMahon Act denied the UK access to American technical developments. The AEA was the consequence of the British reaction to the American position, and a reflection of the British determination to become an atomic power despite her enforced isolation. Its task was to provide the proof of Britain's continued greatness through a demonstration of independent atomic prowess, and the power and resources that it commanded matched the undertaking.

In 1957 the Authority had decided that the successor to the Magnox reactor should be the AGR,[14] and it had a 30 MW prototype working at Windscale by 1962. The AEA expected that commercial versions of the AGR would be a significant improvement on the Magnox, which had limited development potential; the Calder and Chapelcross reactors have a capacity of 50 MW (net) each and an outlet steam temperature of a little over 300°C, and the reactors of the last Magnox station, at Wylfa, are 420 MW and 385°C, but the new AGRs were to be 600 or 660 MW and have steam temperatures approaching 650°C. The AEA's major research effort went into developing the AGR, and it was so confident that it would be chosen for the second reactor programme that an AGR fuel production line was established in the early 1960s, pre-empting a decision by the government and the CEGB.[15]

American PWRs, which use light, or ordinary, water as both moderator and coolant, were, in the early 1960s, beginning a decade of great commercial success. By its end they dominated the market world-wide, although success was short-lived—the last uncancelled reactor order in the US was placed in 1973. But at the beginning of the 1960s PWR sales had not achieved superiority, and AEA saw three principal advantages in its AGR that would enable it to compete for international markets: on-load refuelling (the AGR was designed to be refuelled on load, but the water-cooled reactors have to be shut down for refuelling); steam conditions (the AGR outlet steam temperatures are higher and the steam is drier); and safety (the greater mass of the AGR's core, and its gas coolant, makes it intrinsically safer).[16] Additionally it was originally hoped that the AGR could use natural, unenriched, uranium fuel. These contentions can reasonably be used to argue in the AGR's favour today, but it proved to be impossible to use unenriched fuel. Unexpected problems arose because of the high steam temperatures required, and it was soon discovered that the fuel canning material used in the Magnox reactors (a magnesium alloy, hence the name) would melt at such temperatures. Strenuous efforts were made—£10 million worth—to find a way of using beryllium which, it was hoped, would allow high operating temperatures with no, or very little, fuel enrichment.

The chain reaction in a reactor depends on there being enough neutrons available to sustain U-235 fission. Magnox reactors work without enrichment, though at lower temperatures than those required from the AGR. To attain higher temperatures, more fissions must take place. This can be achieved either by reducing the neutrons absorbed by the internal reactor components, such as the fuel cans, or by increasing the proportion of fissile U-235 atoms in the fuel by enrichment. The experiments with beryllium fuel cans were an unsuccessful attempt to reduce neutron absorbtion in the core, and the AEA also tried to achieve the effect of enrichment by mixing fissile plutonium with the fuel. Efforts with both techniques failed, stainless steel was chosen as the AGR fuel canning material, and fuel enrichment became necessary.

In retrospect, that would have been the moment to abandon the AGR and move into the mainstream of reactor ordering, which was beginning to concentrate on water-cooled reactors. France, the only other country to have an early commercial interest in gas-cooled reactors, switched to an American design of PWR in 1969.[17] Although in Britain there were voices that urged the same course, the AEA decided to continue with gas-reactor development. This was partly because of a genuine conviction as to its merits, partly because the enormous problems of its commercial development were not foreseen, and partly in pride and self-defence. The pride is by now familiar—could the country with the world's first commercial nuclear station and the world's first nuclear power programme, admit that its technological assumptions were wrong? and admit that America's were right?—and it had a powerful ally in the institutional momentum of the AEA itself. Any move away from the AGR, and towards a technology not developed and supported in its own laboratories would 'undermine the fundamental rationale of the AEA'.[18] The whole range of research facilities would no longer be needed, and it would not be able to justify its own expensive existence. The Atomic Energy Authority did not intend to abandon lightly seven or eight years work in favour of an American design.

Dungeness 'B'
In April 1964[19] the government announced the second nuclear power programme, but made no decision as to reactor type, or to the site of the first of the new stations. Tenders were invited for the reactor in the same year, and the announcement that the first site would be Dungeness was made in 1965.[20] The CEGB received seven offers in response to its invitation; three tenders for AGRs, one offer for a BWR, one for a PWR and two priced design studies for PWRs. Two of these, an AGR and the BWR, were shortlisted, and were the subject of the CEGB's Appraisal.[21]

The atomic atmosphere at the time was defensively parochial. The American McMahon Act, which gave legislative expression to that country's post-war atomic isolationism, still rankled, and the competitive reaction to it underpinned the British attitude. There was a strong feeling that Britain should maintain an independent nuclear technology, and keep at least some of the hoped-for international business out of American hands. There was a corresponding fear of an American intrusion into the British domestic reactor market, coupled with a certain resentment at the size of American resources, and a tendency to disparage her successes. There was an emotive atmosphere in British nuclear circles, 'almost a sense of neurosis',[22] illustrated by the story of the British delegates to the 1964 Geneva Conference on the Peaceful Uses of Atomic Energy, who were 'whipped into party line, with early morning brainwashing sessions at their hotel. Once it was only the Russians who did this sort of thing'.[23]

The specifications for the AGR tenders were issued in April 1964, and one requirement was that fuel clusters contain 18 fuel rods arranged in two rings. At this time there

were three consortia still in business, but one, APC, decided
not to bid for the first AGR contract. The AEA therefore
gave to APC the job of costing its new concept of a 36 rod,
three ring cluster; APC finished this work in September 1964.
In the following month APC changed its mind, and decided
to work up an AGR tender after all, based on the 36 rod fuel
cluster. On 30th November, eight weeks before the tender
deadline, the CEGB changed the specifications to permit the
36 rod cluster. APC's was therefore the only design to
incorporate it, as the other consortia could not re-work their
designs in time—this, naturally, caused bitterness.[24] Despite
the fact that the CEGB recognised APC as the weakest of the
consortia, and the fact that APC's tender was a sketch
design, in its own words 'not a tender in depth to the extent
that some of the other tenders were',[25] its design was chosen
as the AGR contender for the contract. Professor Burn
comments:[26]

The CEGB knew what the public was not told, that there
was at this stage only a sketch plan for Dungeness 'B', that
there was much less detail in the APC tender than in the
other tenders offered.

The Appraisal compared APC's AGR design with the BWR
proposal from TNPG.[27] There were several criticisms of this
exercise, but the most significant, in its effect, concerned the
AGR's theoretical ability to be refuelled on-load. The total
cost difference between the two designs was £8.8/kW, and
the availability adjustment, credited to the AGR for on-load
refuelling, was £8.97/kW. The economics of the two reactors
were almost identical; the advantage to the AGR lay solely in
its claimed enhanced availability through on-load refuelling.
This was eventually achieved at Hunterston 'B' on 30 August
1982, and soon afterwards at Hinkley Point 'B', but in both
cases only at 30 per cent load.[28]

The public, and Parliament, were not told until two years
after the contract was let to APC about the extent of the
CEGB's reservations concerning that consortium. In 1967
the Board told the House of Commons Select Committee on
Science and Technology that it was concerned whether APC

could 'tackle and programme' the contract, and it revealed that a condition of the contract with APC was that it should strengthen its resources and recruit some 'very senior personnel';[29] these conditions had been omitted from the published Appraisal two years earlier.

The CEGB's decision in favour of the AGR was greeted with jubilation.[30] The Minister of Power, Fred Lee MP, said in the Commons:[31]

I am quite sure we have hit the jackpot this time. . . I am sorry that the Hon. Gentleman is in such a tizzy about our great success. Here we have the greatest breakthrough of all time. Why does not the Hon. Gentleman rejoice with us?

The Financial Times wrote that 'This nuclear breakthrough is pure gain for the British economy' and *New Scientist* said 'The result is astonishingly satisfying. . . and an initial triumph'.[32] Dungeness 'B' became the worst failure (to date) of the British nuclear industry, possibly the most disastrous contract ever let in Britain. It has yet to commission, 19 years after work started on site. Its cost is 2.67 times the original estimate, according to the CEGB,[33] and 4.07 times, according to the CEGB's critics.[34] The table below shows how the CEGB has maintained its optimism about Dungeness 'B' over the last two decades.

Table 2.1

Source	CEGB's estimated date	CEGB's description of that date
Statement 25.5.1965	1970	brought into service
CEGB Annual Report:		
1965/66 p. 86, 88	1971	completion
1966/67 p. 88	1971	completion
1967/68 p. 87	1971	completion
1968/69 p. 85	1972	completion
1969/70 p. 97	1974	completion

Table 2.1 (cont)

Source	CEGB's estimated date	CEGB's description of that date
1970/71 p. 95	1975	completion
1971/72 p. 92	1975	completion of erection
1972/73 p. 50	1976	completion of erection
1973/74 p. 74	1977	completion of erection
1974/75 p. 54	1977	completion of erection
1975/76 p. 46	1978	completion of erection
1976/77 p. 53	1979	completion of erection
1977/78 p. 61	1980	completion of erection
1978/79 p. 60	1981	probable completion of commissioning
1979/80 p. 18	1981	probable completion of commissioning
1980/81 p. 18	1982	probable completion of commissioning
1981/82 p. 20	1983	probable completion of commissioning
1982/83 p. 18	1984	probable completion of commissioning
1983/84 p. 29	1984	probable completion of commissioning

By 1969 four more AGR contracts had been let; three by the CEGB (at Hinkley Point 'B', Heysham and Hartlepool) and one by the SSEB (at Hunterston 'B'). Thus five large nuclear stations, each comprising two 600 or 660 MW reactors, were ordered on the basis of experience gained from the 30 MW prototype at Windscale and, disastrously,[35] three of the five stations were prototypes of different designs, as the three consortia then extant got a turn for a contract.[36] The Dungeness 'B' order was placed by the CEGB in September 1965, the Hinkley Point 'B' order in March 1967, and eighteen months later the Board decided to order Hartlepool and Heysham. All these stations over-ran severely during construction; the quickest, Hinkley Point 'B', commissioned late in 1978, 72 months behind schedule.[37] But its net design capacity was 1,250 MW[38] and its commissioned capacity was (and is) 1,040 MW.[39] Thus only 83 per cent of it has been commissioned. .

Not until 1972 did a new CEGB Chairman, Arthur Hawkins, in evidence to the House of Commons Select Committee on Science and Technology, feel able to say that the Board had been 'very strongly advised' by the AEA to choose the AGR for Dungeness 'B'.[40] A year later, before the same committee, he commented that the CEGB 'had been under somewhat pretty heavy persuasion' to select the AGR.[41] Commenting on the three different prototype AGRs then being built by the generating board, he said that the AGR record 'was a catastrophe we must not repeat',[42] sentiments shared by Dr Leslie Hannah, the Electricity Council's historian:[43]

> What cannot reasonably be disputed is that the series of decisions of the mid-1960s to invest prematurely and heavily in several different and inadequate designs of AGR stations represented one of the major blunders of British industrial policy.

Professor Burn puts much of the blame on the AEA:[44]

> The AEA made a long string of serious misjudgements. The assurance of those developing the AGR at Windscale in summer 1964 is breathtaking in retrospect. . . it was against the background of these extravagant, unsubstantiated, unjustified claims that the fateful decisions of 1965 and succeeding years, up to the end of 1970, were taken.

The out-turn was certainly a far cry from the AEA's 1961 expectations:[45] 'The main objective of the AGR is to reduce the capital cost of reactor installation.'

As things turned out, the effect on the CEGB's system of these 'fateful decisions' was not as serious as it might have been. Throughout the 1970s the rate of increase of demand for electricity continued to slow down,[46] and a large excess of capacity was retained throughout the decade, despite the failure of three of the four CEGB AGR stations to commission. If the demand forecasts, on which their construction had been justified, had proved accurate[47] —the CEGB's forecasts were, on its own admission, consistently 26 per cent optimistic[48] —there would have been supply disruptions to add to the problems of construction delays and tied-up capital. Conversely, had the four stations been built to time, the amount of spare generating capacity on the system would have become very much larger. No further station was ordered until Heysham II in 1981, and the UK was alone among industrialised countries in that it ordered no nuclear stations during the 1970s. A slowly-dawning realisation of the scale of the AGR disaster, and of the reality of demand trends, saw to that.

1972 and 1973
In 1972 the Select Committee on Science and Technology was considering the future of the consortia. In his evidence to the Committee of that year, the CEGB's chairman, Arthur Hawkins, did not give the impression that his organisation was keen to become the new champion of the atomic industry. He was unenthusiastic about the number of nuclear stations that the CEGB might want to order, and doubted whether it could provide enough work even for one consortium. His evidence contemplated the possibility of a much lower rate of increase in electricity consumption than had been assumed previously. As the annual growth rate in recent years had been only 3 per cent, the CEGB accepted that for planning purposes 3.5 per cent might be more appropriate than the traditional 5 per cent. At the lower figure, only three large generating stations would need to be built in the decade from 1972, of which only one would be nuclear (and that, thought Hawkins, might well be a fast breeder reactor). Even at 5 per cent only four new nuclear stations would be required. As far as reactor choice for the next programme was concerned—a topic also considered by the Select Committee—Hawkins made it clear that AEA pressure had been a factor in the Dungeness 'B' AGR decision, and that the CEGB regarded that reactor as being difficult to build and hastily adopted. The Board, in any case, was not interested in new capacity immediately, but when the time came it

might well favour the PWR on commercial and ease of construction grounds.[49]

By the following year, the CEGB's view had undergone a complete and extraordinary revision. Hawkins was now very clear about reactor choice, and his 1973 evidence marks the beginning of the CEGB's consistently expressed preference for the PWR.[50] Hawkins was clear about the mistakes of the past in ordering AGRs too quickly, from too many suppliers, and from an inadequate prototype: 'But it is ridiculous; you cannot up the size and the temperatures, the fuel ratings and things like that, and expect to get results on a commercial scale.'[51] The AGR programme was going badly wrong, the CEGB wanted a 'bread and butter'[52] reactor system, and it considered that the PWR would fit the bill.

The CEGB's second, and astonishing, change of view concerned the Board's future capacity requirements. The new estimate was that the Board would need to order nine large twin-reactor stations in the period 1974–79, and a further nine between 1980 and 1983—a total of perhaps 34 or 35 reactors—on the assumption of a 4.75–5.25 per cent annual growth rate.[53] There seemed to be no satisfactory explanation for the radically changed expectations (the calculations had been done before the 1973 oil price rise) and the Committee gave Hawkins a 'very rough hearing'.[54] But there was no other official source of demand projections available to the government or to the Select Committee. Whatever the reason for the CEGB's change of view (and the Committee failed to identify it) the new requirements made a decision about the choice of reactor for the next programme urgent.

The advice reaching the Select Committee, and the Minister, Peter Walker MP, was contradictory. The only thing that was agreed by almost everyone was that the next programme should not be based on the AGR, and the choice narrowed down to one between the pressurised water reactor (PWR), which the CEGB wanted, and the steam generating heavy water reactor (SGHWR), which the UKAEA (and some members of the Select Committee) wanted.[55] The SGHWR had been under development for a decade, and was derived from the collaborative war-time research in Canada. It is closely related to the Canadian CANDU reactor: in both, the use of heavy water as moderator enables natural uranium to be used as fuel. A 100 MW prototype was working at Winfrith by 1967.

It was a very difficult political decision, but two pieces of evidence given to the Select Committee may have been important. The first was by the Nuclear Installations Inspectorate, which said that it could well take two years to decide whether the PWR was suitable for a licence in the UK, with no guarantee of success. The second was from Sir Alan Cottrell, the Chief Scientific Advisor to the government and a metallurgist of international reputation, who at the beginning of his maverick relationship with the PWR expressed strong doubts about the integrity of its steel pressure vessel. It was left to Eric Varley MP, the new Labour Energy Minister, to take the decision in July 1974, and partly to provide 'a boost to British technology'[56] he opted for a 4,000 MW programme of SGHWR stations. Confusion reigned for a short period, and again falling rates of demand increase came to the rescue, enabling the implementation of the decision to be deferred for a year. The UKAEA panicked at the prospect of another failure, and in July 1976 told the Minister, by now Tony Benn MP, that it had changed its mind, and advised that the decision should after all be in favour of the PWR.

The PWR

Benn asked the National Nuclear Corporation (NNC), the last consortium, for its reaction. A ten-volume report[57] concluded that there was no case for the SGHWR, that the PWR should be chosen in the future, and that an interim order for an AGR was needed to keep the industry going. By this time the Hinkley Point 'B' and Hunterston 'B' AGRs were working, and Benn decided in January 1978 to countermand the SGHWR decision.[58] He authorised the CEGB and SSEB to order an AGR station each. But because of falling demand the authorisations were not taken up, and work did not start on the Heysham II and Torness power stations until 1981. These were the first orders for the UK nuclear industry since those placed in 1969. Benn also encouraged the industry 'to establish the PWR as a valid option'. In December

1979 the new Secretary of State, David Howell MP, endorsed this statement and made his one-a-year-for-ten-years announcement previously quoted.[59] In 1981 the CEGB applied for permission to build the first PWR on its site at Sizewell, adjacent to the existing Magnox station and on land for which permission to build an AGR had been granted in 1969, and permission to build an SGHWR in 1974.

The Public Inquiry opened in January 1983, a decade after the CEGB had first made plain its preference for the PWR. But in the intervening years the American reactor market had almost collapsed (see Chapter 3), and international competition for PWR orders had become intense. It was clear that the prospect for British PWR export sales was slim and the domestic market, as usual, had not expanded as foreseen. The accident at Three Mile Island in March 1979 had discredited the PWR technology, and had caused American safety standards to be considerably tightened: there was evidence of a renewed American interest in gas-cooled reactors because of their inherently safer characteristics.[60] Ironically by late 1983 it was clear that construction at Torness and Heysham II was going well, and that many of the design and construction problems of the AGR had, at last, been overcome. A body of opinion, which included the South of Scotland Electricity Board, put forward the view that Britain should stay with the AGR. The cost of supporting two major reactor systems, in the context of a much smaller reactor ordering programme than that envisaged in 1979, would be prohibitive, and in any case the Heysham II/Torness design of AGR was price-competitive with the PWR proposed for Sizewell 'B' (see Chapter 7).

The political consensus that nuclear power has enjoyed throughout its history is remarkable. From Magnox to PWR, via AGR, HTR and SGHWR, the British government has remained unwaveringly pro-nuclear, irrespective of political complexion. In 1963 the AEA's Deputy Chairman said:[61]

The momentum which the large costs of nuclear projects necessarily engenders makes frequent changes in major policy difficult and inadvisable.

43

Nearly two decades later his words were echoed by Sir Francis Tombs, writing in 1981, soon after his resignation as Chairman of the Electricity Council:[62]

Most important is the question of institutional momentum, which requires an atmosphere of confidence and determination, and a stable political and industrial climate.

Dr Hannah, whose sponsored history *Engineers, Managers and Politicians* deals with the first fifteen years after nationalisation (1948–63), has commented:[63]

The nuclear power programme has attracted a disproportionate amount of attention for an energy source which played a tiny part in Britain's overall energy economy, a reflection perhaps of the lurid attractions of failure, for few projects can display such a large gap between aspirations and achievements over the timescale of the 1950s and 1960s.

NOTES AND REFERENCES

The Official Histories of the AEA and the Electricity Council do not cover the period discussed in this chapter (except for the final chapter of Dr Hannah's *Engineers, Managers and Politicians*). Primary sources, which are the White Papers, Hansard (House of Commons), the reports and minutes of the Select Committee, the UKAEA journal *Atom,* and CEGB and AEA official publications, are supplemented by two historical studies of nuclear power:

Professor Duncan Burn *Nuclear Power and the Energy Crisis: Politics and the Atomic Industry* (Macmillan, 1978), and Professor Roger Williams *The Nuclear Power Decisions: British Politics 1953–1978* (Croom Helm, 1980).

These are referenced below by the authors' surname.

1. White Paper Cmnd. 9389, 1955.
2. White Paper Cmnd. 2335, 1964.

3. CEGB Annual Report 1969/70, para. 187.
4. *Atom* no. 157, p. 297.
5. CEGB Annual Report 1973/74, para. 224.
6. Hansard, 2 May 1974, col. 1354.
7. Hansard, 10 July 1974, cols. 1360–1366.
8. Hansard, 18 December 1979, col. 288.
9. CEGB Statistical Yearbook, 1983/84, Table 5. See Chapter 5.
10. *Ibid.*, Table 6.
11. House of Commons Select Committee on Science and Technology, Session 1972/73, Q. 284.
12. See *Atom* no. 333, pp. 3–7.
13. House of Commons Select Committee on Nationalised Industries, Session 1962/63, Q. 1025.
14. Burn, p. 118.
15. Williams, pp. 49–50.
16. *Atom* no. 108, p. 202.
17. France also chose Westinghouse, but now manufacture their own PWRs.
18. Williams, p. 313.
19. White Paper Cmnd. 2335, 1964.
20. White Paper Cmnd. 2798, 1965.
21. See *Atom* no. 107, pp. 175–187 (SSBA/S/33).
22. Burn, p. 156.
23. *The Economist,* 5 September 1964.
24. Burn, p. 121, Williams, p. 139.
25. House of Commons Select Committee on Science and Technology, Session 1968/69, Q. 623.
26. Burn, p. 163.
27. APC = Atomic Power Construction Ltd.
    TNPG = The Nuclear Power Group.
28. SSEB and CEGB Annual Reports for 1982/83, p. 15 and para. 59 respectively.
29. House of Commons Select Committee on Science and Technology, Session 1966/67, Q. 898.
30. But the corollary was that the AEA had to be able to supply enriched fuel. In 1965 a £13.5m expenditure was approved for reactivating and modernising the military uranium enrichment plant at Capenhurst (Hansard, 9 December 1965, cols. 323–328).
31. Hansard, 25 May 1965, cols. 237–238. The Hon. Gentleman was John Peyton MP, who had asked: 'Will not (the Minister) now give some facts? Can he tell the House how much cheaper this base load power will be and what are the economic and technical advantages to which he referred?'
32. Both quoted in *Atom* no. 104, pp. 100–101.
33. CEGB/P/8 (ADD 6), Table 1.
34. Professor J.W. Jeffery, one of the CEGB's most effective critics, gives and derives this figure in his SSBA/P/1 (ADD 1), p. 16.

35. Mr Con Allday, BNFL's Chairman, said of Dungeness 'B': 'Not a complete disaster, but it was certainly a disaster.' (Windscale inquiry transcript, day 5, p. 27F.)

36. Hartlepool and Heysham I are closely similar designs, as are Hinkley Point 'B' and SSEB's Hunterston 'B'. Heysham II and Torness are derived from this latter design.

37. Hinkley Point 'B' took 98 months to build from 'Start main foundations' to 'Synchronisation' (CEGB/P/8 (ADD 4 REV), Table 3). This was an over-run of 46 months, on a target of 52. There is a 'representative period of 6 months between synchronisation and commissioning' (CEGB/P/8 para. 35) but, at Hinkley, commissioning followed synchronisation by 32 months (letter from CEGB to Frank Hooley MP, 27 March 1981, reproduced in SSBA/P/1 (ADD 1) pp. 17–18). If the target (i.e. contract) period was to synchronisation, the station commissioned 72 months, or 132 per cent, late. If target was to commissioning, it commissioned 78 months, or 150 per cent late. Hinkley Point 'B' is the only CEGB AGR to have completed interim commissioning by mid-1985. But so far, only 1040 MW of its 1,250 MW design capacity, or 83 per cent, has been commissioned. See Chapter 3 for the consequences in lost production.

38. See Chapter 3, table 3.7 note (a).

39. CEGB Statistical Yearbook 1983/84, Table 5. See Chapter 5.

40. House of Commons Select Committee on Science and Technology, Session 1972/73, Q. 154.

41. *Ibid.*, Session 1973/74, Q. 284.

42. *Ibid.*

43. Hannah, *op. cit.*, p. 285.

44. Burn, pp. 152–153.

45. *Atom* no. 59, p. 23. The proponents of the PWR have similar hopes, see CEGB/P/8, Table 21.

46. In 1973/74 electricity sales fell, as compared to the previous year, for the first time in the industry's 100-year history. It happened again in 1975/76, and again for four years in succession, from 1979/80 to 1982/83. (CEGB Statistical Yearbook 1982/83, Table 2). Sales in 1983/84 increased, but did not reach those of the peak year of 1978/79 (Statistical Yearbook 1983/84, Table 5). See Chapter 5, figure 5.1.

47. However, the CEGB's order for the Hartlepool AGR 'was largely justified not by the increase of load estimates but by our intention to withdraw some 1,300 MW of usable but obsolescent plant'. (Reference 25 at Q. 659.) This seems to have been an early version of the system saving argument developed for Sizewell 'B'.

48. Day 11, page 46C; CEGB/P/4 (ADD 2), p. 2.

49. Reference 40, report para. 43 and Q. 103–160.

50. Reference 41, Q. 286–432.

51. Reference 41, Q. 295. This statement is an extraordinary volte-

face, rendering 'ridiculous' the CEGB's 1965 Appraisal of Dungeness 'B'.

52. Reference 41, Q. 287.
53. Reference 41, Q. 248, 252-255, summarised in Hansard, 2 May 1974, col. 1423.
54. Reference 41, Q. 433.
55. The Select Committee Chairman, Arthur Palmer MP, referred to the SGHWR—which he supported—as 'that poor lonely reactor that goes round and round'. (Burn, p. 228.)
56. Hansard, 10 July 1974, col. 1364.
57. 'The Choice of Thermal Reactor Systems', NNC, 1977.
58. *Atom* no. 257, p. 56.
59. Hansard, 18 December 1979, col. 288.
60. See for example *Science*, 18 May 1984, pp. 699-701 (TCPA/S/274) and 'Nuclear Power in an Age of Uncertainty', US Congress (Office of Technological Assessment) 1984, pp. 99-103 (SSEB/S/2).
61. *Atom* no. 88, p. 40.
62. *Atom* no. 296, p. 162.
63. Hannah, *op. cit.*, p. 316 at note 1.

CHAPTER 3

SUCCESS OR FAILURE? A RE-EVALUATION OF NUCLEAR POWER IN BRITAIN[1] AND THE US

Britain

The first British nuclear programme was announced in 1955, so there is now 30 years experience of building and operating power reactors in this country. The first part of this chapter examines the performance of those reactors in terms of their ability to generate electricity; it assesses how much output capacity (MW) has been provided, and for how long (months and years). It then examines the expected capacity of the reactors that was the basis of investment approval, the capacity that the nuclear designers said would be available and the time for which it would be available. The out-turn performance is compared with the expected performance and a measure obtained of the extent of the success or failure of the nuclear industry in its own terms. The object is to obtain a numerical comparison of the planned performance of British nuclear power with its achieved performance in providing electricity generating capacity.

At December 1984 there were nine commissioned twin-reactor nuclear stations on the CEGB system; eight Magnox and one AGR. The shortfall between their design performance and actual performance in terms of the provision of generating capacity has been caused by two factors. Firstly, every one took longer to build than intended, and secondly they were all (except the very first, at Berkeley) downrated so that, even when built, they were not capable of generating as much electricity as they were designed to. The average construction overrun for the 9 stations was a little less than 20 months, and their average downrating is 139 MW, or about 28 per cent.

Those readers who are prepared to take the author's arithmetic as read will find the conclusion to this section

49

on page 60.

Quantification

The first part of this chapter is exclusively concerned with the capacity of generating stations, or their ability to produce electricity. In the interests of keeping the calculations as simple as possible, it is not concerned with the actual amount of electricity produced. The unit of capacity is the megawatt (MW); here it is used (in accordance with CEGB practice) to mean the capacity of a station net of its own consumption. This is sometimes referred to as the sent-out capacity, or MW so, and sometimes as MW net.

To measure the provision of capacity over time it is necessary to quantify both MW and months, and so the unit 'MW-months' is used.[2] 1 MW-month represents 1 MW of capacity available or unavailable for 1 month. The shortfall in the nuclear programmes is arrived at by comparing the designed or expected MW-months with the actual or out-turn MW-months, both measured until 31 December 1984.

The nuclear industry uses a range·of different definitions of when work starts on a nuclear power station site, and when it ends (see Chapter 5 note 24). In its evidence to the Sizewell inquiry the CEGB used 'synchronisation' as its preferred end-date, which it defined as 'the datum point for the completion of construction'.[3] 'However, it is possible to synchronise a unit without all the support plant being built and commissioned. A unit in this condition could synchronise but could not generate significant power.'[4] The Board defined 'commissioning' as running a unit at full power for 72 consecutive hours,[5] but noted that this has been impossible to achieve in recent years. The CEGB therefore defined the 'less onerous' standard of interim rating commissioning, which is achieved when a unit has run at at least 60 per cent of its design rating for 72 hours.[6] This interim commissioning is considered to follow synchronisation by 'a representative period of 6 months'.[7] Data on power station construction periods were given to the inquiry by the Board as months to synchronisation. In the calculations that follow it has been assumed that the commissioning period was a further 6 months (except at Wylfa and Hinkley

Point 'B' where it was a much longer period, and at Dungeness 'B', Hartlepool and Heysham I where it is presently taking much longer).

A. Magnox
i. Construction overruns
Some Magnox stations were built without a contract being signed. 'It was not unusual for a project to commence and in some cases be completed based on a CEGB Letter of Intent rather than a formal contract.'[8] Those completed without a contract, and therefore without a formal target period, were Berkeley, Bradwell and Trawsfynydd.

Table 3.1 Magnox capacity from scheduled start-up[9]
(i.e. what should have been available to December 1984)

	Target to synchronisation + 6 months	Months to end 1984	Design capacity (MW)	MW-months
Berkeley	Jan 1962	275	275	75,625
Bradwell	Jan 1962[a]	275	300	82,500
Hinkley Point 'A'	Dec 1962	264	500	132,000
Trawsfynydd	Jan 1964[b]	251	500	125,500
Dungeness 'A'	Mar 1965	237	550	130,350
Sizewell 'A'	Dec 1965	228	580	132,240
Oldbury	Dec 1966	216	600	129,600
Wylfa	Mar 1969	189	1180	223,020
				1,030,835

Notes to Table 3.1
CEGB/P/8 (**ADD** 4 REV) Table 2 gives contract periods to synchronisation, to which the 6 months 'representative' commissioning period has been added, except:
   a. CEGB Annual Report 1958/59 pages 154–155 gives 'first generating set in operation' in 1961. July 1961, plus 6 months, assumed.
   b. The same source indicates 1963. July 1963, plus 6 months assumed.

However, target dates in each case were not met, and the scheduled start-ups were delayed because of construction delays or overruns.

Table 3.2 Magnox capacity from actual start-up
(i.e. after construction delays)

	Actual synchronisation +6 months	*Months to end 1984*	*Design capacity (MW)*	*MW-months*
Berkeley	Dec 1962	264	275	72,600
Bradwell	Jan 1963	263	300	78,900
Hinkley Point 'A'	Aug 1965	232	500	116,000
Trawsfynydd	Jul 1965	233	500	116,500
Dungeness 'A'	Mar 1966	225	550	123,750
Sizewell 'A'	Jul 1966	221	580	128,180
Oldbury	May 1968	199	600	119,400
Wylfa	Apr 1972[a]	152	1180	179,360
				934,690

Notes to Table 3.2
CEGB/P/8 (ADD 4 REV) Table 2 gives synchronisation dates, to which the 6 months 'representative' commissioning period has been added, except:
  a. Wylfa did not complete interim commissioning until 1972/73 (CEGB Statistical Yearbook 1972/73 Table 18), but synchronisation is given in CEGB/P/8 (ADD 4 REV) Table 2 as Jan 1971. Thus, even if 1 April 1972 is assumed for the commissioning date, commissioning must have followed synchronisation by at least 15 months, and this figure, rather than 6 months, has been added.

The effect of the construction delays at the Magnox power station sites may be quantified by comparing the MW-months that should have been available if construction targets had been met with the MW-months that were actually available.

Table 3.3 The effect of Magnox construction delays
(assuming no downrating)

	MW-months
What should have been available to generate electricity (Table 3.1)	1,030,835
What was available (Table 3.2)	934,690
Shortfall =	96,145[10]

ii. Magnox downrating

The output from all the Magnox stations (except Berkeley) was reduced because they were found to be suffering from internal corrosion. Their output temperatures (and therefore their capacities) were lowered in two stages, and announcements were made in Parliament by the responsible Minister in October and December 1969.[11] With three exceptions, the calculations below assume that the full downrating was effective from 1st December 1969. The exceptions are Sizewell 'A', Oldbury and Wylfa, because these stations had not completed commissioning when the corrosion problem was discovered. Sizewell 'A' and Oldbury commissioned at a capacity lower than their design capacity, and were then further downrated in 1969. The design rating of Wylfa, which was still some three years from commissioning in 1969, was reduced before construction was complete. Thus these three stations have never operated at their design capacities.

Table 3.4 Magnox downrating
(all units MW)

	Design capacity	Com-missioned capacity	Dec 1969 downrating	Later downrating	1984[a] capacity
Berkeley[b]	275	276	—	—	276
Bradwell	300	300	50	5[c]	245
Hinkley Point 'A'	500	500	40	30[d]	430
Trawsfynydd	500	500	110	—	390

53

Table 3.4 (cont)

	Design capacity	Com- missioned capacity	Dec 1969 downrating	Later downrating	1984[a] capacity
Dungeness 'A'	550	550	140	—	410
Sizewell 'A'	580	500	80	—	420
Oldbury	600	546[e]	112	—	434
Wylfa	1180	840	—	—	840

Notes to Table 3.4
a. See 1983/84 CEGB Statistical Yearbook Table 7.
b. The only British civil nuclear station to have achieved, and exceeded, its design output.
c. Announced in 1979/80 CEGB Statistical Yearbook.
d. Announced in 1977/78 CEGB Statistical Yearbook.
e. Includes 16 MW added in 1974/75, and 18 MW added in 1982/83.

The next Table converts the downratings to MW-months calculated until the end of December 1984, using 1st December 1969 as the date of downrating except as noted.

Table 3.5 Magnox downrating as MW-months to December 1984

	Total down- rating (MW)[a]	MW-months
Berkeley	+1[b]	+264
Bradwell	55[c]	9,365
Hinkley Point 'A'	70[d]	9,850
Trawsfynydd	110	19,910
Dungeness 'A'	140	25,340
Sizewell 'A'	160[e]	32,160
Oldbury	166[f]	35,330
Wylfa	340[g]	51,680
	1040	Shortfall = 183,371

Notes to Table 3.5
a. Figures obtained by subtracting the last column from the first in Table 3.4.
b. Berkeley uprating assumed to start in December 1962, 6 months after synchronisation.
c. See Table 3.4, note c. Mid-year (October 1979) assumed.
d. See Table 3.4, note d. October 1977 assumed.
e. Sizewell 'A' commissioned at 80 MW less than design capacity, date assumed to be July 1966 (Table 3.2). It was downrated by a further 80 MW in the 1969 downrating (see note 11).
f. Oldbury commissioned at 88 MW less than design capacity, date assumed to be May 1968 (Table 3.2). It was downrated by a further 12 MW in the 1969 downrating. It was then uprated twice, (see Table 3.4, note e). Mid year (October) assumed in both instances.
g. From April 1972 (the earliest possible commissioning date, see Table 3.2, note a).

iii. Magnox—summary
The Magnox capacity that should have been available to generate electricity, in MW-months, was calculated in Table 3.1. If shortfalls due to late construction (Table 3.3) and downrating (Table 3.5) are together subtracted from it, the relationship between the capacity designed and paid for, and the capacity actually provided, can be calculated.

Table 3.6 The ratio of design capacity to out-turn capacity

		MW-months
Design capacity		1,030,835
deduct: delay	96,145	
downrating	183,371	
	279,516	279,516
Achievement		751,319

The success of the attempt to provide electricity generating capacity by means of the Magnox programme may be represented as a percentage.

$$\frac{751,319}{1,030,835} \quad X \quad 100 \quad = \quad \underline{72.9 \text{ per cent}}$$

B. Advanced Gas-cooled Reactors
In a similar way the construction overruns and downratings of the CEGB's original four AGR stations can be examined, and a conclusion drawn about their efficiency in providing generating capacity. Data for the fifth AGR, Heysham II, are not included—it was started in 1981 and is due to commission in 1988.[12]

i. AGR construction overruns

Table 3.7 AGR capacity from scheduled start-up
(i.e. what should have been available to December 1984)

	Target to synchronisation +6 months	Months to end 1984	Design capacity (MW)[a]	MW-months
Dungeness 'B'	Nov 1970	169	1200	202,800
Hinkley Point 'B'	Oct 1972	146	1250	182,500
Hartlepool	Mar 1974	129	1250	161,250
Heysham I	Mar 1976	105	1250	131,250
				677,800

Notes to Table 3.7
a. The earliest figures available to the author have been quoted. Dungeness 'B' has been consistently quoted at 1200 MW, in CEGB Statistical Yearbooks from 1967 to 1983/84 'Plant under construction' tables, except in 1978/79 which was presumably a misprint.

Hinkley Point 'B' first appeared in the 1968 Yearbook (Table 13) at 1,320 MW, including 4 gas turbines at 17.5 MW each. The design capacity of the reactors is thus 1,250 MW. In 1972/73 the gas turbine ratings were reduced to 17 MW, giving the reactors 1,252, which has been the figure quoted ever since.

The Hartlepool and Heysham I reactors first appear (1970 and 1972 respectively) at the same 1,250 MW rating as Hinkley Point 'B', and also change to 1,252 MW in 1972/73. In recent years the capacity of the gas turbines at Hartlepool and Heysham I have fluctuated wildly; because total station output (gas turbines + reactors) has been constant at 1,320 MW, the capacity of the un-completed reactors has also fluctuated. In 1981/82 the reactors at both stations were quoted at 926 MW, in 1982/83 at 1,015 MW and in 1983/84 at 1,050 MW. (Statistical Yearbooks Tables 13, 13 and 14 respectively.)

(NB: Prior to 1972/73, the title of the Yearbooks gave only the second year of the financial year to which they referred.)

Hinkley Point 'B' was the only CEGB AGR station not listed as being 'under construction at 31 March 1984'.[13] The position had not changed by December; at year end it was alone in having completed interim commissioning.

Table 3.8 AGR capacity from actual start-up
(i.e. after construction delays)

	Commissioning date	Months to end 1984	Design capacity (MW)	MW-months
Dungeness 'B'	—	—	1200	—
Hinkley Point 'B'				
1st reactor	1976/77[a]	99	625	61,875
2nd reactor	Oct 1978[b]	75	625	46,875
Hartlepool	—	—	1250	—
Heysham I	—	—	1250	—
				108,750

Notes to Table 3.8
a. CEGB Statistical Yearbook 1976/77. October 1976 assumed.

b. Date given in a letter from CEGB to Frank Hooley MP, 27 March 1981, quoted in SSBA/P/1 (ADD 1), pages 17–18. 1st October assumed.

The effect of the construction delays at the AGR sites may be quantified by comparing the MW-months that should have been available if start-ups had been achieved on time with the MW-months that were actually available.

Table 3.9 The effect of AGR construction delays
(assuming no downrating)

	MW-months
What should have been available to generate electricity (Table 3.7)	677,800
What was available (Table 3.8)	108,750
Shortfall =	569,050[14]

ii. AGR downrating

Although Hinkley Point 'B' completed interim commissioning in October 1978, 28 months after synchronisation and 72 months after the intended date of commissioning,[15] its design capacity did not commission at that date. At December 1984 only 1,040 MW had commissioned; the difference constitutes the shortfall in capacity, or downrating.

Table 3.10 AGR downrating as MW-months to December 1984
(all figures refer only to Hinkley Point 'B')

	Capacity (MW)	Commissioning date	MW-months
a. Design capacity	1250	(see Table 3.8)	108,750

Table 3.10 (cont)

	Capacity (MW)	Commissioning date	MW-months	
b. Actual capacity	400	1976/77[a]	39,600	
	400	Oct 1978[b]	30,000	
	200	1979/80[a]	12,600	
	40	1980/81[a]	2,040	
	1040 1040		84,240	84,240
	212		Shortfall =	24,510

Notes to Table 3.10
a. See relevant CEGB Statistical Yearbook. October assumed in each case.
b. See Table 3.8, note b.

iii. AGR—summary
The AGR capacity that should have been available to generate electricity, in MW-months, was calculated in Table 3.7. If shortfalls due to late construction (Table 3.9) and downrating (Table 3.10) are together subtracted from it, the relationship between the capacity designed and paid for, and the capacity actually provided, can be calculated.

Table 3.11 The ratio of design capacity to out-turn capacity

		MW-months
Design capacity		677,800
deduct: delay	569,050	
downrating	24,510	
	593,560	593,560
Achievement		84,240

The success of the attempt to provide electricity generating capacity by means of the AGR programme may be represented as a percentage.

$$\frac{84,240}{677,600} \times 100 = \underline{12.4 \text{ per cent}}$$

C. Summary

The relationship between the CEGB nuclear capacity, both Magnox and AGR, that should have been available, to that which has been provided, can now be calculated.

Table 3.12 CEGB nuclear achievement in MW-months
(This table sums the figures in Tables 3.6 and 3.11)

			MW-months
Total design capacity			1,708,635
deduct:	total delay	665,195	
	total downrating	207,881	
		873,076	873,076
			835,559

The success of the attempt to provide electricity generating capacity by means of nuclear power on the CEGB system may be represented as a percentage.

$$\frac{835,559}{1,708,635} \times 100 = \underline{48.9 \text{ per cent}}$$

These figures and percentages do not measure the success of the CEGB's nuclear stations in generating electricity, but rather their success in providing generating capability. No power station can operate at 100 per cent load year in and year out; refuelling losses, and time off load for maintenance and breakdown, are inevitable. These losses are reflected in a percentage figure called the load factor, which is the ratio between the electricity produced by a station and its theoretical maximum capability. The load factor expected from the Magnox stations varied from 75 per cent to more than 85 per

60

cent, according to source and date of estimate.[16] It was hoped that AGR load factors would be similar, but Hinkley Point 'B' achieved only 67.9 per cent of its design rating in 1983/84.[17]

The CEGB publishes the amount of electricity produced by each of its stations in the annual Statistical Yearbooks. When the Board compares what was actually produced with the theoretical maximum, in order to arrive at the load factor for each station, it ignores the two items quantified above; the years of construction delay and the design capacity lost by downrating. In its evidence to the Sizewell inquiry, the Welsh Anti-Nuclear Alliance (WANA)[18] reworked the load factor calculations to take them into account. As in the calculations above, the reworking assumed that the stations should have started production on time, and at their design capacity. Load factors calculated on that basis could then be compared with the target load factor of 75-85 per cent to provide some measure of the return on the British investment in nuclear power.

WANA calculated Magnox and AGR load factors both for individual years and on a cumulative basis. Its evidence—not disputed in cross-examination—was that the Magnox reactors as a group reached a peak load factor on the cumulative basis of 50.3 per cent in 1980. Figures have stayed close to 50 per cent since then, but if all the CEGB nuclear stations are considered as a group, the load factor has been falling steadily since 1970 because of the disastrous failure to commission the AGRs. In 1983/84 it was 34 per cent, with that of the AGRs alone between 7 and 8 per cent.

The United States

A similar exercise was performed in respect of the PWR reactors sold in America by the Westinghouse Corporation, the major US manufacturer and the vendor of the Sizewell 'B' design. Their performance has been comparable to that of the British reactors. In America stations have been built late, almost without exception, although they have not been downrated. The larger the reactor the longer the delay: the average construction time for reactors of 1,100 MW and over—the group into which Sizewell 'B' falls—is now 134 months, exactly three years longer than the CEGB's central estimate for Sizewell 'B', and four and a half years longer than its target construction period.[19] Only three of the 36 large Westinghouse PWRs have been built in less than the CEGB's central estimate period.

If load factors are calculated for this group of large reactors using the scheduled start date of operation rather than the actual date of operation, the cumulative figure to the end of 1983 is 9 per cent. This should be compared with the average scheduled load factor of 80 per cent for the American reactors, or with the CEGB's 64 per cent expectation for Sizewell 'B'. If load factors are calculated for all Westinghouse PWRs, of all sizes, the average is 28 per cent, again to be compared with the expected 80 or 64 per cent.

The magazines *Nucleonics Week* and *Nuclear Engineering International* are the sources of the American statistics. The former commented, in relation to those statistics:[20]

> Our purpose of showing the unit's performance in relation to what the seller and buyer felt the unit was bought, designed, built and intended to do.

If the performance of nuclear stations is calculated according to the performance that vendors promised and investors expected at the time of the order, nuclear stations on both sides of the Atlantic have proved to be a notoriously bad investment. In Britain the industry is both nationalised and a monopoly, and the effect of the nuclear failure has been primarily reflected in energy costs. In America, the home of competitive capitalism, the technology has been abandoned.

It is difficult to overstate the depth of the nuclear crisis in the United States. *Time* magazine commented in February 1984:

> Says Robert Scherer, the Chairman of Georgia Power and head of the US Committee for Energy Awareness, a pro-nuclear group; 'No utility executive in the country would consider ordering one today—unless he wanted to be certified or committed.'

By 1982 American utilities had cancelled 100 nuclear reactors from all vendors—45 per cent of the capacity that had been ordered. The first cancellation took place in 1972.[21] The last reactor order in the United States that has not subsequently been cancelled was placed in 1973; the last export order, for four modest 800 MW reactors to South Korea, was placed in 1978. Of the 95 non-military domestic orders for Westing-house PWRs, 37 had been cancelled by May 1985, 2 deferred and a further 2 suspended. These cancellations have been concentrated among the larger machines, and half of the orders for reactors of 1,100 MW net capacity or greater have now been cancelled. The capacity of these larger cancellations amounts to 26 Sizewell 'B's. The American reactor manu-facturers, among which Westinghouse is dominant, have enormous economic resilience,[22] but the orders for Sizewell 'B' and the subsequent stations must be necessary for the survival of the industry, if not in direct financial terms then in terms of international approval and acceptability. It is interesting to note that Westinghouse Reactor Division is collaborating with Mitsubishi to design and market the Advanced PWR, the APWR, in an attempt to break the dead-lock. The APWR is not the reactor proposed for Sizewell 'B' (see Chapter 6).

The financial costs of some of the recent cancellations are huge, and a measure of the reaction against nuclear energy in America. The Marble Hill 1 and 2 reactors in Indiana were cancelled, half built, because the budget had risen from $1,400m to $7,000m; $2,500m was written off. The Zimmer station in Ohio, started in 1969 and 97 per cent complete, is being converted to coal firing at a cost of $350m. The biggest financial failure of all, and the best known of the American nuclear economic disasters, is the collapse of the Westing-house Public Power Supply System, known to its customers (whose electricity prices have trebled) as Whoops. Situated in a state with immeasurable hydro-electricity resources, the WPPSS consortium decided in 1971 to build five nuclear power stations at an estimated cost of $6,700m. The last estimate, in May 1981, was of $23,800m plus a debt servicing cost over 30 years of $87,000m, giving a total cost of $110 billion. In January 1982 work stopped on plants 4 and 5; the utility could not afford to mothball them. In April number 1 reactor was mothballed for 5 years and in June work on number 3 was stopped for three years; it was 64 per cent complete. Only number 2 reactor, said to be 98 per cent complete, survived. WPPSS defaulted on its payments in July 1983, work stopped on all the reactors, and none is complete. The affair is bogged down in the courts, with banks, bond holders, utilities and customers all involved. It was caused, essentially, by a combination of spiralling capital costs and an over-estimate of increases in electricity demand. The CEGB's case for Sizewell 'B', too, is predicated on stable capital costs and rising demand (see Chapter 5).

Since WPPSS, the utilities that have stopped building new generating plant are those best able to keep prices down, and those that the banks look upon with most favour. Despite the cancellations, there is still an excess capacity of 36 per cent in America as a whole, and many major utilities such as San Diego Gas and Electric, and Consolidated Edison, have adopted a policy of buying in spare electricity from other utilities or from Canada.[23] This option is open to the CEGB. There is a 1 GW transmission link with Scotland, a country which will have an excess capacity of more than 100 per cent when Torness is commissioned in 1988. A 2 GE link with France is under construction and will be operational in 1986 —France, with its huge nuclear programme, is actively seeking to export electricity to its neighbours. Exploitation of these resources, which together could supply the equivalent of 2.7 Sizewell 'B's, would enable us to defer a decision about new plant construction until a decision was actually required. By that time, some of the uncertainties discussed in Part 2 may have been resolved.

NOTES AND REFERENCES

1. No attempt is made to examine the SSEB's stations at Hunterston.
2. The industry sometimes uses 'reactor-years', but MW-months reflects the 4.5-fold difference in nuclear design capacities, from 275 to 1,250 MW.
3. CEGB/P/8, para. 28
4. *Ibid.*, para. 29.
5. *Ibid.*, para. 29.
6. *Idem.* The CEGB comments: 'It is believed that no other major utility uses a similar definition of commissioning.'
7. *Ibid.*, para. 35.

8. *Ibid.*, para. 23.
9. In this and all Tables in this chapter, when an event is reported as taking place in an accounting year, e.g. 1979/80, the assumed date is mid-year, e.g. 1 October 1979. When the calendar year is given, 1 July of that year is assumed.
10. It is interesting to note that the design capacity of the Sizewell 'B' PWR station is 1,155 MW, and its lifetime for appraisal purposes 35 years. This gives an expectation of 485,100 MW-months.
11. Hansard, 13 October 1969, col. 38 and 1 December 1969, col. 188–189. 5½ months after the first of these announcements to the House of Commons, and 4 months after the second, the CEGB Statistical Yearbook 1969/70 quoted the un-downrated capacities at its Table 6. The Yearbook for 1970/71 published the downrated figures. The calculations assume downrating effective 1 December 1969.
12. CEGB Annual Report 1983/84, Table 17.
13. *Ibid.*
14. See note 10.
15. Assuming that the 'representative' commissioning period was intended. See CEGB/P/8 (ADD 4 REV), Table 3.
16. 1963–'An 85% load factor would be a conservative estimate'
    Sir William Cook, *Atom* no. 78, p. 77,
    1965–'. . . More than 80% of the hours in every year'
    Sir William Penney, *Atom* no. 99, p. 9,
    1968–'. . . the design intention of a lifetime load factor of 75%'
    Silverleaf and Weeks, *Atom* no. 141, p. 161.
17. CEGB/P/8 (ADD 11), Table 6.
18. WANA/P/2. See day 145, and day 313, pp. 2–17.
19. Day 313, p. 15. CEGB estimates taken to be 98 and 80 months respectively, to include 8 months site preparation.
20. *Nucleonics Week*, 20 January 1983, p. 12.
21. 'Nuclear Plant Cancellations: Causes, Costs and Consequences', USDOE. April 1983 (CEGB/S/785).
22. *Nuclear Inc* by Mark Hertsegaard (Pantheon, New York, 1983) is good on the structure and resilience of the US reactor industry.
23. *Business Week*, 29 October 1984, pp. 64–68.

PART 2

THE SIZEWELL INQUIRY

'This inquiry is undoubtedly of enormous value to the Board. We are better for it. . . that I believe. We may not be brilliant now, but we were worse before.'

(Senior CEGB witness, day 136, p. 42B)

CHAPTER 4

SNAPE MALTINGS

A dozen miles north of Aldeburgh the extraordinary shifting coastline of this part of Suffolk submerged the large medieval town of Dunwich, where sometimes, after closing time on still summer evenings, the bells of the town's eight or nine drowned churches can faintly be heard. But south of Aldeburgh the sea has added, not taken away, and a shingle spit runs a dozen miles down the coast, a mile wide at Orford Ness but only a few yards wide at its beginnings just below the town, and at its end. The River Alde, running sea-wards from the village of Snape, is prevented from reaching its destination by these few yards of shingle and turned inland again, and is forced to run parallel to the sea down to Shingle Street.

This is the place where a planning inquiry was held into the CEGB's application to build a pressurised water reactor at Sizewell, during the two years 1983 and 1984. The reason that the inquiry was held there, rather than somewhere more easily accessible by public transport, is that natural justice dictates that the hearings of a public inquiry into a planning application should be held reasonably close to the site for which application is made. Local people, it is assumed, are those most directly affected and their ease of access to the hearings should be a prime consideration. Snape is only ten or eleven miles from Sizewell and halls large enough to seat the hundreds expected to attend, with adequate and adjacent office space, meeting rooms and car parking are few and far between in East Anglia. Despite the lack of public transport, and despite the appeals of those who wanted to take part but who lived some distance away that it should be held in Ipswich or even in London, the Maltings was chosen as the venue. Two considerations may have been significant; firstly that the initial estimates of the inquiry's duration were about nine months, so the inconvenience of Snape was not going to last very long, and secondly that the Aldeburgh Festival Foundation was in a parlous financial state, and a grateful recipient of the Inquiry's rent.

But this was no ordinary planning inquiry. It was to serve a special purpose, going far beyond the examination of local environmental and social effects that constitute the concern of a normal inquiry. In July 1981 the Secretary of State for Energy made a statement concerning the proposed power station:[1]

. . . On the information so far available to me it appears that the following points will be relevant:

a. The CEGB's requirement for the power station in terms of the need for secure and economic electricity supply and having regard to the Government's long-term energy policy;

b. The safety features relevant to the design, construction and operation of the station and in particular the views of the Nuclear Installations Inspectorate as the licensing authority;

c. The arrangements for waste management, in the light of the views of the authorising Departments;

d. The implications of the proposed development (including both construction and operation) for:
1. agriculture and fisheries
2. local employment
3. water supply and disposal
4. transport requirements
5. coast protection
6. housing and public services generally
7. local amenities and in particular areas of special landscape value or nature conservation interest.

Although this statement did not define the subjects to be discussed at the inquiry it was a clear indication that the Secretary of State expected a very wide-ranging discussion of the issues involved, a discussion that would encompass the CEGB's economic case for the station, the safety of the

PWR design that the Board wanted to build, and the controversial area of radioactive waste management, in addition to those factors that might be of particular relevance to the local community. It seemed that the Secretary of State was asking a planning inquiry to do something that it was not designed to do: conduct a searching examination of a technical and complex proposal, and advise him accordingly.

Many individuals and organisations opposed to nuclear development, and many opposed to the PWR in particular, were surprised by such broad parameters and welcomed them. The appointment of Sir Frank Layfield QC as inquiry Inspector was also well-received, or more accurately it was recognised as an astute choice, as Sir Frank had represented one of the objectors at the Windscale inquiry in 1977. Some people considered that the whole thing was a public-relations exercise, that the government's fondness for nuclear projects would see Sizewell 'B' built however sound the arguments against it, and they decided that participation in the inquiry would be a waste of their resources. Many others took the opposite decision, not necessarily because of any greater faith that the eventual outcome would be to their liking but because they saw the inquiry as a forum where their views could be publicly stated and debated, and as an opportunity to probe the nuclear assumptions, and to examine the technical background, that might not be repeated for some years.

The government, like its predecessors, had not made a secret of its hopes for nuclear expansion. The announcement of the PWR programme made in December 1979[2] was followed in the next month by promises to Parliament, repeated twice in the same day, that the Sizewell inquiry would be 'full and thorough'.[3] Two years later, when announcing the arrangements and starting date for the inquiry, the Secretary of State for Energy stated:[4]

The Government are convinced that nuclear power has an increasingly important role to play in electricity generation in Britain.

Four months later, the Parliamentary Under Secretary,

commented to an American audience:[5]

> It goes without saying that the whole process will be fair
> and impartial. I expect that the accompanying public
> debate will be wide ranging and thorough. Overall it will be
> a very elaborate exercise absorbing a great deal of time.
> Nevertheless I am sure that it is a very important part of
> the battle to gain public acceptance of nuclear power.

Many decided not to participate in the inquiry because of the
government's role as both prosecutor and judge. They felt
that this was incompatible with a 'fair and impartial' inquiry,
and with the principles of justice.

As well as having the government committed to its cause,
the CEGB had the inestimable advantage of apparently
limitless funds. The CEGB was not only responsible for its
own expenses, which must have been £1 million a year, but
also for the whole expense of running the inquiry. For the
first time in planning history the applicant, rather than the
Department of the Environment, was responsible for the
Inspector's fees and expenses, the Secretariat and shorthand
writers, Counsel to the Inquiry, the accommodation, the
documentation, and the coach which daily met the 7.15 from
Liverpool Street at Ipswich, and returned in time to catch
the 6.28. Informed estimates of the total cost lie between
£15 and £25 million, a cost met by the electricity consumer.
A modest enough sum if the prize is a series of orders for
power stations at £1,172 million each, perhaps, but the
disparity between the resources available to the CEGB and
those available to its opponents[6] was gross; a disparity
underlined by the fact that the Board felt able to spend
£200–250 million on the Sizewell 'B' project before a decision
was announced.

In the three preliminary meetings convened by the
Inspector between June and October 1982, he was under
great pressure to try and arrange some funding for *bona fide*
objectors. Sir Frank Layfield wrote to the Secretary of State
at some length, if belatedly,[7] setting out with some clarity
the reasons for, and strength of feeling behind, the objectors'
request for funds. The reply—both letters were published—

was a refusal, primarily on the grounds of precedent, and the objectors were left with the problem of paying for legal representation, expert witnesses and supporting research from income generated by jumble sales; a problem that had the merit, if nothing else, of being familiar.

Of those groups who remained involved after the final decision on funding, only two voluntarily-funded organisations retained counsel. The rest decided to do the job themselves, and did it well, but the Board's ability to maintain a permanent team of four barristers and 30-odd support staff gave it an overwhelming advantage. Lawyers are both swords and shields, whose skills are in acting offensively and defensively in their clients' interests. The British legal aid system implicitly recognises that an imbalance in legal representation can affect the outcome of proceedings irrespective of the merits of the case, but there is no legal aid for participants at planning inquiries. The importance of this inequality can be tested by postulating a reversal of roles. Would the inquiry be regarded as 'full and thorough' or 'fair and impartial' if CEGB employees had to present their case at their personal expense, during unpaid leave from their work, and aided by such lawyers as their jumble sales could pay for, while opponents salaries and expenses were fully met from public funds, as were those of a resident team of QCs? Such a situation would challenge the perceptiveness of any Inspector, in distinguishing between the merit of the case and the quality of its presentation.

As well as doubts about government impartiality and financial constraints there were added problems to do with the remoteness of Snape Maltings. The venue was chosen for the convenience of local people, but the breadth of concern, and the scope of the issues as outlined by the Secretary of State in 1981, ensured that a wide range of individuals, groups and organisations wanted to participate. Most of the inquiry was devoted to generic, rather than local, issues, and the venue was inappropriate for much of the time. Only two locally-based voluntary organisations took part, the Suffolk Preservation Society and the Stop Sizewell 'B' Association, and only two groups, the SSBA and the Town and Country Planning Association, took advantage of the office accommodation provided to maintain a full-time presence. Despite the attractions of the scenery and the beer, the Maltings was an inconvenient venue for most participants, and especially so for those without expense accounts.

Between 11 January 1983, when the main hearings opened, and 7 March 1985, when they closed,[8] the number of times that the audience exceeded 20 could be counted on the fingers of two hands. After an initial flurry of interest members of the public were rarely seen in the 850-seat concert hall at the Maltings, and when they did come they could usually be identified by the obvious inability to follow the proceedings that soon showed on their faces. From time to time a class from a local school, or some college students, turned up, but their teachers invariably failed to check the programme with the secretariat and they too had no comprehension of what was going on. Interest was not greatly stimulated by the inquiry's first three months, which were taken up by the CEGB reading its previously-published evidence on to the transcript, but even when things became more purposeful the subject matter was so technical, the documentation so huge and the quasi-legal inquiry parlance so removed from everyday reality, that following the inquiry inevitably became a full-time job. Even with its £3.9 million public relations and publicity budget,[9] the CEGB could not drum up any significant interest among local people who, sadly, were almost totally excluded from this important public inquiry, not by intent but by obscurity.

There was often no audience at all except for the two ushers on duty, and as proceedings were transmitted by loudspeaker to the various offices on site, even the small band of regulars had no need to attend in person unless 'performing'. The inquiry became the small, formal group on the stage. The Inspector sat at a slightly raised table facing the hall, with his complete set of inquiry documents in cabinets behind him, and the shorthand writers, coming and going every ten minutes, in front. Proponents sat at a table to his left, and opponents and neutrals to his right. The witness or witnesses sat at a table directly in front of him, and at his extreme right a member of the secretariat was always present. Behind the witness, from the Inspector's point of view, the rows of empty seats banked up, almost meeting the new wooden roof.

NOTES AND REFERENCES

1. Hansard, 22 July 1981, col. 126.
2. Hansard, 18 December 1979, col. 288.
3. Hansard, 14 January 1980, col. 1192.
4. Hansard, 20 January 1982, col. 284.
5. Speech to a conference at the Edison Electric Institute, Los Angeles, 5 May 1982 (day 13, p. 39B).
6. Except the South of Scotland Electricity Board.
7. See day 3, pp. 87–89.
8. The inquiry formally opened at the start of the second pre-inquiry meeting, 26 July 1982. The first day of the main hearings, 11 January 1983, was day 5, and the last, 7 March 1985, was day 340. The Windscale inquiry of 1977 lasted for 100 days; the Sizewell 'B' inquiry finished in its 100th week.
9. CEGB Annual Report 1983/84, p. 57.

CHAPTER 5

ECONOMICS

The December 1979 announcement by David Howell, the newly appointed Energy Secretary, that 'the next power station should be a PWR'[1] was preceeded by a statement made by Tony Benn, the Labour Energy Secretary, in January 1978, that 'We must develop the option of adopting the PWR system in the early 1980s'.[2] In applying for consent to build a PWR at Sizewell, the CEGB was therefore acting on the express wishes of two consecutive governments, although inevitably those wishes were largely dictated by the Board's consistently-expressed preference for the PWR.

But forecasts for electricity demand fell severely between 1978/79 and 1982, and a new generating station could not be justified on grounds of forecast capacity shortfall in 1982.[3] On the CEGB's central estimates a shortfall would not arise until 1997, implying a start on site in 1989 or 1990.[4] The case for Sizewell 'B' thus did not rest on the immediate expectation of power shortages if the station was not built. Instead, it rested on the proposition that electricity generated by the PWR over its lifetime would be cheaper than that generated by any other method—so much cheaper that the station would provide significant savings on the system. It would achieve these savings by enabling coal and oil fired plant to be used less, or retired altogether, avoiding the use of fossil fuels. Less coal and oil would be burned on the generating system, and over its lifetime, these savings would outweigh the high capital costs of building a nuclear power station. Moreover, the savings would be so significant that it would be worth building the station as soon as possible, to obtain the benefit as quickly as possible.

This system benefit argument, which had already been deployed in a simplified form at Hartlepool (see Chapter 2, note 47), is useful in that it enables orders to be placed for new generating capacity at a time when short-term demand projections cannot justify them. But the argument does depend crucially on long-term forecasts of economic activity, in particular of electricity demand and fuel prices. In the case of Sizewell 'B', forecasts up to the year 2030 had to be made, as it was possible that the station would be in service until that time.[5] It is relevant to look at the historic record of electricity supply industry forecasting.

Demand and forecasting
The Electricity Council has made short-term forecasts of electricity demand since its inception in 1957, and these are adopted by the CEGB and published annually. In recent years the usual forecasting period has been seven years ahead; the Board's evidence to the Sizewell inquiry was the first time that an extensive range of long-term forecasts had been published.

The industry experienced a continually expanding demand for its product for almost a century. But as the left-hand side of figure 1 shows,[6] the annual increases have been getting smaller since the 1950s, and between 1973/74 and 1983/84 demand actually contracted in six years out of the ten (see Chapter 2, note 46). The electricity supply industry's forecasts have been late to recognise this trend. Projections made in the middle and late 1960s were regularly 30 per cent, and sometimes 50 per cent, optimistic,[7] and the most recent forecast for which, at the time of writing, we know the out-turn (1976/77 for 1983/84) was 28.5 per cent too high.[8] As confirmed by the Board, this percentage error was typical of those of the preceding decade,[9] and the industry's record earned it this comment from the Monopolies Commission:[10]

> Demand forecasting by the Board and by the Electricity Supply Industry as a whole has been seriously inaccurate.

Although more recent forecasts have been more modest, the record in short- and medium-term forecasting suggests that the CEGB's long-term projections should be grounded in caution rather tham optimism.

The forecasts for the Sizewell inquiry were made in the context of five scenarios, or assumptions, of future UK economic activity. The intention was to provide a range of credible assumptions against which to test the PWR proposal.

Table 5.1 Scenario definitions
[CEGB/P/4 Table 2]

	GDP growth rate: % p.a. to 2000
A — high growth based on services	2.6
B — high growth based on manufacturing	2.6
C — medium growth	1.0
D — stable low growth	-0.4
E — unstable low growth	-0.4

The Board commented that 'With the exception of scenario C, and in some respects D, the scenarios all represent relatively extreme views',[11] but throughout the inquiry much more emphasis was placed on C, as the 'least unlikely'[12] scenario, than on D. The considerable difference in long-term demand projections between the two scenarios can be seen from the table below; this difference, based on the difference in GDP growth rates, was central to the case for Sizewell. It was maintained in spite of the statement from the Department of Energy that:[13]

The Department has never seen. . . a close or deterministic relationship, a direct relationship, between the rate of GDP and the rate of growth of energy demand.

Table 5.2 Electricity demand projections (GW)
[CEGB/P/4 Table 3]

Scenario	1979/80	1983/84	1990	2000	2030
A	44.1	43.5	48.9	51.3	54.9
B	44.1	43.5	51.1	61.7	93.9
C	44.1	43.5	43.7	46.9	57.1
D	44.1	43.5	38.6	37.9	37.9
E	44.1	43.5	35.9	35.1	32.2

Note to Table 5.2
CEGB/P/4, table 3, updated in CEGB/P/4 (ADD 3) to include data for scenario D. All figures are restricted ACS maximum demand, except 1983/84 which is unrestricted demand from 1983/84 Annual Report, p. 16. (The unrestricted figure for 1979/80 was 45.5GW). Demand growth in scenario B is so high that it 'would present a severe task to the CEGB as to the provision of adequate generating capacity'. (CEGB/P/4 para. 51).

It can be seen that demand in the central scenario C is modest until 2000, but increases rapidly until 2030, demonstrating the Board's central view that static or declining demand will prove to be a temporary phenomenon. The extent to which these projections run counter to the historic trend is shown in figure 5.1, and the long-term scenario C projections are essential to justify a large power station ordering programme in the 1990s (see below). Should scenario D be thought more likely, that justification would largely disappear.

As well as the scenarios, the CEGB postulated three future mixtures of coal and nuclear generating stations on the system. These plant mix backgrounds were the High Nuclear Background, the Medium Nuclear Background and the No New Nuclear background.[14] The first two represented the economic effect on the system of nuclear programmes, and the third the effect of all future capacity being coal-fired. As PWRs were deemed to be cost-saving investments, and thus might be built ahead of capacity need, and coal stations were not, the different background assumptions gave different forecasts of station commissionings.

Table 5.3 Station commissionings 1991–2010, scenario C[15]

HNB		MNB		NNNB
PWR	Coal	PWR	Coal	Coal
39	1	23	10	22
= 46.9 GW		= 45.3 GW		= 41.2 GW

Note to Table 5.3
A new coal station is assumed to be 1,875 MWso (MW sent out, i.e. net of station consumption), a PWR 1,155 MWso. The HNB figure involves commissioning 3 PWRs in each year from 2001 to 2010.

The central scenario C involves building up to 39 PWRs by 2010.

System benefit—net effective costs (NEC)
Long-term forecasts formed the basis of the system benefit argument for Sizewell 'B', and the net effective costs was the method used to evaluate that benefit. It is, in principle, an equation with the total costs of the proposed power station over its lifetime on one side, and the total savings it would make on the other. If savings are greater than costs, the result of the equation is a negative number, indicating that the station would be of benefit. If costs are greater than savings, the station would be a cost to the system.

For any power station proposal, the main parameters of the NEC are the same. On the costs side, the two main ones are:
— the capital cost of building the station (per kW) and interest during construction,
— fuel costs over the station's lifetime.
The only significant component of the savings side is:
— the value of the fossil fuels which would not be burned in older, costlier stations if the new station is built.
The CEGB constructed NECs for the PWR proposal, for a new AGR station and for a new coal-fired station, for comparative purposes. The NEC for the PWR, on the Board's figures, was more negative, under all scenarios and backgrounds, than those of the other two station types. The challenge to the components of the NEC for the AGR is briefly described in Chapter 7. The NEC for a new coal station looks rather different to that for either nuclear design, because its capital costs per kW 'are lower but its fuel costs are higher. Although it would save much the same amount of coal and oil from being burned in less efficient stations (again, per kW), its own fuel costs are higher. The Board's

79

FIGURE 5.1

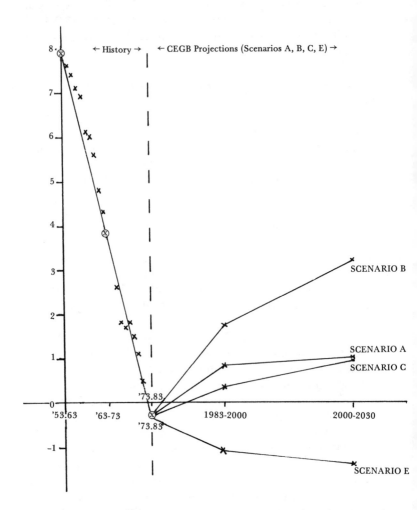

The yearly rate of increase of Average Cold Spell (ACS) maximum demand on the CEGB system, as restricted by load management. The final years of three 10-year periods, ending in 1962/63, 1972/73 and 1982/83 are plotted. From 1982/83 the plotted increases to 2000, and then from 2000–2030, are those of the CEGB scenarios A, B, C and E. In the historical section points are given for all the intermediate years except 1973/74, the year of the coal strike. Data from CEGB (letter of 5 July 1983, SSBA/S/32). Projections from CEGB/P/5, Tables 46 and 50.

assumptions on future coal prices were disputed at inquiry, and that debate clearly had a significant effect o the calculation of the NEC for a coal station. However, in this brief introduction, no further mention will be made of NECs other than that of the PWR.

Under scenario C, capital costs made up some 64–68 per cent of the total on the costs side of the NEC, and fuel costs 21–26 per cent.[16] The balance is made up of decommissioning costs at 0.5 per cent, and 'other works costs' and 'overhead costs' which together account for some 9 per cent.[17] The savings were made up of coal and oil, in quantity terms 92–94 per cent coal[18] although the value of the oil savings was greater than its quantity would suggest (see below). All the assumptions, judgements and forecasts that defined the components of the NEC were examined at the inquiry, some several times. This process occupied most of its first year, and is clearly impossible to recount in any detail. However it might be of interest to examine some of the debate that took place around two or three of the NEC parameters, and as construction, or capital, costs are the major component on the costs side, and fossil fuel prices the only component on the savings side, these items are briefly discussed below.

Construction costs
These were estimated at £1,172 million[19] at March 1982 prices.[20] As the station was designed to generate 1,155 MW so,[21] this cost was expressed as £1,015/kW in the NEC. In this form the capital cost figure was affected by a number of plant performance parameters, including assumptions about lifetime, rating and availability. Another parameter which had an obvious bearing on construction costs was construction time, since costs would be affected by delays on site. The target construction period for Sizewell 'B' was 72 months, and the central estimate used for economic appraisal purposes was 90 months.

The CEGB was vulnerable to charges of optimism even over the central estimate, because of the record of construction times at its AGR power stations. The average of the construction times of the first four AGRs was 176 months

site to commissioning;[22] this record was
ir Alaistair Frame (see Chapter 6) among
GB could do little except point to improved
arrangements and progress at Heysham II
and at the same time remind critics that the
greater 'constructibility' of the PWR was one of the
reasons why it was preferred.[23]

But PWR construction experience in the United States did
little to provide support for the Board's 90 month estimate.
Its own evidence showed that the average construction period
of all US 4-loop Westinghouse stations is 103.5 months,[24]
and that of all US 1,000–1,300 MW PWRs started in or after
1972 is 190 months.[25] Fifty-four Westinghouse power
reactors are operating or under construction in the United
States. It is true that by no means all of these are both
4-loop and large, and it is also true that the American data
base is a shrinking one because of cancellations. Nevertheless, many objectors at the inquiry felt that it was unwise
to assume that a first British example, built to British safety
standards, would be constructed more quickly than the
appropriate American average.[26]

Coal prices
During the inquiry's first year, when most of the economic
evidence was heard, more time was spent discussing coal
prices than any other subject, and more evidence was presented on that than on any other.[27] This reflected the fact
that the price of fossil fuels, of which coal is the largest
component, was the most significant parameter of the NEC,
as the CEGB confirmed.[28] Forecasts of coal prices increasing
in real terms were essential to the system benefit argument
for Sizewell, to the extent that if coal prices increase only
at the rate of inflation during the lifetime of the plant, it
would not be profitable.[29] High coal prices were advantageous
to the nuclear NEC, because they maximised the savings
side of the equation.

The coal price forecasts provided to the inquiry by the
Board were lower than those provided to the House of
Commons Select Committee in 1980/81,[30] but still repre-

sented large real increases in coal costs over the lifetime of
the station.

Coal price forecasts—scenario C (in p/GJ)

1980/81	1990	2000	2030
164	195	230	385

Thus a 19 per cent increase in prices in real terms is expected
before 1990, 40 per cent before 2000 and 135 per cent
before 2030.[31] However, PWR savings were further maximised
because the CEGB used a different set of price assumptions
when calculating coal costs for existing stations to those it
used when calculating coal savings. The latter, known as
'marginal' prices, were an average of 18 per cent higher than
the prices of NCB coal delivered to a central power station
quoted above.[32] The CEGB's assumptions for coal price
increases, when calculating PWR benefit, thus becomes a 40
per cent increase before 1990, 90 per cent before 2000 and
180 per cent before 2030.

These increases were foreseen despite the Board's assumption of static or falling labour costs in the coal industry from
1980-2000, and falling costs in all scenarios from 2000-
2030.[33] They were also foreseen despite the two consecutive
Joint Understandings between the CEGB and the NCB
governing the NCB's purchases of power station coal. In the
second of these, the CEGB agreed to buy 70 million tonnes
in each year up to 1987 at prices that will increase at less
than the rate of inflation. Any additional purchases (the
'marginal' coal referred to earlier) will be even cheaper.[34] The
CEGB is by far the NCB's biggest customer, and as such must
have a considerable influence on the price it pays for coal.
Indeed, the Joint Understandings reflect that influence, and
it is in the commercial interests of both Boards to continue
them. As the CEGB said in evidence:[35]

> Whatever decisions are taken with regard to new plant over
> the next few years the CEGB will continue, because of its
> existing plant mix, to be committed to coal as the major

element of its fuel supplies beyond the end of the century.

Another witness remarked, less formally, that 'Cheap coal is a jolly sight better than expensive coal, that is certainly true'.[36] In addition to its commercial interests, which would cause it to actively seek to constrain coal prices, the CEGB has a statutory duty 'to develop and maintain an efficient co-ordinated and economical supply of electricity in bulk. . .'[37] The Board is in the position of wanting to constrain coal prices, because about 80 per cent of the electricity it supplied in 1983/84 came from its coal-fired stations,[38] but at the same time forecasting that they will increase, in order to justify Sizewell 'B'.

A senior energy resources analyst, D.C. Ion, was asked by the Inspector to give independent evidence on the future availability and prices of world energy resources. His summary comment on coal demand and price was:[39]

> Therefore, in the next century, it would seem probable that:
> a. demand for coal will grow slowly but steadily,
> b. the price of coal will also rise only slowly because of
>   i. competition between exporters
>   ii. the availability of petroleum.

He also commented, in answer to a question from the Board:[40]

> I do not agree with the tenor of the [CEGB evidence] that coal prices must rise in real terms inexorably and substantially.

Oil prices
The CEGB's original evidence was that between 9 and 12 mtce of oil would be saved by Sizewell 'B' over its lifetime in scenario C,[41] but by October 1983 this figure had been reduced to 5 mtce.[42] The Board's assumption was that Sizewell 'B' would only be able to save oil during the early years of its life, because only during the early years would oil still be used on the system. However the expected com-

missioning date for Sizewell 'B' had to be put back for 2 years (because of the length of the inquiry, among other factors), and so the calculated oil savings had to be reduced correspondingly. It was noted above that oil was a more significant component of the NEC that the quantities involved might indicate; this is largely a reflection of the higher price of oil, but was also because all the oil savings were early, and their value was magnified because of the effect of discounting (see Appendix 5).

Objectors argued that all savings should be considered to be of coal, and this difference was articulated in one of the few 'agreed documents' produced during the inquiry produced by the Stop Sizewell 'B' Association/Ecoropa and the CEGB:[43]

> The basic difference lies in the demand projections. On [objector's] projections. . . the 4 mtce [pa] of oil being used at present will be taken out of the system by the impending 5 large power stations, plus Dinorwig and the French link, long before Sizewell B could be operating. . . The CEGB is working on the assumption that demand will get back to the scenario C projections, and that all these new sources of power will be required to satisfy the large increase in demand, so that the oil would still be there for Sizewell B to save.

When discussion of the Board's economic case for Sizewell 'B' finally came to an end, many participants considered that, at the very least, the NEC had been shown to be less favourable than the CEGB had at first proposed. The Electricity Consumers Council, itself with statutory duties,[44] concluded that the economic case for Sizewell 'B' was 'marginal verging towards adverse'.[45] The Council's summary was:[46]

> The most obvious and immediate conclusion is that there is no narrow system economic case for seeking to build a Westinghouse PWR as a one-off project ahead of capacity need. . . The best estimates of the ECC suggest that consumers will not benefit economically to any large or direct extent by the construction of Sizewell B in advance of capacity need.

85

As conclusions such as this were reached, the Board began to lay more emphasis on its strategic arguments than it had when the inquiry opened.

Strategic arguments
Two were put forward by the Board to reinforce its system benefit case. The first was that a further nuclear station would reduce, although not greatly, the preponderance of coal generation on the system. It would increase fuel diversity, and thereby security of supply. The CEGB saw itself as vulnerable to disruptions in both supply and price of fuels, and considered that an increased nuclear component would reduce this vulnerability. Clearly, this argument only becomes significant in the context of a number of new nuclear stations, and the case for Sizewell 'B' was designed to be convincing whether or not further PWRs are built. It was not deployed in any quantitative way during the inquiry, although it may have appealed to those who are responsible for making energy policy decisions in this country. It was countered in two ways; some pointed out that the choice of the PWR necessarily involved remote siting, and consequent transmission losses and increased vulnerability of the grid.[47] Others noted that an increased nuclear generation involved importing more fuel:[48]

These strategies recommended for security. . . do have implications for a greater dependence upon overseas sources of fuel, which many other countries would regard as a somewhat bizarre way of approaching the question of security.

The second strategic argument for Sizewell 'B' openly presupposed a programme of PWRs and, like the first, was not quantified in any detailed way at the inquiry. It became known as the 'door opening quality':[49]

There are certain reasons why Sizewell might be judged to have a less attractive NEC, because of learning effects. . . One would not expect those disbenefits to carry on to later stations and then one might well make the judgement

86

that one could incur those relative disbenefits in order to make a greater profit on what was going to follow.

Objectors who felt that they had made some progress in persuading the Inspector that the system benefit argument for Sizewell was not as conclusive as claimed were now beginning to get the measure of the Board's economic defences. But the sustained challenge to the economic case for a single station ahead of capacity need achieved a shift towards a greater reliance on the strategic arguments. These by definition depended for their efficacy on a programme of PWRs, and the Board's intentions in this regard became clearer.

The programme
The announcement made by the Secretary of State for Energy in December 1979,[50] in which he referred to 'a programme of the order of 15,000 MW over 10 years', was mentioned in Chapter 2. That programme was based on 'cautious assumptions' from the industry, and remains government policy. Although running late, it has not, at the time of writing, been superceded or withdrawn.

The leading role that the nuclear industry has played in maintaining British national self-esteem for more than thirty years has already been discussed (Chapters 1 and 2). The industry did not receive a single order throughout the 1970s, and in 1979 the government saw the situation as urgent:

> The British nuclear programme has been in decline over the past decade. . . If we are to reverse this trend and ensure that the industry is on a sound footing, we must act now.

Despite the AGR 'catastrophe', and despite the failure of the industry to export its product, the government had evidently decided that the survival of the industry was necessary. As consecutive administrations have done since the war, the government provided support to the nuclear industry at the highest level, despite its complete failure to succeed in normal commercial terms. The maintenance of this industry, for what can only be reasons of national prestige, is one of the most remarkable features of recent British industrial history.

A way had to be found of reconciling the level of ordering that the government and the CEGB said that they wanted, with the reality of falling demand. The solution in the short term was the net effective cost methodology, used to justify power station orders ahead of need on cost-saving grounds. This would clearly suffer from diminishing returns, and in the longer term a programme based on sizeable forecast capacity shortages was necessary.

In evidence to the House of Commons Select Committee on Energy during its 1980/81 hearings, the then Chairman of the CEGB was clear as to his intentions:[51]

> Q. So the CEGB in fact is not going to wait until there is operational experience of the reactor. . . but are going right into the programme of ordering further PWRs a year from the time they have started work on site. That seems to me to be quite fantastic.
> A. . . . We do not need, in our view, to obtain operating experience at all. . . We would be happy one year later to start on the second.
> Q. Without any operating experience at all?
> A. Indeed yes.

There was some confusion, early in the inquiry, as to whether or not a formal programme existed. The Department of Energy witness, speaking for the government, was clear that one did not:[52]

> Q. There is no government programme for the ordering of nuclear power stations?
> A. Correct.
> Q. Either by reference to number or timescale or both?
> A. That is now the position, yes.

It is impossible to judge whether or not the word 'now' was intended to imply that the government had changed its mind about the 1979 programme. Certainly Parliament has not been informed of any such reversal of policy.

The CEGB's position was stated in its evidence:[53]

> The CEGB has no commitment as to the number of subsequent stations to be built, their timing, whether they should be conventional or nuclear and, if the latter, what type of reactor should be adopted.

However, the next paragraph comments:

> From the information presently available the CEGB therefore believes that, subject to gaining consent for Sizewell 'B', there is likely to be a strong case for further stations to be of the PWR type.

The following page is more specific:

> The CEGB has already announced its intention to seek consent for a further nuclear station [Hinkley Point 'C']. . . The CEGB's present intention is that the site for any consent application subsequent to Hinkley Point 'C' would be chosen from Druridge, Northumberland, Dungeness, Kent; Sizewell; and Winfrith UKAEA, Dorset.

In oral evidence the Board made it clear that 'to build one alone is not a likely management decision, but one might have a small group',[54] since 'the concept of a single PWR stuck on the system, if that is a real risk, is not an attractive concept'. What the Board wanted from the inquiry was 'to have reasonable confidence. . . that we would be able to replicate the plant let us say two or three times to produce a minimum family at least on our system.'[55] At least in its evidence to the inquiry, the CEGB was anxious to give the impression that it had learned from its earlier over-optimism:[56]

> We have had any number of leaders of the electricity industry and the nuclear industry who have [made] bold statements about how many reactors of such and such a type are going to be done in such and such a period, and it has its attractions. I think it is also, in some respects, a

89

touch naive. . . My own judgement is that one could use-fully have some certainty which might cover, let's say, a credible five year period.

Two leaked documents helped to throw some light on the question of the programme. The first was the CEGB's 1983 Capital Investment Memorandum to the Department of Energy, which was passed to the Council for the Protection of Rural England. The other, a 'secret' CEGB memorandum of July 1982 called 'A strategy for the next power station developments', was given to the Suffolk Preservation Society. Both became inquiry documents.[57]

The Capital Investment Memorandum commented in its opening paragraph that (emphasis added):

The estimates for later years show the consequences for capital expenditure of *the CEGB's present plans,* although, as far as uncommitted expenditure is concerned, these plans are liable to modification in reaction to changes in circumstances.

The assumed starting dates for seven nuclear stations subse-quent to Sizewell 'B' were listed, and ranged from June 1987 to June 1991,[58] but no sites were specified other than Hinkley Point.

The second document discussed further nuclear sites at some length, their advantages, the site selection criteria used and the costs of building at each site. Appendix 1 gave a 'Notional PWR Programme', with keydates for a 12-station, 12,210 MW programme 'which meets the higher feasible nuclear development for scenarios A and C'. The last two stations on this programme are assumed to start on site in 1993 and commission in 2000. The document concludes with a 'Public Relations Strategy for the Next Nuclear Power Station Sites'.

From its analysis of the CEGB's future capacity require-ments, the Electricity Consumers Council concluded that most of the new stations assumed to commission by 2010 under scenerio C will not be needed on the grounds of supply shortfall. They will be justified as cost-saving investment:[59]

Beyond that date (the late 1990s), nearly three-quarters of the 44 GW of generating investment expected by the CEGB to commission up to the year 2010. . . is 'optional' or cost-saving investment. . . (Given ECC's NEC estimates) it appears that a substantial programme of cost reducing investment based on the Westinghouse PWR is difficult to justify.

When Counsel for the ECC made his closing speech to the Inspector, his first and last substantive comments concerned the intended PWR programme, and he clearly laid some emphasis on the subject. His closing comment was:[60]

It is now clear, and it was ambiguous at the start of the Inquiry, that the intention is to build a series of reactors rather than just one reactor.

The use of the system benefit argument, rather than the capacity need argument, to support the case for Sizewell 'B' rested on the calculation of net savings over its lifetime. Whether or not the station would make money in 20 or 25 years time, its large capital costs will certainly increase electricity costs in the short and medium terms. Beyond Sizewell, the case for the programme of PWRs rests entirely on the assumption that the range of long-term forecasts associated with scenario C will prove accurate. If that scenario's electricity demand increases for 2000–2030 are not realised, the central feature of the CEGB's hopes and plans will have no foundation. As the Board's senior witness remarked:[61]

I am far from clear that it would be possible to pursue the thermal reactor strategy in any meaningful way against a background. . . moving towards scenarios D and E.

If the growth needed to justify the thermal reactor strategy does not materialise, we can only hope that the institutional momentum which has been a characteristic of the nuclear establishment since the earliest days can be stopped in time.

NOTES AND REFERENCES

1. Hansard, 18 December 1979, col. 288.
2. Hansard, 25 January 1978, col. 1392.
3. The CEGB's Statement of Case was published in April 1982, and the case for Sizewell 'B' effectively fixed, except in details, from that date.
4. CEGB/P/4 (ADD 6), Table 5.
5. The CEGB hoped for a 40 year life, but assumed 35. (CEGB/P/8 para. 195). With planning inquiry and construction, forecasting into the second quarter of the next century was necessary.
6. From SSBA/P/1, figure 1.
7. The most inaccurate seems to have been that made in 1964/65 for the year 1970/71, which was 60.4 per cent optimistic.
8. Referring to CEGB Annual Reports 1976/77, p. 18, and 1983/84 p. 16 we can derive:

1976/77 demand was	42.1 (A)
1976/77 forecast for 1983/84 was	55.1 (B)
1983/84 demand was	43.5 (C)
thus over-estimate (B–C) was	12.0 (D)
% error in forecast ($\frac{D}{A} \times 100$) =	28.5%

   (All figures are unrestricted ACS maximum demand, in GW).

9. Day 11, p. 46C; CEGB/P/4 (ADD 2), p. 2.
10. Monopolies and Mergers Commission: Report on the Central Electricity Generating Board, 1981, p. 285.
11. CEGB/P/5, para. 158.
12. Day 67, p. 21F. See also CEGB/P/4, para. 50.
13. Day 44, p. 18H.
14. High Nuclear Background—PWRs built as quickly as possible up to 70 per cent of total capacity.
   Medium Nuclear Background—PWRs built to 40 per cent of total capacity.
   No New Nuclear Background—no new nuclear construction after the Heysham II AGR (i.e. Sizewell 'B' not built).
15. Derived from CEGB/P/4, Table 26C.
16. Depending on background. See CEGB/P/4 (ADD 6), Table 14.
17. Other works costs—salaries and maintenance.
   Overhead costs—training, safety, rent, rates and insurance.
   CEGB/P/4, pp. 154–5 and 121.
18. CEGB/P/4 (ADD 6), Table 15. Oil measured in mtce (million tonnes of coal equivalent).
19. Capital costs were £1,172 million when the evidence was published in April 1982, had risen to £1,184 million by October 1983 (CEGB/P/4 (ADD 6), para. 22), and subsequently returned to £1,172 million (CEGB/P/4 (ADD 21), para. 2).

20. March 1982 values were adhered to throughout the inquiry.
21. Output was originally 1,110 MW so, but was subsequently raised to 1,155 MWso (CEGB/P/4 (ADD 6), para. 30).
22. CEGB Statistical Yearbook 1983/84, Table 14 gives start on site to probable completion of commissioning for Dungeness 'B' as 18 years, Hartlepool as 16 years and Heysham I as 14 years. Hinkley Point 'B' took 130 months to commissioning, see Chapter 2, note 37.
23. This view did not go unchallenged; see SSEB/P/1, para. 62.
24. The Sizewell 'B' proposal was for a Westinghouse 4-loop reactor. For data, see CEGB/P/8, Table 4. The figures for Callaway, Wolf Creek and Diablo Canyon were corrected by CEGB/P/8 (ADD 1). Table 4 does not include data for Indian Point 1 and 2, but data are given (using slightly different criteria) in CEGB/P/8 (ADD 4 REV), and do not make a material difference to the average. CEGB/P/8 and its addenda 'might have been designed for ambiguity'; they are a minefield of different definitions of when work starts on a power station site, and when it ends. One example was given in Chapter 2, note 37. CEGB/P/8 (ADD 5) was produced in response to the Inspector's expressed confusion on this subject, and can only have increased it. Various attempts were made to sort it out during cross-examination, see for example day 121, pp. 99E to 105D.
25. CEGB/P/8 (ADD 7), p. 13.
26. See for example CPRE/P/1, ECC/P/2.
27. See for example CPRE/P/2, ECC/P/4, SSBA/P/1, TCPA/P/2, TCPA/P/3.
28. Day 136, p. 27E.
29. Day 136, p. 25E. This refers to CEGB/P/4 figures 5-8, which show that NECs in all scenarios are positive on zero fossil fuel price increases in real terms. Scenario C is marginal on half the postulated increase.
30. House of Commons Select Committee on Energy, 1980/81 Report (CEGB/S/26B), p. 560.
31. All figures are NCB prices delivered to a central coalfield power station, as given by CEGB in SSBA/S/6. NCB prices delivered to Thames are higher (CEGB/P/6, Table 24) but the percentage increases are similar.
32. SSBA/S/14.
33. CEGB/P/6, Table 13.
34. SSBA/S/6 details the second understanding.
35. CEGB/P/1, para. 68 (ii).
36. Day 136, p. 25B.
37. Electricity Act, 1957, Section 2.
38. CEGB Annual Report 1983/84, p. 7 gives 14.7 as the percentage of nuclear electricity produced in that year. Oil fired plants were used only to meet peaks because of high fuel costs.

39. ION/P/1, p. 36.
40. ION/P/1 (ADD 1), p. 9.
41. CEGB/P/4, Table 15, NNNB and HNB respectively.
42. CEGB/P/4 (ADD 6), Table 15 revised.
43. SSBA/P/1 (ADD 6), p. 2.
44. Energy Act, 1983, Section 21.
45. Day 200, p. 33C. Day 200 records ECC's closing speech.
46. Day 200, p. 34D, 34H–35A.
47. See WANA/P/2, paras. 2.4–2.6.
48. Day 112, p. 38C.
49. Day 98, p. 66F-G.
50. Hansard, 18 December 1979, col. 288.
51. Reference 30, Q. 1801, 1802.
52. Day 40, p. 65D.
53. CEGB/P/1, para. 132.
54. Day 106, p. 40D.
55. Day 285, p. 23.
56. *Ibid.*, p. 20B, D.
57. CPRE/S/113; SPS/S/10.
58. Two in 1990 and in 1991.
59. Day 200, p. 39 E-F.
60. *Ibid.*, p. 50F.
61. Day 285, p. 64D.

CHAPTER 6

TWO PROCEDURES AND TWO DESIGNS

One of the duties of the Nuclear Installations Inspectorate (NII) is to decide whether the design of a proposed civil nuclear installation conforms to UK safety standards, and can therefore be licensed for construction.[1] That necessitates a lengthy dialogue with the designers, which might be expected to be especially protracted if the proposed design is for a type of nuclear plant new to this country. This dialogue was not finished when the public inquiry into the application for planning consent for Sizewell 'B' opened. The two examinations had to be conducted in parallel, despite the obvious fact that there was not much point in the inquiry discussing whether or not planning consent should be given, if an NII licence was not forthcoming.

FOE's application for an adjournment
The government recognised that the licensing process should precede the planning inquiry in November 1979, when the Secretary of State for Energy said in the Commons:[2]

> At the same time it must be right that full safety clearance is given by our well-tried and laid down safety procedures through the Nuclear Installations Inspectorate, before any new reactor design is placed before an inquiry in this country. That is understood.

In the following month he said:[3]

> On the question of the public inquiry, we are, of course, giving full consideration to the type of inquiry that would follow safety clearance. There could be no inquiry until we had full safety clearance.

These two statements represent an unequivocal commitment by the government that the inquiry would be consecutive to, and not concurrent with, the NII's safety assessment. The commitment was further repeated by the Secretary of State in evidence to the Select Committee on Energy in July 1980,[4] and by Mr Dunster, the Deputy Director-General of the Health and Safety Executive, the NII's parent body. Mr Dunster said to the Energy Committee in March 1980:[5]

It is a policy decision on the part of the Executive, and I suppose the Department of Energy, that we wish to go to this inquiry with a complete picture. We wish to appear before it saying that we are now in possession of the information that would enable us to licence the plant.

When the inquiry's main hearings opened on 11 January 1983, it was clear that these assurances given to Parliament would not be fulfilled. Not only was the NII unable to indicate whether or not the PWR could be licensed before the inquiry opened, it also became apparent that it would still be unable to do so at its end. In a letter to the inquiry Secretariat, the CEGB stated:[6]

The licensing process, which involves the provision of further detailed analyses and further material to meet the NII's requirements, will continue well beyond the time-scales for the public inquiry.

Counsel for Friends of the Earth (FOE) directly addressed the inquiry Inspector, Sir Frank Layfield:[7]

The most that you will be able to report, even if you accept the Board's case down to the last dot and comma, is that you are confident that at some time in the future the Board will be able to produce a design for the PWR which it could show to be safe.

FOE, which had brought the Inspector's attention to the commitments quoted above, applied for an adjournment of those parts of the inquiry concerned with safety, until such time as the NII was in a position to make its decision. As counsel remarked:[8]

> If the Inquiry proceeds without the adjournment applied for, those repeated and unequivocal commitments will be broken.

FOE made their application on 25 January 1983, two weeks after the start of the main hearings. On 8 February the Inspector announced that he would not at that time make a ruling, although he did say that 'The applicants have legitimate cause for complaint'.[9] He invited FOE to reapply after 15 March, which they did on 10 May.[10] The Inspector finally rejected the adjournment application on 14 June. In his summary of FOE's case he referred to the statement made by Mr Dunster to the Select Committee,[11] but made no reference to the earlier statements by the Secretary of State, on which the application centrally relied. The Inspector said:[12]

> It is said that the Select Committee, and Ministers, adopted and relied upon the force of Mr Dunster's commitment.

This seems to have been an important misunderstanding, as Mr Dunster's statement was made four and five months after the Secretary of State's two statements to Parliament. The Minister could not have adopted and relied on Mr Dunster's statement. The Inspector rejected the application with these words:

> My concern at the position, and my sympathy with the position, in which Friends of the Earth find themselves is of a nature and scale entirely different, however, from the force of argument that would be required to justify adjourning an important part of a major Public Inquiry, in which many parties and the public have a proper and real interest in ensuring its steady progress to its conclusion.

By this time, five months into the inquiry, no-one was surprised at the decision. As the Inspector implied, the hearings had acquired a momentum of their own.

The two designs

Ministers do not renege on assurances given to Parliament without good reason. In this case, the reason was that the NII could not finish its safety assessment of the design before the start of the inquiry, if the inquiry was to begin when the Secretary of State and the CEGB wanted it to begin. The reason that the NII could not finish the assessment in time was largely because the CEGB withdrew the design which the NII had been assessing for some months and replaced it with another. And the reason that the CEGB changed the design was that a power station built to the first design would have been too expensive.

In April 1978 the CEGB authorised the National Nuclear Corporation (NNC) to prepare a design for the Sizewell 'B' station based on a large Westinghouse 4-loop reactor. The reference design took three years to produce, and it is impossible that the CEGB could have been anything other than intimately involved with every stage of that design. The Board's design teams were as responsible for the design as the NNC's. The design was presented formally to the CEGB in April 1981, and rejected by the CEGB's executive board. It was rejected because it was too expensive, would take too long to build, and did not make best use of American experience.[13] It was not rejected on safety grounds.

Following the rejection of the April 1981 design the Secretary of State set up a Task Force under the chairmanship of Dr Walter Marshall, at that time Chairman of the UKAEA and later, knighted, to take over at the CEGB. The Task Force began work in July 1981, and the new reference design was adopted by the CEGB and NNC in September. The pre-construction safety report (PCSR) was, in this instance and against precedent, based on the reference design and was made available to the NII in draft at the end of December 1981. Both the PCSR and the reference design were published in April 1982. Because of the great pressure on time the normal processes of design evolution were short-circuited—usually a preliminary safety report (PSR) is produced from the reference design. The PCSR should be based on the fully-detailed contract design, which is the design for construction, and in normal circumstances the NII expects to be provided with this full PCSR as the foundation for a licensing decision. The PCSR for the April 1982 design was in fact the PSR, because the design process had not progressed to the contract design stage—there had been no time to work at that level of detail. The contract design and the PCSR proper for Sizewell 'B' will presumably be made available in due course.

NNC had taken three years to arrive at a design which satisfactorily—in its view—adapted American PWR technology to British standards. The Task Force took less than three months to do the same, and it did so only by relying heavily on US designs. Bechtel, an American firm of architect/engineers, was represented on the task force (as was Westinghouse) and has been retained as consultant to the project. Bechtel's experience in designing power stations to satisfy American safety standards replaced NNC's experience in designing stations to satisfy British standards.

The NII was asked to license, for the first time, a power station based on a PWR, a reactor with fundamentally different safety characteristics to the Magnox and AGR reactors. Inevitably the examination leading to a licensing decision was a long one, but in the beginning the NII was at least dealing with a designer who had many years experience of UK standards and of the NII's requirements. When the first design was rejected and an American-based one substituted, it was obvious that the NII would require even longer to make a decision as to the licence.

Licensing and planning inquiry in parallel
In June 1980 the CEGB and the NII agreed a programme that would enable an NII decision to be made by May 1982. This required that the first draft of the PCSR be issued to the NII by February 1981. The Board's decision to reject the April 1981 design meant that the agreed programme was impossible to maintain. Regardless of the wishes of the Secretary of State, licensing could not be completed before the inquiry began. A way had to be found of enabling the two processes to take place concurrently.

They did not co-exist happily. The inquiry felt obliged to keep a close, almost supervisory, watch on the safety assessment; the Inspector was keenly aware that his inquiry would become a joke of historic proportions in legal circles if the NII found against the design. During the hearings' second year day-long sessions were regularly devoted to reviewing progress between the CEGB and the NII, and it was obvious that the Inspectorate was under considerable pressure from several directions, in a situation that was not of its making. Although many observers felt some sympathy for the NII during this period, it was apparent that a major problem was that the two organisations could not communicate effectively with each other. The Inspector lost patience with them both, and announced that one day, 16 March 1984, would be devoted to:[14]

> understanding why it is that exchanges between two expert, well-informed parties wishing to arrive at a single conclusion appear to have been unfruitful on a number of occasions.

On that day the inquiry came closer than usual to providing some courtroom drama. A small audience gathered in the concert hall; some very senior staff from most of the nuclear organisations were present. On the stage the witness table was extended to provide space for six; three senior CEGB staff, led by the project director, were joined by three Inspectors, led by the Deputy Chief Inspector. They directly faced the Inspector at his raised table, and two QCs were on their feet, one on either side of the stage; Lord Silsoe for the Board and Michael Howard (now MP) for the Inspectorate. For the first and last time counsel for the NII took the opportunity to cross-examine CEGB witnesses.

But the excitement never quite materialised, and the sparks never quite flew. Soon afterwards the Inspectorate came to the conclusion that it was going to be able to license the PWR and that any design changes that it did insist on would not involve large-scale capital expenditure. The CEGB breathed again—it looked as though its gamble in pushing through the April 1982 design at full speed was going to pay off.

National Nuclear Corporation
The CEGB's rejection of NNC's April 1981 design for Sizewell 'B' had an effect on the timescale of the NII's assessment, on the ability of the public inquiry to fulfil its function, and on the credibility of the Secretary of State. It also, obviously, had an effect on NNC. The Corporation is the last nuclear design and construction organisation in Britain—the last of the consortia. It was established in 1973 with 50 per cent of the shares held by GEC, 35 per cent by a group of other interested companies, and 15 per cent by the UKAEA. In 1975 the Nuclear Power Company was set up as the operating arm of NNC, and GEC took on the management of this company. GEC was thus the last British company to have an active interest in the nuclear construction business. However in 1976 it reduced its holding to 30 per cent and, because no other buyer could be found, the AEA increased its to 35 per cent. In October 1980 GEC also withdrew from its commitment to manage NPC. There is no doubt that GEC was intimately involved in the CEGB's extraordinary announcement of 1973 (see Chapter 2). When the orders then envisaged did not materialise, the company pulled out.

NNC was capitalised at £10 million in 1973, which has not been increased. It is unable to take on the risk of building entire nuclear stations for the Board, as its consortia predecessors had tried to do, and a CEGB board member said:[15]

It would be unrealistic to expect a substantial share of the financial risk [of Sizewell 'B'] to be borne other than by the CEGB.

NNC was unable to bring significant financial resources to the project, and it seemed that it was unable to bring very much design expertise either. Its experience in gas-cooled reactors was irrelevant, and following the rejection of the April 1981 design, it seemed that its experience in station design was also irrelevant. Its role in the British nuclear future was becoming increasingly hard to define.

101

The estimates given by the CEGB for the construction time, and therefore capital cost, of Sizewell 'B' were vulnerable to criticism because of the construction record of the AGRs. The precedent was poor, and the Board had to demonstrate that its record of construction site management would be improved. The Inspector was not convinced by the evidence on project management given by NNC and the Board, and he decided to call further evidence to enable him to:[16]

> judge whether the cost figures for the construction of Sizewell B can be regarded as reliable, having regard to the degree which successful control of the project can be anticipated with confidence.

He invited Sir Alaistair Frame to give his views on the management proposals for Sizewell 'B' in the light of his extensive experience of large project management. Sir Alaistair was Deputy Chairman and Managing Director of Rio Tinto Zinc, and has been a part-time member of the CEGB and the director in charge of fast reactor development for the AEA.

He came twice to the inquiry, once to present his evidence and later to be cross-examined on it. His second appearance was the more interesting, as the criticisms delivered under cross-examination were even more forthright than those contained in his prepared evidence. His comments about the quality of CEGB construction management was uncomplimentary:[17]

> One is bound. . . to question whether the Board has people of adequate abilities to manage a project of this nature. The record is there for all to see. . . What I like to see, when I am looking for a man to run a project, is a man with a proven track record of achievement, and I do not see that in the Generating Board's performance in the last 10 years, on major capital sites in this country.

His advice, that the CEGB should hire the best PWR man available in the world to run the project, was not accepted by the Board. However, his comments and recommendations concerning the definition of project management responsibilities were. In this context his evidence had a profound effect on both the Sizewell 'B' project and on the structure of the industry. He noted:[18]

I regard this as very important. I would seek that either the CEGB take control of this project or the NNC, that they have one design office, one physical location, not several physical locations throughout the country. If this is not done there will be delays.

Sir Alaistair's perception of the relationship between the CEGB and NNC as being blurred, and his suggestion for resolving the problem, were significant:[19]

I think probably the CEGB man should be in charge on site, CEGB site manager with the NNC or whoever does the nuclear island having the responsibility for that area but responsible to the CEGB man.

This proposal, coming as it did from an independent witness who had been invited by the Inspector to give evidence, suited the Board. It reinforced the views that it already held about the redefinition of responsibilities between the two organisations, and legitimised them. The proposal was accepted, and the project management strategy for the project revised to reflect the controlling role now to be played by the Board.[20] Thus it moved, with Sir Alaistair's help, one step closer to a monopoly in civil nuclear power.

This was directly contrary to the wishes of the Secretary of State for Energy and the Prime Minister, expressed during a meeting of the Cabinet Ministerial Committee on Economic Strategy on 23 October 1979. The minutes of that meeting, reproduced as Appendix 4, record that:

He also proposed that the [nuclear] industry should be reorganised, to strengthen the role of the National Nuclear Corporation relative to the CEGB. The aim would be that by the time the first PWR could be constructed the NNC would be in a position to assume full responsibility for the station, and not merely for the 'nuclear island'.

This was agreed by the Prime Minister and the Committee, and the Energy Secretary's subsequent statement to the House contained a clear reflection of that agreement:[21]

It is the Government's wish that the company [NNC] should take on total project management responsibility for the first PWR.

A final irony
In both April 1981 and April 1982 designs the reactor is contained within a domed containment building circular in cross-section, and in both the required level of redundancy of safety systems is designed to be achieved by the provision of four sets, or trains, of key safety machinery. An important difference between the two is in the layout and segregation of those trains. In the earlier design the reactor containment is completely surrounded by an auxiliary building housing the four trains, which are grouped annularly within it. The later design has all the trains grouped on one side of the containment, with a consequent reduction in their independence and segregation and a diminished resilience to common cause failures.[22]

The 1981 design followed normal UK practice for the AGR stations, but was rejected because of the greater quantities of materials involved, and because the containment and the auxiliary building could not be built simultaneously. The later, adopted, design follows current US practice, but it was noted in Chapter 3 that that practice may be changing. Westinghouse and Mitsubishi are collaborating on the design of an Advanced PWR, the first example of which, Tsuruga-2, is being built in Japan.[23] The APWR, which reflects demands in both American and Japan for greater inherent safety in reactor design, has its trains of safety equipment arranged in the manner of the April 1981 design and the AGRs. Thus at the same time as the UK is abandoning its nuclear safety practices, the US, conscious of the need for greater demonstrated safety, is turning to them.

The design adopted for Sizewell 'B' was out of date before the inquiry started. Any hopes that Britain might be able to compete successfully in the international PWR market must be without foundation. The Department of Trade and Industry, in its submission to the inquiry, maintained that:[24]

Construction of a PWR at Sizewell would provide the British power plant industry with a singularly important element in their export strategy which hitherto has been denied to them, namely a 'home reference' for an exportable nuclear power station.

Even ignoring—as the Department did—the worldwide overcapacity in PWR production facilities, it must be obvious that a demonstrated ability to build an out-of-date PWR will not be very useful as a 'home reference'. America and Japan have moved on, adopting British safety standards as they went, and the UK has chosen obsolescence.

On the available evidence, NNC and the CEGB developed a design for an Advanced PWR which might have gone some way towards relieving legitimate concerns about PWR safety, and would have put British designers in the vanguard of safer reactor development. It was rejected in favour of an elderly, imported American design with a tarnished reputation, in a decision of classic expediency.

NOTES AND REFERENCES

1. This does not apply to UKAEA installations.
2. Hansard, 26 November 1979, col. 859.
3. Hansard, 18 December 1979, col. 291.
4. House of Commons Select Committee on Energy, Session 1980/81, Q. 1842 (30 July 1980).
5. *Ibid.*, Q. 606 (26 March 1980).
6. Letter dated 9 December 1982.
7. Day 13, p. 35C.
8. *Ibid.*, p. 33E. FOE's application, including the text of references

2-6 above, is recorded on pp. 21-58 of day 13.
9. Day 21, p. 5C.
10. Day 66, pp. 8-57.
11. See note 5.
12. Day 76, p. 6.
13. CEGB Statement of Case (CEGB 01), para. 16.14.
14. INQ/69.
15. CEGB/P/1 (ADD 1), p. 2.
16. Day 109, p. 2B.
17. Day 134, p. 9 A-B.
18. Day 109, p. 21E.
19. *Ibid.*, p. 24E.
20. See CEGB/P/46 'The Revised Project Management Arrangements for Sizewell 'B'.'
21. Hansard, 18 December 1979, col. 289.
22. See FOE's cross-examination of the PWR Project Director for a full discussion of the differences, day 176, pp. 24-64.
23. Tsuruga-2 is described in *Atom* no. 355, pp. 11-12.
24. DI/S/1, para. 10.

CHAPTER 7

THE AGR CONTROVERSY

The CEGB's disastrous experience with Advanced Gas-cooled Reactors was briefly described in Chapter 2. It was a disaster of the Board's own making. Perhaps, in the 1960s, the UKAEA was a very much more influential organisation than it is now, and the CEGB a less powerful one, but the series of decisions to order four large twin-reactor AGR stations in as many years, on the basis of experience with one small prototype reactor at Windscale, was the Board's. Perhaps it was too dependent on the Authority for assistance in evaluating the various designs, but the CEGB knew, as it awarded the Dungeness 'B' contract, that the successful design was a sketch design, and that the successful tenderer was under-strength and very possibly unable to complete the contract. With hardly a pause for breath, the Board then proceeded to order three further stations, using two new designs, but without going to tender. By 1970 it was attempting to build four large stations, three of which were prototypes. Whatever the division of blame between the CEGB and the AEA, the AGR suffered very badly from what must have been one of the worst periods of large project mismanagement in British industrial history.

And yet, if you must have power reactors, the AGRs have a great deal to recommend them, particularly in terms of availability and intrinsic safety characteristics (see below). If the Hinkley Point 'B' design, the only first generation AGR on the CEGB system to have a hope of commercial viability, had been adopted from the beginning, and if further orders had been replicas or developments of that design, the AGR story would be radically different. Hinkley's performance would have been better, because the CEGB's resources would have been concentrated on that design, and the embarrassments of Dungeness 'B', Hartlepool and Heysham I would not have happened.

The South of Scotland Electricity Board, whose Magnox station at Hunterston 'A' consistently has a higher availability than any other British nuclear station and the fifth highest in the world,[1] was also persuaded by the AEA to build an AGR. Whether by good luck or good design evaluation, SSEB chose the Hinkley Point design, and has found Hunterston 'B' to be a successful station. Had the CEGB's experience paralleled that of the Scottish board, it is unlikely that its PWR lobby would have achieved and maintained such prominence.

So the AGR presented a dilemma for the CEGB at Sizewell. As the inquiry proceeded it became clear that construction of the latest AGR stations (Heysham II and Torness in Scotland) using designs directly descended from the Hinkley 'B'/Hunterston 'B' design, was going well.[2] The Board was therefore vulnerable to the accusation that it wanted to abandon the AGR at the moment when its success was imminent, when the national investment might begin to show a return. It was pleased with progress at Heysham II, because it substantiated the claim that it could after all build nuclear stations to time and cost—a claim central to the case for the Sizewell PWR—but at the same time the reasons for its historic preference for the PWR were being eroded. This preference had acquired its own institutional momentum within the Board, so it was happy that the latest AGRs were looking as though they would be successful, but at the same time it was concerned in case they were so successful as to challenge the PWR.

Ron Round
The Board did not offer the inquiry a comparison between the safety features of the AGR and the PWR, and stated:[3]

> The submission of evidence on AGR safety to the Inquiry would not be helpful to the Inspector. . . the question that the Inspector is considering is whether the safety of the PWR is acceptable.

There the matter might have rested, had not Mr Ron Round submitted two proofs of evidence to the inquiry on behalf of the Norfolk County Labour Party. Mr Round had recently retired from the position of Deputy Chief Engineer of the Eastern Electricity Board, and he was one of a small group of participants who, while having reservations, did not object to nuclear power on principle but to the PWR in particular. He might not have taken part had the Board applied for an AGR (or, more accurately, had it sought to activate the AGR consent for the Sizewell 'B' site, granted in 1969). His views were thus of considerable interest because they reflected the views of those parts of the nuclear industry that felt that the CEGB had understated the merits of the AGR.

In his first proof[4] Mr Round concluded that the performance parameters used by the Board to evaluate the economics of the AGR were pessimistic. Using more realistic parameters he found that there was no significant difference between either the capital or the running costs of the two reactors, and that the AGR had the potential to out-perform the PWR. His second proof, which examined comparative safety, argued that:[5]

> The PWR has a greater inherent potential for disaster than the AGR, which cannot be compensated for entirely by additional devices to ameliorate the consequences of breakdown, or of operator failure.

The conclusion of his evidence as a whole was:[6]

> The safety case cannot be isolated from the economic case. Only in the event of a significantly more favourable economic case could a marginally lower safety case be discounted. Where the economic cases are closely balanced, the reactor with the lower safety case, however marginal, should be discounted.

The first proof found that four of the parameters in particular were pessimistic. The most significant of these was the CEGB's assumption that the load factor of a new AGR would be 65 per cent. This figure was based on the early experience of the Hinkley Point 'B' station, and ignored the later experience both there and at the SSEB's Hunterston 'B' that demonstrated that load factors of 85 per cent and higher could be achieved. He therefore suggested that a central figure for a new station should be 80 per cent, and commented under cross-examination:

> Come what may, the PWR will be refuelled off-load. That puts a limit on its availability, which does not exist for the AGR.

The effect of that single change, making no change in the other assumptions made by the Board, is to make the economic difference between the two reactor types marginal.

Mr Round looked at three further parameters. He suggested that the 25-year lifetime assumed for the AGR was too low, and submitted an AEA research paper in support. This paper concluded:[7]

> Relative improvements indicated by the research programme suggest a life extension to 40 years at 85% load factor.

He suggested that a 35-year assumption—the same as that for the PWR—was more appropriate. Mr Round also expressed the view that the 20 per cent contingency allowance for the AGR was too high, as a new AGR would be a replication of an existing design, although that figure was appropriate for a first British PWR. He suggested a 10 per cent contingency for the AGR. Finally Mr Round proposed an increase in the efficiency parameter (see Appendix 1, Glossary) for the AGR from the CEGB's 39.6 per cent to 41.5 per cent, a figure lower than the efficiency of 41.6 per cent that the CEGB expects to achieve at Hinkley Point. Mr Round also made allowance for the fuel ratings that are already being achieved, a 33 per cent improvement on the CEGB's assumed fuel rating for a new AGR. The cumulative effect of these changed assumptions was, in Mr Round's evidence, to make electricity from the AGR some 10 per cent cheaper than that from the PWR.

His second proof of evidence examined the design of the AGR, in so far as its intrinsic features have an effect on safety. Two major design principles are relevant; firstly the massive reactor core which is the result of using graphite as the moderator, and secondly the use of a gas, carbon dioxide, as the coolant. These two principles of design govern the way in which the AGR deals with heat loads in normal and accident situations, and contribute to a stability that is not found in the PWR.

Significant quantities of heat continue to be generated in a reactor for many hours after the fission process has been stopped and the reactor shut down. This 'decay heat' is caused by the continued decay of fission products within the core, and is unstoppable. Most of the safety precautions in a reactor are designed to deal with it, and the continuing production of decay heat was the cause of the week-long struggle to control the damaged reactor at Three Mile Island after the accident in March 1979.

Immediately after shut-down, decay heat generates about 7 per cent of the heat generated under normal operating conditions, and after one hour, 1.5 per cent.[8] In the case of the Sizewell design, 1.5 per cent of the thermal power is about 50 MW of heat, or the power of the largest steel melting furnace in Britain. For 24 hours after shut-down the decay heat produces more than 15 MW, or the power of a large, 60 tonne, steel furnace, and for a month the heat remains above 5 MW.[9]

If the reactor's cooling system is working, such quantities of heat are obviously not difficult to deal with. But if the coolant flow is interrupted or stopped, the rate at which decay heat causes core temperatures to rise depends on the characteristics of the reactor in question. At Three Mile Island core temperatures of 2,200°C were reached after three hours, despite the automatic operation of the emergency core cooling system.[10] The melting point of PWR fuel cladding is 1,850°C, and of the fuel itself 2,790°C. Television pictures of the inside of the core show clear evidence of molten fuel.[11]

The speed at which temperatures in the core rise after an interruption to coolant flow depends partly on the mass of

111

the core assembly and its ability to absorb heat, and partly on the behaviour of the coolant. The PWR was conceived as a propulsion unit, and lightness and compactness were important design criteria. Even large commercial reactors have a relatively small mass, with the core, fuel and pressure vessel weighing about 720 tonnes. The all-important heat capacity of this mass is the equivalent to some 65 tonnes of water. An AGR core is far heavier, consisting of about 1,450 tonnes of graphite, 100 tonnes of fuel, and 2,000 tonnes of steel baffle and liner, all of which has a heat capacity of 650 tonnes of water. This ignores the additional heat sink provided by the mass of concrete surrounding the AGR pressure vessel, and it should be remembered that, as there are two AGR reactors to a power station, and only one PWR, the heat produced in an AGR core is a little over half of that produced in a large PWR core. In the event of a coolant accident, an AGR core produces much less heat and has a far greater capacity to absorb it, which ensures a very much slower rate of temperature increase and the virtual impossibility of melting the fuel.

The behaviour of the coolant itself under accident conditions is important to considerations of intrinsic reactor safety. PWR cooling is effected by superheated water, under sufficient pressure to prevent boiling, circulating through the core. An accident involving loss of pressure or of flow rate could result in the almost immediate formation of steam bubbles inside the core. The behaviour of 'two-phase' cooling cannot be predicted, but the one certainty is that steam is a less efficient coolant than water (in a water-cooled reactor), and so temperatures would rise further and more steam would be formed. Additionally, steam reacts with the PWR fuel cladding material (a zirconium alloy), producing hydrogen and more heat, as happened at Three Mile Island. Carbon dioxide, as used in the AGR, does not change state on a change of pressure, and does not react with the fuel cladding. In the event of a complete loss of coolant flow, carbon dioxide in the AGR has the additional great advantage of being able to cool the core by natural circulation alone for more than 11 hours.[12]

Mr Round concluded that the internal temperature of an

PWR can rise to critically dangerous levels within minutes of a loss of coolant accident, but in the worst possible conditions the core temperature of an AGR would remain well within the limits of safety for many hours. Safety features, with sufficient redundancy to satisfy the NII, may reduce the chance of a PWR catastrophe to acceptable (in technical terms, incredible) levels. But events with very low probability do occur,[13] and Mr Round questioned the wisdom of exchanging intrinsic stability and resilience for add-on safety devices, especially if the economic advantage is at best marginal. He caught the attention of the Inspector, who invited the South of Scotland Electricity Board, as the only body other than the CEGB to have experience of building and operating AGRs, to give evidence on the economic merits of that system. Mr Round thus became one of the few individuals who materially affected the course of events at the inquiry; his evidence led directly to an expert challenge to the CEGB's PWR proposal, the more effective for being completely unexpected.

The South of Scotland Electricity Board
Mr Donald Miller, the SSEB's Chairman, personally accepted the Inspector's invitation and gave evidence on 28 and 29 June 1984.[14] He challenged the CEGB's comparative economic assumptions with considerable authority, and publicly demonstrated the lack of unanimity within the industry on the question of reactor choice. Mr Henry Brooke, Counsel to the Inquiry, commented:[15]

No doubt in due course research students can write theses on the approach of two different nationalised Boards on exactly the same material and the different conclusions that they reach.

Later in the same day he put this proposition to Mr Baker, the senior CEGB policy witness, who agreed with it:

It is quite clear that there is a fundamental difference of approach between you and the Scottish board about the way one ought to look at the performance which is now

113

currently being achieved by the Hinkley Point and Hunterston stations.

A recurrent theme of Mr Miller's evidence was that a new AGR would be based closely on the latest Heysham II/ Torness design for which all contracts had been let and at which work was well advanced. Although the performance of a new station would be an improvement, no design changes would be required. It would be a replicated design for which manufacturing facilities already existed, and the design could therefore be accurately costed. Mr Miller was clear about the extent of the failure to replicate:

> I hesitate to embark on a lecture about the follies that we have embarked on during my working career in building power plant. . . we have singularly failed to replicate plant and this has been a national characteristic through my 34+ years. Every one of these stations here, and you find a similar situation anywhere you look in the United Kingdom, that everyone was a prototype.

He clearly saw the PWR as yet another prototype, and as a failure to take advantage of AGR experience and facilities; he was also clear that, in the context of a limited programme of reactor construction, 'possibly between 5 and 7 units of 1,300 MW capacity in the next two decades in the UK', only one reactor type could be supported. He commented:

> Therefore, the outcome of this inquiry and the subsequent Government decision is seen by SSEB as determining the future reactor system of the United Kingdom for the next two decades or more. Our concern is, therefore, that we run the risk of losing the option of building further AGR stations in the future.

In January 1978 the Labour Energy Secretary, Tony Benn, said that 'We must develop the option of adopting the PWR system in the early 1980s'.[16] As usual there was bipartisan agreement on nuclear policy, and in December of the following year David Howell, the new Conservative

Energy Secretary, said that 'The next power station should be a PWR'[17] and announced the recent nuclear programme described in Chapter 2. But later in his speech Mr Benn commented that it would be 'highly irresponsible. . . to write off all the experience we have in gas-cooled technology',[18] and backed his support for the AGR by authorising the construction of Heysham II and Torness. The policy of having two reactor systems available for ordering—the 'dual reactor strategy'—was thus instituted, and it is a classic political compromise between British technology, expertise and pride on one hand, and the CEGB's persistent preference for the PWR on the other.

As a policy it is indecisive and impracticable, and only sustainable on the assumption of a high level of power station ordering. Although the CEGB's forecasts for future capacity requirements were much more bullish than those of the SSEB, it too, in its preferred future, envisaged only one reactor type. The CEGB's evidence was that:[19]

> Subject to gaining consent for Sizewell 'B', there is likely to be a strong case for further stations to be of the PWR type.

Both Boards saw the dual reactor strategy as unsatisfactory, but they differed in their choice of the reactor that should win the race. Mr Miller also made it clear that he was concerned for the future of the NNC. Clearly conscious of the events described in the last chapter, he considered that the Corporation, as the 'centre of AGR design expertise', could not survive a decision in favour of the PWR.

Mr Miller was concerned that a PWR at Sizewell would ensure the demise of the AGR. He and his board were convinced that, if there was to be only one reactor system available in the UK, it should be the AGR. Not only were existing designs capable of producing competitively-priced electricity, but there was a good prospect of AGR costs coming down in future. Partly this was because no new investment is needed in manufacturing or support facilities, partly because of the advantages of replication, and partly because the AGR's performance is capable of being enhanced within the existing design. His comparative costings were based on this 'enhanced AGR', which would have a net output of 1,3600 MW(e)–680 MW per reactor—rather than the 1,300 MW of the Heysham II/Torness design. On the SSEB's assumptions, such a station would be slightly more expensive to build than the PWR but cheaper to run.

The CEGB reacted to Mr Miller's evidence as only a very wealthy monopoly utility could:[20]

> The CEGB has indicated to NNC that the Board would wish to see NNC maintain sufficient design and engineering resource to enable the AGR option to be sustained to 1990 in the absence of an order, and that it is prepared to support the retention of these resources.

The dual reactor strategy is thus to be maintained, at least for a few years, at the expense of the electricity consumer. Mr Baker, a CEGB board member, gave three reasons for this. Firstly a general prudence of the part of the CEGB, and an uncertainty as to reactor preferences in the short-term future, especially in a party political context.[21] Secondly Mr Baker considered that it was not impossible that electricity demand would pick up to such an extent as to require that AGR, PWR and coal stations be available for construction. Thirdly, he recognised that the SSEB might want to order a further AGR in about 1990, but did not have the resources to maintain the option on its own until that date. He commented: 'If I were Mr Miller running the Scottish system, I might well be inclined to stick with gas reactor technology.' He agreed that a single PWR on the system 'is not an attractive prospect', and indicated that the CEGB was expecting to order at least two or three more after Sizewell, to take advantage of replication. The SSEB, with its lower order rate, could not expect to establish a series of PWRs, and so the CEGB would keep the AGR option open for the SSEB for a few years.[22]

Perhaps the most significant part of that cross-examination of Mr Baker came when he hinted at another reason why the Board wanted to build a PWR rather than another AGR; a reason additional to those economic and strategic arguments which had already been put forward. He suggested that that the CEGB's AGR software resources were under 'enormous pressure':

> Undoubtedly, manufacturing industry would be capable and glad to start building another one tomorrow. However. . . the coincidence of work on the existing operational AGRs, the very difficult commissioning phase for Dungeness 'B', Hartlepool and Heysham, and pursuing the front-end design on Heysham II. . . One would hope, and we are obviously working hard towards it, that one would get over the hump. I have every hope that Heysham II and Torness[23] are going to prove easier to commission than the prototype stations. Therefore one can see a position in about three years time, but it will not be much before that, when one might be saying that there is a free resource capability in AGR technology which is available.

The idea that the CEGB might not have enough software resources to support the design and construction of another AGR was a new one. The implication was that one advantage of the PWR was that much of the necessary support could be bought from America, along with the reactor. In this way the CEGB could build a new nuclear station at a time when its own resources were fully stretched.

Many people were taken by surprise by the strength of the Scottish board's support for the AGR, none more than the CEGB. SSEB's closing submission[24] was a trenchant defence of the British system, and concluded:

> In short, the SSEB has faith in the AGR system as operating at Hunterston/Hinkley, both now and in the future. It stands comparison in terms of economics and of performance with any other system in the world. It is British, and supported by British expertise and British industry. [SSEB] believes most strongly that this country cannot support two different systems at the same time. . . It is misleading to talk of options. There is no choice—except to maintain the AGR system or to introduce the PWR. . . SSEB are concerned that permitting just a single station

117

would inevitably have the effect of ending the AGR system there and then.

NOTES AND REFERENCES

1. *Nuclear Engineering International,* October 1984 Supplement, p. 64.
2. CEGB Annual Report 1983/84, p. 30, for Heysham II.
3. Letter from CEGB to Norfolk County Labour Party, 10 February 1984.
4. NCLP/P/1, presented and cross-examined on day 146.
5. NCLP/P/2, presented and cross-examined on day 224.
6. *Ibid.,* para. 31.
7. *Atom* no. 323, pp. 188–191 (NCLP/S/1).
8. CEGB Statement of Case (CEGB 01), para. 15.9.
9. Figures from SSBA/P/4 paras. 21–23. They assume a 3 year old core.
10. 'Core Temperature Transient in the Early Phase of Core Uncovering at TMI-2' in *Progress on Nuclear Energy* Vol. 7, pp. 197–228.
11. *Spectrum,* April 1984 (NCLP/S/9).
12. 'The Safety of the AGR', CEGB 1982, p. 84 (CEGB/S/56).
13. A letter to the East Anglian Daily Times, shortly before the Sizewell inquiry opened, read:
    'The deputy chairman and chief executive of UKAEA, and his scientists, whilst "believing" that there is now only a 1 in 100 million chance of a major Sizewell B disaster should bear in mind that the chance of combining eight draws in one line on a treble chance football pool is 1,217,566,350 to one, and it happens frequently.'
14. Days 241 and 242. He was not asked to comment on AGR safety.
15. Day 285, p. 8G. Mr Brooke may have read FOE's Autumn 1984 Newsletter: 'The SSEB's importance was that, on the basis of exactly the same information and experience as the CEGB, it could come to precisely different conclusions. This is a supreme example of the political nature of the arguments for the PWR.'
16. Hansard, 25 January 1978, col. 1392.
17. Hansard, 18 December 1979, col. 288.
18. Reference 16, col. 1398.
19. CEGB/P/1, para. 133.
20. CEGB/P/1 (ADD 8), p. 5.
21. Day 284, p. 23 D–E, p. 24D.
22. Or was Mr Baker looking forward to a reorganisation, or rationalisa-

tion, of the UK electricity supply industry?

23. Day 285, p. 36. This is Mr Baker's second reference to Torness, in a proprietorial sense, in the full transcript of this answer.
24. Day 319, pp. 88–107.

PART 3

THE CONTEXT

'It seems to me that the putative enemy in the East would not change its plans materially if it knew that the CEGB's reactors had produced either 10, 20 or 30 tonnes of plutonium. . . it does not seem to me that this is a sensitive area in the context of national security.'
(Dr Ross Hesketh, speaking for CND, day 284, p. 15C.)

Chart II.—Nuclear Power Unit and Ancillary Plant

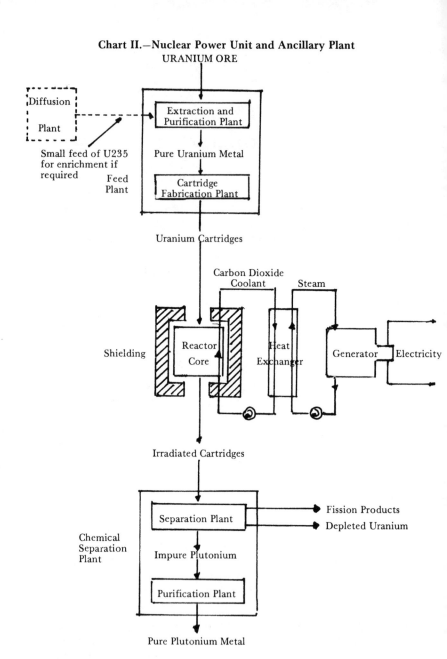

URANIUM ORE

Diffusion Plant

Small feed of U235 for enrichment if required

Extraction and Purification Plant

Pure Uranium Metal

Feed Plant

Cartridge Fabrication Plant

Uranium Cartridges

Carbon Dioxide Coolant

Steam

Shielding

Reactor Core

Heat Exchanger

Generator

Electricity

Irradiated Cartridges

Separation Plant

Fission Products

Depleted Uranium

Chemical Separation Plant

Impure Plutonium

Purification Plant

Pure Plutonium Metal

From the 1955 White Paper, 'A Programme of Nuclear Power' (Cmd. 9389), p. 16.

CHAPTER 8

PLUTONIUM[1]

This is the metal at the heart of nuclear technology—the urgency to manufacture it was the stimulus from which all the rest was developed. The challenge was immense, and success indicated that two prerogatives previously regarded as divine had been usurped by men; creation, and massive destruction. For the scientists plutonium was powerful evidence of a new phase in scientific method, in which they might understand, and make adjustments to, creation itself. For the soldiers its significance was that it provided a weapon amenable to their control, as terrible as any natural calamity. Politicians, seeing both creative and destructive potential, recognised that possession of and competence in the new element would define post-war status and international relationships, and could, perhaps, provide limitless energy for the new society. The early story of plutonium was therefore different in breadth and depth from earlier scientific and military developments. Never before had science created something entirely, chemically, new, and never before had a weapon been so absolutely efficient. It is not surprising that the minds of men were entranced, and have stayed entranced in some measure, ever since.

As noted in Chapter 1, two types of fission bomb were developed by the Manhattan Project teams during the Second World War, using the two fissile substances available, then as now. The one using uranium-235 was in a direct line of descent from the British MAUD report of 1941, and depended on the separation of that isotope from the non-fissile uranium-238 that makes up the bulk of the naturally-occurring metal. The second depended on building a reactor (formerly called a pile) in which to manufacture the plutonium, and a reprocessing plant in which to separate it.

Uranium isotope separation proved to be immensely difficult, despite early British optimism,[2] although enough U-235 was separated to make the Hiroshima bomb, it was even then clear that the plutonium route was the easier option.[3]

The manufacture of plutonium depends on the presence, in a reactor, of the U-238 isotope that is an impurity in a uranium fission bomb. When bombarded with neutrons, the U-238 transmutes to plutonium-239.[4] A reactor that uses as fuel a mixture of the two uranium isotopes is, therefore, a very neat arrangement in terms of plutonium production, because a fissioning U-235 atom emits, on average, 2.5 neutrons. This is enough to fission another U-235 atom and ensure that the chain reaction is self-sustaining, and to transmute a U-238 atom into Pu-239. There is even an allowance for neutrons to escape from the system without having collided with either.[5] By chance, it was found that the ratio of U-235 to U-238 that is found in the naturally-occurring element (0.7:99.3 per cent) was found to be satisfactory for this process.[6]

Such a brief description cannot do justice to the theoretical and technical problems of reactor physics that were encountered and solved. (See Appendix 2.) The process was made to work, both at Hanford during the war and at Windscale after it, by scientists of great ability and motivation, helped by national priorities and unconstrained budgets. Two problems in particular are of interest here: one concerns the immense amount of unwanted heat given off by U-235 fission, and the other concerns the extraction of plutonium from the discharged fuel.

The heat from the earliest plutonium production piles was simply dispersed, by river water at Hanford and by cooling fans at Windscale. Later, when the military urgency had diminished somewhat, this heat enabled the reactor technology to be adopted for electricity generation, and provided the basis for one of the world's largest and most powerful industries. In Britain the beginnings of the civil programme was inextricably bound up with the military programme, because the first reactors in the world to supply significant quantities of electricity were the military plutonium reactors at Calder Hall and Chapelcross. For good pragmatic reasons the fission heat from these eight reactors was and is used to run turbo-generators. The British civil programme stayed bound up with the military programme because, again for good pragmatic reasons, it used reactors based on the Calder Hall design for the first 9 power stations. Because of this line of development, even when optimised for electricity production, Magnox reactors continue to produce more plutonium, with a higher proportion of the 239 isotope, than other types of commercial reactor.[7] The continued extraction and stockpiling of this plutonium provides powerful evidence that the political will does not yet exist to demonstrate the separation of the two programmes.

Optimisation and isotopic composition
All reactors, whatever their primary purpose, produce both plutonium and heat. If the primary purpose is plutonium, heat is the by-product. If the primary purpose is electricity, plutonium is the by-product. Optimisation for plutonium production involves ensuring that as much Pu-239—the fissile isotope—is obtained. Under prolonged irradiation, Pu-239 will transmute to Pu-240, and then to even higher isotopes which, being non-fissile or spontaneously fissile, are impurities in military terms. Thus the fuel rods in a reactor operating under a military regime are withdrawn fairly quickly, before unacceptable quantities of the higher isotopes of plutonium are produced. Optimisation for electricity production involves leaving the fuel rods in the reactor until almost all the U-235 has fissioned and the maximum heat has been obtained. This does not significantly change the quantity of plutonium produced, but it increases the quantities of the higher isotopes in relation to Pu-239. Calder Hall and Chapelcross have been optimised for electricity production since 1967,[8] but have still produced plutonium which has been required by the UK military, as well as some for the USA.[9]

Plutonium with a high proportion of the 239 isotope is therefore expensive to produce because less electricity is generated to off-set production costs. In 1954 discussions in a US Congressional Sub-committee indicated that the price of plutonium for weapons, that is almost pure Pu-239, was

123

then 30 dollars a gram, but the price of plutonium for fuel, that is for civil research, was 12 dollars a gram.[10] Three 'grades' of plutonium are commonly recognised, and they are differentiated by the proportion of Pu-240, the main non-fissile isotope, that they contain. Weapons grade has less than 7 per cent Pu-240, fuel grade between 7 and 19 per cent, and reactor grade more than 19 per cent Pu-240.[11] Early specifications for military plutonium were even more exacting, but as techniques for overcoming the problems of spontaneous fission were overcome,[12] the presence of the non-fissile isotopes became less important. In 1977 a bomb made from reactor grade plutonium was detonated in the United States, and a scientist from the Livermore Laboratory commented that:

> It is likely that a nuclear explosive designer would choose to minimise the Pu-240 concentration, given the choice. However, an entirely credible national nuclear explosives capability could be constructed using only reactor-grade plutonium.

Claims that the plutonium produced by power reactors is unsuitable for weapons use are untrue. Special optimised facilities to make high purity Pu-239 are not necessary to acquire 'an entirely credible national nuclear explosives capability'. All that is required is an off-the-shelf nuclear power station and a separation process on a large laboratory scale. It is certain that many of the countries listed in Table 8.1 have ensured that they are capable of diverting civil plutonium to weapons, should the perceived need arise. Those that are signatories to the Non-Proliferation Treaty (NPT, see Appendix 6) may not yet have done so. But that fragile, confused document, which seeks to encourage the proliferation of nuclear power but discourage the proliferation of nuclear weapons, provides for the signatories' withdrawal at three months notice if their national interests so demand.

Table 8.1 Power reactors in operation under construction and planned, December 1983[a]

Country	Units operational	Units under construction	Units planned
USA	80	49	2
USSR	43	41	39
France	36	25	3
UK	35	7	1
Japan	28	10	10
West Germany	16	11	10
Canada	15	8	1
Sweden	10	2	—
Spain	6	9	4
Belgium	6	2	—
India	5	5	4
East Germany	5	—	—
Taiwan	4	2	4
Bulgaria	4	2	2
Switzerland	4	1	—
Finland	4	—	—
Korea, Rep of	3	6	4
Italy	3	3	—[b]
Czechoslovakia	2	9	5
Argentina	2	1	3
Netherlands	2	—	—
Hungary	1	3	4
Brazil	1	1	7
Pakistan	1	—	1
Yugoslavia	1	—	1
Austria	1[c]	—	—
Poland	—	2	4
Romania	—	2	3
Cuba	—	2	—
Mexico	—	2	—
South Africa	—	2	—
China	—	1	6
Phillipines	—	1	—
Egypt	—	—	4
Libya	—	—	2

Table 8.1 (cont)

Country	Units operational	Units under construction	Units planned
Iraq	—	—	1
Israel	—	—	1
Thailand	—	—	1
Turkey	—	—	1

Notes to Table 8.1
From *Nuclear Engineering International,* October 1984 Supplement, p. 3.
   a. All commercial, dual purpose and large research reactors which supply power to a national system are included.
   b. Italy has tentative plans, unconfirmed at the end of 1984, for 6 large PWRs.
   c. Unit complete but not approved for operation.
If any pattern can be discerned in this table, it is that the countries that are most ambitious in their planning are the developing countries. The period of nuclear enthusiasm in Western Europe and North America seems to be coming to an end.

Reprocessing
As BNFL's Managing Director told the Sizewell inquiry:[13]

The purpose of the original Windscale reprocessing line was to make plutonium for weapons.

As nuclear weapons states, or states which have already proliferated into nuclear weapons, the United States, the Soviet Union, Britain, France and China are not constrained in their civil nuclear activities by the NPT. However the attitude towards proliferation held by the UK and the US, the two countries that primarily concern the present work, are markedly different. As noted in Chapter 1, the Americans have never reprocessed significant[14] quantities of irradiated fuel from their civil reactors—it is stored unreprocessed until a decision is made about disposal. President Carter's support for the US Nuclear Non-Proliferation Act of 1978 'demonstrated the strength of our concern here at home for the hazards of a plutonium economy'.[15] The non-reprocessing of civil fuel remains national policy, as much because it would be uneconomic in private hands as for reasons of international policy.

Such a clear distinction between the military and civil fuel cycles cannot be made in the United Kingdom. All the plutonium produced in the civil reactors has been, and on present intentions will continue to be, separated out of the irradiated fuel. This is done despite the fact that the UK, with America and Russia, is a depository signatory to the Non-Proliferation Treaty. The use of plutonium in commercial fast reactors is at least 25 or 30 years away,[16] and so the only possible present short and medium-term future use for it is in warheads. For as long as civil reprocessing continues, the electricity supply industry will be bound up with a process which has an exclusively military purpose.

The result is that the CEGB owns the largest unallocated stockpile of separated plutonium in the non-communist world. It is the largest stockpile because the Magnox stations were among the earliest in the world, and because they produce more plutonium per unit of electricity than other reactors.[17] It is the largest separated stockpile because the Americans have not reprocessed their civil fuel. It is the largest separated unallocated stockpile because the CEGB has no use for it.

Two arguments have been employed to defend the reprocessing of civil Magnox fuel. The first is that, unlike PWR fuel and to a lesser extent AGR fuel, it corrodes under water and so cannot be stored for long periods: some treatment is needed. This is no longer a reason to reject long-term storage as a policy, because the CEGB is a world leader in dry storage, and built the first large dry stores for Magnox fuel at Wylfa in 1970. These can keep the irradiated fuel indefinitely in an inert gas environment. (See Chapter 10.) If there was once a requirement to reprocess Magnox fuel, for management reasons, there is no longer.

It has also been said that reprocessing reduces the total quantity of radioactivity that is generated by nuclear operations. The truth is that the most active waste category, the heat-generating liquid wastes, arises solely as a result of the chemical operations involved in reprocessing. The quantities of intermediate-level wastes are also significantly increased. Long-term storage does not give rise to these additional wastes.

Reprocessing is also the more expensive option of the two. It adds to electricity costs.[18] Its sole advantage is that it reduces the volume of irradiated wastes that have to be stored. The continued reprocessing of Magnox fuel, which results in unnecessary wastes being created, and two tonnes of plutonium a year being produced (see below), seems inept and irresponsible, an activity apparently compelled by its own momentum, whose only result is to foster suspicions about the continued intimacy between the civil and military fuel cycles.

The Windscale Inquiry of 1977 concerned an application by BNFL to build a new reprocessing plant, THORP, to handle irradiated fuel from reactors that use slightly enriched uranium oxide fuel, such as AGRs, PWRs and BWRs. At that time the establishment assumption was that reprocessing was a necessary and inevitable part of nuclear power operations, even for fuel which does not have the problems of corrosion under water that Magnox fuel has.[19] Since then, opinion has shifted, and the CEGB was careful to make clear to the Sizewell inquiry that:[20]

What I am saying is that there are two options [i.e. reprocessing and long-term storage] . . . both of which are probably perfectly satisfactory, and you are going to choose whichever one you want in the light of the economic circumstances and the environmental circumstances at the time.

At the time of writing, the Board has yet to sign a contract with BNFL for the reprocessing of its existing and future AGR irradiated fuel, or for its PWR fuel, should any ever arise. The quotation above would seem to imply that it has no immediate intention of doing so.

BNFL, however, operates in an international market, and has secured enough foreign business to justify the THORP plant without the CEGB contract.[21] The reprocessing of foreign fuel appears to be a lucrative business—Counsel for objectors at the Windscale Inquiry were shown the contract with Japan, which one described as very profitable for BNFL[22]—the price charged by BNFL was, (at 1977 prices) £160,000 per tonne of irradiated fuel.[23] Despite BNFL's claim at that inquiry that THORP was needed quickly,[24] its construction did not begin until 1984, and it is not expected to be operational until 1990.

The advantages to the client nations are obvious. The part of nuclear power operations that generates the greatest public disquiet is the management of the irradiated fuel. It is 'back-end' processes, whether involving long-term storage or reprocessing, that necessitate decisions about the permanent locations of radioactive waste, and which give rise to the greatest part of the radioactivity involved. The service that BNFL offers is to remove the irradiated fuel from the territories of the client countries, together with the associated discharges, wastes and public concern, so that those countries may operate nuclear power stations as though the problems of irradiated fuel management do not exist. BNFL's traditions and investment are in reprocessing; it is obviously more difficult to compete in the international market for thermal oxide reprocessing if the national utilities do not themselves use the service. The CEGB's eventual decision may well have an effect on the long-term profitability of a large nationalised concern.

Co-processing
The only commercial reprocessing plant that is operational in the UK is BNFL's Magnox plant at Sellafield.[25] This handles the irradiated fuel from the military reactors at Calder Hall and Chapelcross (which are owned and operated by BNFL) as well as that from the civil Magnox power stations. (The latter includes the CEGB and SSEB stations, and the only two British nuclear power station exports at Tokai Mura in Japan and Latina in Italy.) The reprocessing plant is therefore a dual-purpose one, and is the point at which the civil and military fuel cycles meet.

Because plutonium for weapons, whenever it is required,

is produced there, no safeguards authority is allowed access to the plant—it is not safeguarded.[26] It is not on the list of nuclear facilities which may be nominated for inspection under the voluntary safeguards agreement with the International Atomic Energy Agency to which Britain, as a nuclear weapons state, has subjected herself (see Appendix 6). Inspectors representing the Euratom safeguards organisation, to which Britain became subject on her accession to the European Community in 1973, have been refused access to the plant since that date. This refusal is 'a difficulty between Euratom and HMG', and a witness for BNFL at the Sizewell inquiry commented:[27]

> I'm sure you will appreciate that it is a very difficult problem to resolve.

If the difficulties arose simply because the same plant is used for civil and for military purposes, they could presumably be resolved by allowing inspection during the periods when the plant is on civil work. It is not, after all, the role of safeguards to prevent nuclear weapons states from making weapons. But access is refused at all times, because military and civil fuel is co-processed; that is to say that batches of irradiated fuel from Calder Hall and Chapelcross are mixed with batches of fuel from the civil stations. The military reactors have been optimised for electricity production since 1967,[28] but:[29]

> Optimising them for electricity production does not inhibit their capability of producing plutonium for weapons.

Their spent fuel is co-processed with that from the power stations (but the resultant plutonium is added to the military, not the civil, stockpile) except when an order for plutonium with a high proportion of Pu-239 has been received. When that happens the fuel is discharged early from the reactors, and the reprocessing line stopped and washed out. 'This fuel would then be reprocessed separately in order to preserve its identity and avoid degradation of its isotopic content by

130

mixing with fuel from other stations.'[30]

Except when such special campaigns are required by the military,[31] fuel from Calder Hall and Chapelcross and from the civil reactors is reprocessed together. One consequence of co-processing is that it is impossible to trace the source of the plutonium in the civil and military stockpiles. As BNFL agreed under cross-examination at the Sizewell inquiry, it is 'highly likely' that some of the plutonium that was produced in civil reactors has ended up on the military stockpile.[32] This is difficult to reconcile with the CEGB's categoric assurance that:[33]

> The current position is accordingly quite clear; no plutonium produced in CEGB reactors has been applied to weapons use either in the UK or elsewhere.

or with the Secretary of State's subsequent assurance to Parliament:[34]

> No plutonium produced in any of the CEGB's nuclear power stations has ever been used for military purposes in this country, and there are no plans to use it thus in the future. Further, no plutonium from the CEGB nuclear programme has ever been exported for use in weapons.

Because specific material cannot be traced through the reprocessing line, co-processing necessitates a system of accounting between military and civil, and between the CEGB's, SSEB's and the foreign Magnox stations. Although the British power stations have not been selected for inspection by the IAEA, they are inspected by Euratom.[35] (The military reactors are unsafeguarded.) Therefore the volume of irradiated fuel discharged from the civil reactors, and its estimated plutonium content, (all isotopes) is known to Euratom. When the fuel enters the reprocessing plant it leaves safeguards, and the plutonium that is separated re-enters safeguards on its arrival at the civil stockpile. The Inspectors, whose only concern is to detect and deter the diversion of nuclear materials to military use,[36] are able to check that the amount of plutonium that left the power stations in the discharged fuel matches the amount that arrived at the stockpile. But the Inspectors are not permitted to know the isotopic content of that plutonium,[37] nor to inspect the reprocessing line. They can only inspect the efficiency of the accounting system that allocates plutonium arisings between the civil and military reactors in terms of total volumes. They are quite unable to check on whether the system of allocation is accurate with regard to the isotopic composition, and thus the military usefulness, of the plutonium. They are unable to detect if high-grade civil plutonium has been swapped for the same mass of low-grade military plutonium in the reprocessing plant.

The problem was described in the following way by the Campaign for Nuclear Disarmament in its evidence to the Sizewell inquiry:[38]

Using figures that are of a reasonable magnitude in regard to the United Kingdom, I postulate a civil system and a military system which produced over the same, undefined, short period of time the following quantities of plutonium:

	Civil	Military
Weapons grade	8 kg	1 kg
Fuel grade	72 kg	9 kg
Reactor grade	0	0
Total plutonium	80 kg	10 kg

In this hypothetical case, only the figure of 80 kg would be available to the Safeguards Authorities. Although the plutonium might originate as shown above, the Safeguards Authorities would be none the wiser if the plutonium which arrived at the plutonium store had the following composition:

	Civil	*Military*
Weapons grade	0	9 kg
Fuel grade	80 kg	1 kg
Reactor grade	0	0
Total plutonium	80 kg	10 kg

Only the figure of 80 kg appearing in this second table would be available to the Safeguards Authorities and they would have no evidence of diversion. All they would know was that 80 kg of plutonium had originated under safeguards (first table) and that 80 kg of plutonium had arrived at the civil stockpile under safeguards (second table).

In the example cited in the previous paragraph, up to 8 kg of weapons grade plutonium can be transferred from the civil system to the military, providing that an equal mass of fuel grade plutonium is transferred in the reverse direction. Of such transfers the Safeguards can have no knowledge. . . [such diversion] is an act which lies within the limits set by the Safeguards agreement.

The Managing Director of BNFL agreed:[39]

What the system of auditing does not do is deal with the isotopic composition. . . he is perfectly right in principle, that one could do the sort of exchange within the plant that is implied.

The UK/US Mutual Defence Agreement

By 31 March 1983 the eight civil Magnox stations operated by the CEGB and the one operated by the SSEB had produced 35.5 tonnes of plutonium plus an undisclosed amount exported to the United States. 9 tonnes were still in the reactors, and of the 26.5 tonnes plus the exported material that had been discharged, 17 tonnes were in the stockpile and another 0.5 tonne in the process of joining it.[40] Fifteen months earlier the stockpile had stood at 14.5 tonnes, and the total amount produced had been 33 tonnes.[41] It therefore seems that the civil stockpile of plutonium grows by about 2 tonnes each year.

The quantity exported to America may be deduced by calculating the amount of plutonium that should have been discharged from the power stations by 31 March 1983, and subtracting from it the 26.5 tonnes given in the Parliamentary Answer quoted above. The calculation requires a knowledge of reactor physics and is complex; it was done in 1984 by a nuclear physicist from Imperial College, London, and two colleagues.[42] Their conclusion was that the total discharged by 31 March 1983 was 33.4 tonnes, ± 1 tonne. They therefore concluded that 6.9 tonnes, ± 1 tonne, have been exported to the United States from British power stations. The CEGB contested this figure at the Sizewell inquiry, but refused to release details of plutonium production for national security reasons. As the Inspector remarked, the 6.9 tonnes figure was 'the only figure, I think I am correct in saying, based on a reasoned footing that I have in the Inquiry'.[43] The Board has, however, admitted that the amount of exported civil plutonium is 'about four tonnes'. This figure was given (four times) in a speech by the General Secretary of the Electrical Power Engineers Association (EPEA) to its 1984 Conference, the contents of which had been agreed between the EPEA and the CEGB.[44]

The generating boards own the plutonium that was discharged from their reactors after 31 March 1969. That discharged before then is, or rather was, the property of the UKAEA, which was then responsible for all military and civil fuel cycle activities except power production but including bomb manufacture. The export of civil plutonium to America ceased on 31 December 1970;[45] since that date the trade has been in military plutonium from Calder Hall and Chapelcross.[46] Allowing 20 months for reprocessing, it is possible that the civil plutonium exported to America was UKAEA-owned plutonium, as the total production of power station plutonium to 31 March 1969 was about 4.5 tonnes.[47] If the CEGB/EPEA figure of 'about 4 tonnes' is correct, virtually all the pre-April 1969 production must have been exported. If the 6.9 tonnes figure is correct, the UKAEA plutonium must have been supplemented by either some military plutonium or by some post-April 1969 electricity board plutonium. The question of ownership is, in any case, academic in the context of the uses to which the Americans may have put this material; the Parliamentary Answer quoted above[48] speaks of 'plutonium produced in any of the CEGB's nuclear power stations', and not of plutonium owned by the CEGB.

Although it is specifically a defence treaty, the Agreement for Co-operation on the Uses of Atomic Energy for Mutual Defence Purposes (Cmnd 537, 1958) and its Amendment (Cmnd 733, 1959) was the means whereby this civil plutonium was exported to the United States. It has been regularly renewed since, and in September 1984 was renewed until 1994 (Cmnd 9336). It is the essence of the 'special relationship' between the two countries. It reflects the recognition in America that Britain had developed atomic technology to the point at which she could do, or would soon be able to do, something that America could not do. That something was to produce quantities of plutonium high in the Pu-239 isotope. The effect of the amended Agreement was that British plutonium would be bartered for American tritium and highly enriched uranium, which would be wanted in Britain for thermonuclear bombs and as fuel for submarine propulsion reactors respectively. It was signed in expectation of large quantities of plutonium becoming available from the Magnox programme in the mid-1960s; the US Congressional Sub-Committee responsible for drafting the Mutual Defence Agreement recorded that:[49]

When the Joint Committee was in England, British representatives indicated that plutonium would be produced in great quantities beginning about 1965.

A letter from the Chairman of the Congressional Joint Committee on Atomic Energy to the Acting Chairman of the US Atomic Energy Commission of 13 March 1959 notes that:[50]

At that time [i.e. 1958] we were told that 11,000 kg of plutonium would be obtained from Euratom and the United Kingdom at the weapons price.

Britain was then the major plutonium producer in Europe, and references in the rest of the letter are exclusively to the UK. It seems likely that the Americans expected a large proportion of that 11 tonnes to come from Britain.

There is no doubt of the military purpose of the Mutual Defence Agreement. The preamble recognises that:

... the common defence and security [of the two countries] will be advanced by the exchange of information concerning atomic energy and by the transfer of equipment and materials for use therein.

Article V, paragraph C of the Agreement reads:

Except as may be otherwise agreed for civil uses, the information communicated or exchanged, or the materials or equipment transferred, by either party pursuant to this agreement shall be used by the recipient party exclusively for the preparation or implementation of defence plans in the mutual interests of the two countries.

Despite the kudos that would have been gained, and the embarrassment that would have been saved, no announcement has ever been made to either Parliament or Congress that the caveat contained in the first clause above has been exercised. This was confirmed by Mr Donald Hodel, the United States Secretary of Energy, in 1984:[51]

The US/UK Mutual Defense Agreement permits the use of any plutonium obtained thereby for defense purposes.

His statement clearly includes the pre-1971 plutonium from the British civil power reactors, and may be compared with statements made to Parliament, of which the following is typical:[52]

The balance of the plutonium produced in the Boards' reactors was consigned to the United States before 1971 under the United States/United Kingdom Defence Agreement and... was used by the United States for civil purposes.

The British plutonium sent to the US after 1970 has been from the military reactors at Calder Hall and Chapelcross. Parallel statements were made in both countries. From Mr Hodel in March 1984:[53]

In summary, the United States received several shipments of plutonium, through barter, from the United Kingdom military stockpile between 1971 and the present which were used for United States weapons.

In Parliament, in the following month:[54]

Plutonium derived from the UK's military reactors, has been supplied to the US under the 1958 US/United Kingdom Mutual Defence Agreement during the last 13 years. The United States has been free to put this material to such uses as it has decided.

Both these statements make it clear that military plutonium was not exported to the US until 1971; they therefore confirm that all the pre-1971 plutonium came from the civil reactors.

This export of civil plutonium under the Agreement has become controversial. The metal is used in the research and development of fast reactors (an activity considered to be civilian) as well as in weapons. The United States has only two fast reactor research sites, and in 1984 abandoned its plans for a commercial fast reactor at Clinch River. The two sites are FTFF, whose plutonium inventory is 600 kg,[55] and ZPPR, whose inventory is 3.8 tonnes.[56] Despite the fact that such use is contrary to the terms of the Mutual Defence Agreement, Parliament was told in July 1982 that:[57]

The bulk of the. . . plutonium produced in the generating Boards' Magnox reactors and consigned to the United States before 1971. . . is in the form of 'coupons'. . .

of fuel for these two reactors. If, as the CEGB states,[58] several core loadings for the FTFF totalling almost 3 tonnes have been manufactured, and if these, plus the ZPPR core loading, are almost exclusively made up from British civil plutonium, then 'the bulk' of that plutonium could be resident in those reactors. It is, however, impossible to be certain, in the face of the uncertainty expressed by Mr Hodel:[59]

> The Department of Energy is not aware of which United Kingdom reactor(s) was the source of the plutonium acquired under the 1958 Mutual Defense Agreement.

The US Department of Energy is responsible for both nuclear energy development and for the supply of fissile material to the military. What therefore is certain is that if, despite the wording of the Agreement, several tonnes of British civil plutonium are resident in the fast reactor cores, a similar quantity of US plutonium has been released for use in weapons.

The Mutual Defence Agreement is more than a quarter of a century old, and it is not surprising that public attitudes about the use of power station plutonium have changed over that period. The Agreement has surfaced from time to time in the House of Commons, and it can be seen how the changing attitudes have been reacted to by the government of the day in its Parliamentary statements. A week after the Amendment to the Agreement was announced, the then Prime Minister said, in May 1959:[60]

> Any plutonium which we may exchange with the Americans will come either from the civil nuclear power stations or from the Atomic Energy Authority's own reactors at Calder Hall or Chapelcross.

By March 1963 Berkeley and Bradwell, the first two CEGB nuclear power stations, were producing plutonium, and Parliament was told that:[61]

> Plutonium is being supplied to the USA for military purposes under the terms of the Amendment of 7 May 1959 to the Agreement. . .

This is an important statement, since it was noted above that all plutonium supplied before 1971 came from the civil power stations. It is therefore clear that civil plutonium has been supplied to America for military purposes.

A Prime Ministerial statement of April 1964 shows an awareness that controversy might be developing:[62]

> Our plans do not envisage the use of any of the plutonium produced by our civil reactors in the United Kingdom weapons programme, and I am informed by the United States Government that they have no intention of using the plutonium obtained from us for weapons purposes.

These words do not announce an American commitment to divert the UK plutonium to civil uses, and they do not constitute an agreement between the two countries to exercise the caveat contained in Article V of the Mutual Defence Agreement. The words refer only to an informed intention. Nevertheless this 1964 statement was relied upon until February 1983, when a new assurance was given to Parliament:[63]

> No plutonium from the CEGB nuclear programme has ever been exported for use in weapons.

It is difficult to reconcile this statement with Article V of the Agreement, which states that the materials exchanged:

> shall be used by the recipient party exclusively for the preparation and implementation of defence plans;

and it is difficult to reconcile with Mr Hodel's statement that the Agreement:[64]

> permits the use of any plutonium obtained thereby for defense purposes.

The assurance is impossible to reconcile with the 1963 statement that:[65]

Plutonium is being supplied to the USA for military purposes. . .[66]

Mr Hodel has failed to give absolute assurances that British civil plutonium will not be used in American weapons, and thereby failed to let the British government off the hook. In a series of answers to Representative Ottinger,[67] Mr Hodel uses the phrase

The DOE is not relying on the United Kingdom plutonium supplied between 1964 and 1971 to meet weapons requirements.

or

The UK-origin plutonium will not be relied on to meet weapons requirements.

a total of six times, as though he hopes that repetition will strengthen his words. Nowhere does he make the simple statement that UK plutonium supplied before 1971 will not be used in US weapons. Matters came to a head when Section 214 of bill HR 5048 was due to be discussed in the US House of Representatives. HR 5048 was an authorising bill for USDOE's 1985 and 1986 expenditure on its civil activities, and Section 214 was an attempt to maintain a clear distinction between civil and military in both finance and materials. It read in part:[68]

No plutonium used or produced in, or obtained from, any civilian energy research, development, demonstration or test facility of the Department of Energy. . . may be transferred, reprocessed, used, or otherwise made available for any nuclear explosive purpose.

Mr Hodel, the Energy Secretary, in a letter to the Chairman of the House of Representatives Energy and Commerce Committee, urged against Section 214. His letter constitutes a clear statement of the attitude of the US government to the British civil plutonium:[69] (original emphasis)

Section 214 (b) would affect future use of Government-owned defense plutonium. This includes both the plutonium produced in US Defense Programmes reactors *and* the plutonium obtained from the UK prior to 1971 under the US/UK Mutual Defense Agreement. This agreement stipulates that the plutonium, obtained from the UK in exchange for US defense materials, is to be used for defense activities. The Department's Defense Programmes has loaned this plutonium to DOE energy supply R&D activities with the knowledge of the UK. The terms of the Mutual Defense Agreement, however, remain unchanged. This agreement has been reviewed and approved by the Congress every 5 years since 1958. The loan of this plutonium during the past two decades has been with the understanding that, if required, it would be returned to its owners—Defense Programmes. As I have stated previously, the Department's policy has been and continues to be not to use this material for weapons.

Mr Hodel concludes his letter:

If shortages of defense plutonium critical to national security were experienced at some future date, it would not be in the national interest to prohibit the utilisation of this very valuable and essentially irreplaceable defense material in defense activities.

The position of the American government is therefore quite clear. It will not rule out the possibility of using the British civil plutonium for weapons; it is not the government which wishes to change the terms of the Agreement by which it was obtained. It has decided that America's perceived defence needs have a higher priority than saving the face of the British government, which is embarrassed because its assurances are seen to be empty. Once again British atomic prowess, which was intended to maintain national prestige and status, has provided instead discredit and disrepute.

Although America's position is legally correct, the Mutual Defence Agreement affair has brought disapprobation on both countries. Despite being depository signatories to the

Non-Proliferation Treaty, they have found it expedient to blur the distinction between the civil and military technologies. The Campaign for Nuclear Disarmament, making a application for the disclosure of information at the Sizewell inquiry, said:[70]

> The fragile system of international safeguards. . . rests on establishing a clear distinction between civil and military nuclear systems throughout the world. It is never going to be easy for nuclear weapons states like Britain, France and America to persuade countries with nuclear ambitions like Argentina, Israel, South Africa and Pakistan to resist from making bombs from civil nuclear facilities. The task, however, will become impossible if the line between civil and military is seen to be blurred in the weapons states. If Britain has used its civil reactors to fuel the arms race in America or anywhere else, how can we expect to dissuade other countries from doing the same?

NOTES AND REFERENCES

1. This chapter owes a considerable debt to the Sizewell Working Group of the Campaign for Nuclear Disarmament, in respect of both the cross-examinations that it conducted, and the evidence that it presented, at the Sizewell inquiry.
2. This was the main reason why Churchill decided against attempting an independent British uranium bomb, and agreed to co-operate on the Manhattan Project.
3. Although it is interesting to note that, having obtained the materials, the uranium bomb is easier to make. The rate of spontaneous fission is lower in U-235 than in Pu-239 and so the engineering is simpler. The spontaneous fission rate of Pu-239 increases further with the presence of Pu-240.
4. U-235 is fissile, as is Pu-239. U-238 is fertile.
5. In order to increase the chance of hitting the nuclei of their target atoms, the neutrons are slowed down to thermal speeds by collision with atoms of the moderator. As Gowing remarks (Appendix 2): 'Atoms consist largely of empty space, and if an atom were magnified to the size of a house the nucleus would still appear to be smaller than a pinhead; the wonder is that neutrons ever hit nuclei.'
6. Given a moderator and internal reactor components made from materials with low neutron capture. Many power reactors (AGR and PWR, not Magnox) use fuel slightly enriched with U-235 to increase

the rate of fission.
7. Hansard, 27 July 1983, col. 437 (some copies 439) gives:

	Tonnes Total Plutonium per GWey generated (net)	*% Pu-239*
Magnox	0.80	60–80
AGR	0.25	50–60
PWR	0.30	55–60

8. Day 274, p. 52E; letter from BNFL to the author 2 October 1984.
9. Hansard, 25 April 1984, col. 506.
10. Amending the Atomic Energy Act of 1954: Hearings before the Subcommittee on Agreements for Co-operation of the Joint Committee on Atomic Energy, 85th Congress of the United States, 1958, p. 75 (being CND/P/1 ref. 142).
11. Magnox reactors in normal operation produce fuel grade plutonium; AGRs and PWRs produce reactor grade.
12. See note 3.
13. Day 274, p. 39D.
14. See Chapter 1, note 44.
15. President Carter, cited in Committee on International Relations, 95th Congress of the United States, 5 August 1977 (being CND/P/2, ref. 48);
16. Sir Peter Hirsh, Chairman of the UKAEA, in evidence to the House of Commons Public Accounts Committee, 1984, and cited by the House of Commons Energy Committee, Session 1983/84, ninth report, para. 22.
17. See note 6.
18. See *The Guardian*, 15 April 1985.
19. PWR fuel seems capable of indefinate storage under water; BNFL/P/1, para. 3.3 notes that it has been stored for 23 years without problems, presumably in the US. AGR fuel may be kept under water for at least 10 years, but the CEGB assumes long-term storage in dry stores (*ibid.*, para. 3.4).
20. Day 126, p. 54D.
21. 'BNFL would not proceed [with building THORP] if, in the event, the company was unable to obtain sufficient foreign business to make the project worthwhile.' Windscale Inquiry Report, para. 9.17.
22. *Ibid.*, para. 9.18.
23. *Ibid.*, para. 9.15.
24. *Ibid.*, para. 8.6.
25. Prototype Fast Reactor (PFR) fuel is reprocessed at Dounreay.
26. It is the only not exclusively military plant on the Sellafield site which is not inspected by the safeguards authorities. Day 274, p. 64A.
27. *Ibid.*, p. 62F.
28. *Ibid.*, p. 52E.
29. *Ibid.*, p. 53G.

30. Letter from BNFL to CND, 18 July 1983, quoted on Day 274, p. 52A.
31. There was one civilian order for high Pu-239 material from Japan during the early 1970s. It was fulfilled partly from Wylfa and partly from the military reactors. *Ibid.*, pp. 50B–51E.
32. *Ibid.*, pp. 54G–55E.
33. CEGB/P/1, para. 162.
34. Hansard, 4 February 1983, col. 206.
35. See Appendix 6. In the UK, as a weapons state, the IAEA nominates nuclear sites for inspection from a list prepared by HMG. Two are currently nominated; neither are power stations. Euratom, on the other hand, inspects all European civil nuclear sites (but see note 26).
36. Day 274, p. 56F.
37. Agreement between the United Kingdom of Great Britain and Northern Ireland, the European Atomic Energy Community and the International Atomic Energy Agency for the Application of Safeguards in the United Kingdom of Great Britain and Northern Ireland in connection with the Treaty on the Non-Proliferation of Nuclear Weapons, Cmnd 6730, 1977. Article 8(b) (i) and Article 92(2) sub-paragraphs D(a) and G(a).
38. R V Hesketh, *Nuclear Power UK, Nuclear Weapons USA*, being CND/P/1, paras. 119–120, 151.
39. Day 274, p. 70B.
40. Hansard, 27 July 1983, col. 438 (some copies 440) gives figures ± 0.5 tonne at 31 March 1983. In addition to the 9 te still in the reactors and 3.5 te awaiting reprocessing, 5 te had been sold or leased to UKAEA and 0.5 te exported to countries other than USA. Figures exclude plutonium produced in the Hankley Point 'B' and Hunterston 'B' AGRs, and that produced in Calder Hall and Chapelcross, even though the latter have been optimised for electricity production since 1967 (note 8).
41. Hansard, 1 April 1982, col. 169.
42. 'The Production and Destiny of UK Civil Plutonium' by Barnham, Hart and Stevens (CND/S/151).
43. Day 284, p. 2G.
44. *Electrical Power Engineer*, Summer 1984, pp. 163–164 (CEGB/ S/1264).
45. There are several references in Hansard, for example footnote (g) to references 40 and 41.
46. Hansard, 25 April 1984, col. 506.
47. See note 42.
48. Reference 34.
49. Reference 10, p. 204.
50. *Ibid.*, pp. 58–59.
51. Letter and enclosures from Mr Donald Hodel, Secretary of Energy, to Representative Richard Ottinger, Chairman of the House of

Representatives Sub-committee on Energy Conservation and Power, 5 March 1984 (being reference 26 to CND/P/1).

52. Footnote (g) to reference 41.
53. See note 51.
54. See note 46.
55. The Fast Flux Test Facility at Richland, Washington, a civilian development facility. Inventory from reference 44.
56. The Zero Power Plutonium Reactor in Idaho, a civilian research facility. Inventory from reference 51.
57. Hansard, 27 July 1982, col. 439.
58. See note 44.
59. See note 51.
60. Hansard, 14 May 1959, cols. 1426 and 1427. Ownership of the reactors passed to BNFL in 1973, see Chapter 2.
61. Hansard, 27 March 1963, col. 168.
62. Hansard, 21 April 1964, col. 1098.
63. Reference 34. The (UK) Department of Energy provided to the Sizewell inquiry a document containing the statements from Hansard concerning plutonium made between 14 May 1981 and 9 March 1983 (DEN/S/11). Curiously this statement was omitted.
64. See note 51.
65. See note 61.
66. Another statement relevant in this context was made by two senior AEA staff, writing in a professional journal in 1966 about the future production and use of British civil plutonium. They clearly recognised that things would change after the generating boards assumed ownership of their plutonium in April 1969:

    'Magnox plutonium produced after 1969 is no longer committed to weapons production.' (*Nucleonics,* September 1966, p. 67.)

    This passage was quoted by CND at the Sizewell inquiry in support of its contention that civil Magnox plutonium produced before 1969 was so committed. To clarify matters, one of its authors wrote to a senior CEGB board member:

    'With hindsight, it would have been better if we had been more precise and said "no longer committed to the requirements of the UK/US Defence Agreement", but you will realise that this was not an aspect which excited any particular public interest at that time. . . To the best of my knowledge, no plutonium from UK civil stations was ever used for weapons or defence purposes except as an item in the defence agreement.' (Letter from N Franklin to J Baker, 7 November 1984 [CEGB/S/1969].

    The author was apparently concerned that his 1966 words might have been construed as meaning that civil plutonium was used in British bombs. He wished to make it clear that the plutonium was only used in American bombs.
67. See note 51.
68. Quoted in CND/P/1, p. 78.

69. Letter from Mr Hodel to Representative John Dingell, Chairman of the House of Representatives Committee on Energy and Commerce, 3 May 1984 (being reference 158 to CND/P/1).
70. Day 193, p. 9 B–D. See Appendix 6.

CHAPTER 9

DISCHARGES, DOSES AND CANCER INDUCTION

Sellafield
In the mid 1970s, when discharges from Windscale, as it then was, were at their peak, they amounted to more than those from all other published sources in the world put together. In 1984 the local MP commented that the Magnox reprocessing line:[1]

Is recognised as being responsible for 75 per cent of the entire radiation dose received by the European Community from all nuclear installations.

Until THORP is operational in 1990, the Magnox line is the only reprocessing line at Sellafield, and 70 per cent of its discharges are attributable to British civil power stations.[2] In the absence of adequate dry storage facilities, in which it can be stored indefinitely, Magnox spent fuel can only be stored under water for two years before corrosion releases dangerous quantities of fission products into the cooling water, thus increasing sea discharges. In 1973/74, for reasons that included industrial action, some of the spent fuel in the Magnox storage ponds was kept under water for too long. Discharges to the Irish Sea reached their peak soon afterwards—in 1973 almost 5,000 curies of alpha-emitting material, and in 1975 250,000 curies of beta-emitting material,[3] were discharged. (The curie, a relatively large unit of radioactivity, is being superceded by the very much smaller Becquerel. See Appendix 1.) The consequences of this incident have persisted for more than a decade; the Black report notes that:[4]

Beta discharges from the site are still dominated by the arisings from the Magnox storage ponds.

147

As noted below and in Chapter 10, dry storage technology, which enables the safe long-term storage of spent Magnox fuel and renders reprocessing unnecessary, has existed for more than 15 years. Until the decision is taken to stop reprocessing, the generating boards will continue to be responsible for the great bulk of the Sellafield discharges, and for their consequences.

Since the mid-1970s discharges to sea have been steadily reduced, and by 1983 they had come down to 378 curies of alpha, and 67,200 beta.[5] 1985 figures are expected to show further reductions to 200 and 30,000 curies respectively, a new £30m salt evaporator being instrumental in the alpha reduction, and the £110m SIXEP ion exchange plant having a large effect on the beta. In terms of the doses received by those members of the public most at risk, in 1982 the 'critical group' received 56 or 61 per cent of the maximum permissible dose, according to the definition of the critical group, and in the following year they received 41 or 51.5 per cent of the maximum.[6] The 1985 figures are expected to show that these latter percentages have been halved.[7] Continuous public concern has kept up the pressure on BNFL to reduce discharges still further, and in June 1984 the company announced:[8]

> . . . the launch of an urgent study into ways by which the Company could reduce its discharges of radioactivity to sea to 'as near zero as possible', taking account of the available technology, cost benefit considerations and time-scales for introducing new plant and equipment.

By December 1984 this urgent study resulted in government approval for:[9]

> . . . the company's proposal to build a floc precipitation plant, costing £150m, which would be in operation by 1991. The target is to reduce discharges to less than 20 curies a year of alpha activity and about 8,000 curies a year of beta/gamma activity (excluding tritium). The latter figure is below the level currently achieved by the only plant in any way comparable, the newer French reprocess-

ing plant at Cap de la Hague, and the alpha figure is approximately equal to the current figure for that plant.

The statement went on to point out that the situation would further improve when Magnox reprocessing stops in the early years of the next century.

Three expressions of public disquiet have had a particular effect on BNFL:

— the accidental discharges of 11–17 November 1983, one of which was encountered by Greenpeace on 14 November. These discharges have resulted in criminal proceedings being brought against the company,
— the consistently better record of the French reprocessing plant at Cap de la Hague in terms of both discharges and doses to workers, which was brought to the attention of the Sizewell inquiry by the Stop Sizewell 'B' Association and Ecoropa, which led directly to the statement quoted above,
— the evidence of increased cancer rates in the under-25 age group in West Cumbria, which was brought to prominence by Yorkshire TV's film 'Windscale—the Nuclear Laundry', and which was subsequently investigated by Sir Douglas Black's inquiry.

There can be little doubt that the company has responded to this pressure at least partly because of the growing public awareness that reprocessing is an unnecessary part of the civilian nuclear fuel cycle. Magnox fuel can be stored indefinitely in dry stores, as it is at Wylfa, and its reprocessing could be discontinued. AGR and PWR fuel can be stored in the same way, rendering THORP unnecessary. The reluctance of the generating boards to sign contracts with BNFL for the reprocessing of this oxide fuel indicates that the boards are aware that public pressure may force the stoppage of the activity that will still, after all the improvements, give rise to more radioactive discharges than any other. BNFL has made and is making considerable efforts to clean it up, and the company is undoubtedly aware that its future is at stake.

Accidental discharges
Sellafield, or Windscale as it was known until 1981, is a

large industrial site, containing the Magnox reprocessing line, spent fuel storage ponds for Magnox and for oxide fuel, a fast reactor fuel assembly plant for Dounreay, the plutonium stores, the high-level and intermediate-level waste storage tanks, as well as the four Calder Hall reactors. THORP, and a vitrification plant for high-level waste are under construction, and the Drigg dump site for low-level solid waste is nearby. Work commenced on the site in September 1947, and the first major project to be completed was the laying of the first two discharge pipelines to sea in June 1950. These extend 2.5 km beyond the high water mark into the Irish Sea. The first of the air-cooled plutonium piles was operating by October 1950, and the second eight months later (they were closed after the fire of October 1957), and the first reprocessing line opened in January 1952, to be closed, again after an accident, in 1973. The first of the Calder Hall gas-cooled reactors, (the prototype of the Magnox's), was operational in August 1956, and all four were working two years later. They are expected to 'operate certainly through the mid-1990s and maybe beyond'.[10] The second, present, Magnox reprocessing line started up in 1964, and facilities for storing spent oxide fuel opened four years later, in expectation of gaining consent to build an oxide reprocessing plant. A third pipeline was laid in 1976, and consent for THORP was in fact granted in 1978, after the Windscale Inquiry.

In the early years experiments were conducted to find out both the geographical distribution of the liquid discharges once in the sea, and their rate of entry into the food chain. Mr Dunster, now Director of the National Radiological Protection Board (NRPB) and a member of the International Commission on Radiological Protection (ICRP) but then a scientist with the UKAEA, reported to a UN conference in 1958 that:[11]

> In general terms the intention has been to discharge fairly substantial amounts of radioactivity as part of an organised and deliberate scientific experiment, and the aims of this experiment would in fact have been defeated if the level of activity discharged had been kept to a minimum.

The best-known incident involving unplanned discharges from Sellafield remains the 1957 fire. This incident, described above,[12] released quantities of iodine-131 and polonium into the atmosphere from one of the original air-cooled plutonium piles, and resulted in the closure of both piles. The major incident immediately preceding the discharges of November 1983 involved the discovery in March 1979 of a ground leak that had been in existence at least since 1976—throughout the Windscale inquiry. The Health and Safety Executive/ Nuclear Installations Inspectorate report on that leak, published in August 1980, criticised the safety standards and professional judgement of BNFL in 'the strongest attack ever made by the HSE on a public utility'.[13] 100,000 curies were thought to have seeped into the ground, and Norman Lamont MP, then at the Department of Energy, was reported to have said that only the previous good record of the plant, and the prompt remedial action taken by BNFL, saved the company from a prosecution for negligence.[14]

The November 1983 discharges did result in prosecution, but not for negligence. Although the discharges did not breach the authorisations, and were in fact only a small proportion of them, the main charge brought against BNFL was that it was in breach of a requirement imposed in February of that year that discharges should be kept 'as low as reasonably achievable'.[15] They occurred during the re-processing plant's annual maintenance shut-down, when it was being washed out in order to reduce doses to operators doing maintenance work. Washings typically consist of aqueous waste, solvent waste which floats on the aqueous, and a solid material known as 'crud' between the two liquid layers, 'all of which may be highly radioactive, particularly the solids'.[16] Solvent waste is the residues from the solvent, tri-butyl phosphate (TBP), which is used to separate the plutonium from the rest of the fission products during re-processing. It has the peculiar chemical property of attracting plutonium to itself. As for crud:[17]

its nature is not fully understood, however it is known to contain degradation products of TBP, produced by the intense radiation to which the solvent is subjected.

151

It is known that crud is very radioactive.

Clearly neither solvent waste nor crud should ever be discharged to sea; radioactive waste management depends crucially on them being separated from the aqueous waste, which is then either discharged if of a low enough activity, or retained for storage on site.

There are six HAPW (high active plant washout) tanks available to receive washout wastes, but they do not, or did not in 1983, contain any equipment to detect the presence of solvent or crud. Only the activity of the aqueous layer could be measured, and the only way of ensuring that solvent or crud was not sent to the sea tanks for disposal was by administrative checks and log-book records, a fact that the Radiochemical Inspectorate found 'of particular concern'.[18] In any case it seems that, on this occasion, no attempt was made to float off the solvent; contrary to the Standing Instructions a hand-written note was added to the Plant Washout Instructions for 1983 reading 'For this shutdown it is proposed not to float off and recover solvent from HAPW's'.[19]

The practice is to send the contents of the HAPWs to the sea tanks for flushing to sea, having first ascertained that they contain material of suitably low activity. At the time only two of the nine sea tanks were functioning, so they were alternately filled and flushed. On this occasion the HAPW to sea tanks transfer began at 21.15 on 10 November 1983. Sea Tank 2 was full by 22.30, and flow was switched to Sea Tank 1. At 00.45 on 11 November a radiation monitor on the transfer pipework sounded an alarm and registered full deflection. At about the same time transfer stopped of its own accord because of a blockage in the pipe, which 'usually indicates the presence of solvent or blockage by solids'.[20] Low-level wastes were used to flush the pipework, and by 05.30 radiation levels were acceptable. In all, 720 cubic meters of waste had been sent to Sea Tank 1, including 16 cubic meters of high-active liquids and solids containing an estimated 4,500 curies of mainly beta activity.

It was decided to pump the contents of Sea Tank 1 to the intermediate-level storage tanks via a small bore emergency pipe provided for that purpose. However the rate of transfer was so slow that it would have taken a week to empty the sea tank. After about 2½ hours, sampling suggested that the active material had floated to the top of the sea tank, and had therefore been pumped out. On this incorrect assumption[21] the decision was made to flush the remainder of Sea Tank 1 to sea. Flushing began at 21.30 on 11 November, and continued until 00.15, when activity levels at the discharge pipe rose sharply and pumping was stopped. BNFL subsequently estimated that 600 (of the 4,500) curies were discharged at this time. The small amount of wastes remaining in the sea tank were then transferred to the intermediate-level storage tank along the small bore pipe; this took place from 01.00 to 04.00, and from 10.30 to 19.00, on 12 November. In between, the contents of Sea Tank 2 were flushed to sea, involving a further discharge of high-activity waste from a short length of common pipework.[22]

On 13 November it was decided to flush the sea discharge pipework to sea, causing the second major discharge. It is possible that the small bore pipe was also drained to sea at this time.[23] Workers at the sea line valve had to be urgently evacuated as radiation levels rose, and activity levels continued to fluctuate until midnight on 16 November. BNFL management was particularly criticised for this further discharge.[24] Another discharge of solvent seems to have occurred on 17 November when Sea Tank 2 was emptied more completely than usual; this may have been the second slick observed (see below).

At 10.00 on 14 November members of Greenpeace were near the end of the pipelines in an inflatable boat, and saw a long narrow slick which appeared to be welling up from beneath the surface. They sailed into it and monitored it; they and their boat were subsequently decontaminated at Sellafield. This incident was reported in *The Guardian* of 17 November 1983. On the 16th a DOE inspector working at Sellafield was told of the discharge, but it was not thought serious enough by either the inspector or BNFL management to warrant a formal report. On 18 November BNFL staff noticed a second slick, but by the time a boat crew was sent to disperse it the wind had changed to on-shore and the slick could not be found. Before dawn on the following day contamination was found on the beach. UKAEA police were used to warn the public away, and BNFL informed the appropriate government department at midday. On the 19th, after measuring the activity on the beach, BNFL concluded that there was no further risk and withdrew its advice to avoid the area.

Radioactive debris was deposited in increasing quantities, over an increasing area, and a ten-mile stretch of coastline remained closed for six months. The Radiochemical Inspectorate's report made it clear that solvent and solid discharges are inadequately controlled, and that solvent discharges are not uncommon. Crucially, it concluded that:[25]

> Solvent discharges to sea may in part be responsible for the reported enrichment of plutonium in the sea surface and the sea to land transfer of that material.

Its recommendations included the installation of adequate instrumentation to detect solvent and crud, and a demand that BNFL cease to discharge bulk quantities of solvent to sea forthwith; a demand echoed in the Black report.[26] The RCI also called for:[27]

> Further research to be carried out to investigate any link between solvent discharges to sea and radioactivity transfer from sea to land.

Both the RCI and the parallel Health and Safety Executive/ Nuclear Installations Inspectorate report[28] criticised notification procedures, and concluded that breaches of statutory provisions may have taken place.

Clearly, Sellafield's inability to properly control solvent and crud discharges is of fundamental concern. Estimates of doses to the local people, and of the uptake of radioactivity into the food chain, depend absolutely on calculations of the way that the sea around Sellafield disperses and dilutes the discharges. If discharges of plutonium, even at the permitted levels, are followed by discharges of solvent, proper dispersion will not take place due to the solvent's property of attracting plutonium to itself. As it floats on water, it will be the first substance to be returned to shore in sea spray in any kind of on-shore weather. It is thus likely that solvent discharges account for the higher than expected levels of plutonium found in spray as compared to the surrounding sea water, and they also support the thesis that people who use the beach at Sellafield have received very much higher radiation doses than they would have done if discharges had been dispersed as planned.

The series of accidents that led to BNFL's prosecution involved the transfer of 4,500 curies of radioactive wastes to the sea tanks. By all accounts not all of that was in fact discharged, but the beaches were closed for six months, and the daily eating and recreational habits of the local people inevitably affected. And yet 4,500 curies is 1.5 per cent of the annual discharge limit for Sellafield that was then in force, and 5 per cent of the beta that was actually discharged in 1983.

Authorisations and discharges—Sellafield and Cap de la Hague
Discharge authorisations for Windscale/Sellafield remained unaltered, except for one amendment from 1971, until the reports on the incidents described above forced a change at the end of 1984. The limits were 2,000 curies of alpha in any three-month period, to an annual maximum of 6,000 curies; and 75,000 curies of beta in any three-month period, giving an annual maximum of 300,000 curies. There were specific restrictions on ruthenium-106 and strontium-90. In February 1983 a new condition was added:

> that the company shall limit the amount of radioactive elements discharged and the rate of their discharge such that radiation exposures are as low as reasonably achieve-able and shall use any means that shall be approved for that purpose by the Secretary of State.

It was for breaches of this condition that BNFL was prosecuted.

There has been growing pressure on the government both to reduce the numerical maxima and to replace the words 'as low as reasonably achievable' by 'as low as technically achieveable'. That pressure has resulted, firstly, in the new lower discharge limits, and secondly in BNFL's use of the phrase 'as near zero as possible'.[29] The new authorisations, which came into force on 1 January 1985, reduced both alpha and beta limits, and for the first time limited short-term discharges. Alpha was limited to 30 curies in any two days, 200 in any three months and 600 in a year, and beta to 7,000 curies in any two days and 50,000 in any three months, giving an annual permissable total of 200,000. Ruthenium and strontium were further reduced, and for the first time the authorisations included new strictures on the discharge of solvents and solids. 'Liquid radioactive waste' was defined by the Department of the Environment as being aqueous, and free 'as far as is practicable' from solids and solvent.

The present discharge authorisations for Cap la Hague have been in force since October 1980, and permit liquid discharges of 90 curies a year of alpha and 45,000 curies a year of beta. Thus the Sellafield limits in force at the time of the November 1983 accidents were 6.6 times greater than those at la Hague in respect of beta emissions, and 66.6 times greater in respect of alpha. Both sites have kept actual discharges well within the respective authorisations, and a comparison between discharges is as striking as a comparison between authorisations, especially in terms of alpha. Total liquid alpha discharges from 1967 to 1981 from Sellafield were 31,583 curies and from la Hague 141.6 curies, the Sellafield total being more than 220 times greater. The peak year for Sellafield was 1973, when 4,728 curies of alpha were discharged; the peak year for la Hague was 1974, when 27 curies were discharged.[30]

Annual beta discharges from Cap la Hague between 1977 and 1980 averaged 27,270 curies,[31] and from Sellafield 152,846 curies, although the former figure includes plutonium-241 discharges and the latter does not. When the Pu-241 (which, unlike the other plutonium isotopes, is a beta emitter) discharges are added to the Sellafield figure, BNFL's record is nearly seven times worse, a statement with which the company's deputy managing director agreed under cross-examination at the Sizewell inquiry.[32] But Pu-241 is important because it transmutes to the alpha emitter americium-241, and the 185,687 curies of Pu-241 discharged from Sellafield between 1976 and 1981 will, over 100 years, become nearly 6,200 curies of americium. This is an important addition to the alpha-emitting plutonium isotopes and americium already discharged, and brings the total of alpha material in the Irish Sea to some 40,000 curies.[33]

Despite the fact that discharges have been very much lower, and that therefore more radioactivity has been retained on the site, doses to operators at la Hague have also been lower than those at Sellafield. The average individual dose to workers at Sellafield was halved between 1975 and 1982, but the total collective dose remained the same, indicating the use of a larger workforce. This collective dose was, in 1982, more than five times higher than that at la Hague. If only Magnox operations are considered, and adjustments made for the different quantities and irradiation levels at the two sites, BNFL has agreed that doses to workers at Sellafield per unit of electricity generated are a little more than double those at la Hague.[34]

The company suggested under cross-examination that the reason for the lower doses at la Hague 'is a reflection in essence of a more modern plant'.[35] But the French Magnox line was operational in 1967, only two or three years after that at Sellafield, and it seems more likely that different management targets and attitudes are the dominant cause, especially in view of the much greater off-site discharges at Sellafield. It is interesting to note that average doses to workers in the new THORP plant, due to become operational in 1990, are projected to be twice those currently being achieved in the present UP-2 plant at la Hague. Having agreed that this is the case, BNFL commented:[36]

Clearly, they could be lower—let's make no bones about it. If one spends enough money you could get them down almost without limit. In our judgement that level [the target for THORP] represents an average which is acceptable within the terms of the licence and within the as low as reasonably achievable criterion.

157

Magnox reprocessing will continue to provide the bulk of discharges and doses at both sites until those reactors cease operation and the last of their fuel is reprocessed (assuming no change in current practice) in 2000 or soon afterwards. BNFL's recent reductions in the sea discharges are to be welcomed, especially the commitment to bring them down to French levels,[37] and there can be no doubt that discharges from future oxide reprocessing in the new plants, if it takes place, will be considerably lower than the Magnox discharges. But these improvements are costing hundreds of millions of pounds, and result in increased costs to the generating boards. The increased costs must further doubts about continuing with a process that is unnecessary for the satisfactory operation of a nuclear programme. But there is growing evidence that the price in terms of human lives is already unacceptable. If Sellafield were to close down tomorrow, the three-quarters of a tonne of plutonium already on the bottom of the Irish Sea will be washing and blowing ashore for years to come.

Cancer incidence at Seascale
Coincidentally, the Yorkshire TV film 'Windscale—the Nuclear Laundry' was shown on 1 November 1983, just 10 days before the series of accidental discharges described above began. The film dealt with the incidence of cancer in people aged under 25 at diagnosis, and resident in areas adjacent to the Sellafield works. Researchers found details of seven young people living in Seascale, the nearest village, who had contracted leukaemia between 1956 and 1983. They identified a further twenty five who had contracted cancer in the larger Millom Rural District, a number which included the seven leukaemia cases in Seascale. The leukaemia rate of children under ten was particularly high, being ten times greater than the national average.[38] The film also provided evidence of radioactive discharges returning to shore; plutonium, americium, caesium and ruthenium were found in dust collected in a vacuum cleaner at a house in Ravenglass, 9 km from Sellafield.

The government reacted quickly, and established an independent inquiry under Sir Douglas Black, which first met on 22 November 1983. Its report was published in June

1984. Early in the hearings Sir Douglas commented to the Director of Greenpeace that the purpose of his inquiry 'was to reassure the Cumbrian public', and, in his report, he did feel able to come to the conclusion that:[39]

> The Seascale incidence and Millom Rural District mortality rates for leukaemia among young people are unusual, though not unparalled.

He stated:[40]

> We have found no evidence of any general risk to health for children or adults living near Sellafield when compared to the rest of Cumbria, and we can give a qualified re-assurance to the people who are concerned about a possible health hazard in the neighbourhood of Sellafield.

Sir Douglas based his 'qualified reassurance' on his findings that, among 765 electoral wards in the Northern Children's Cancer Registry region, Seascale came 6th in its incidence of all cancers per 1,000 children, and 3rd in its rate of leukaemia per 1,000 children.

The Seascale figures are distorted because Sir Douglas restricted his analysis to the years 1968–1982. He did not consider the high childhood cancer rates in the village before or since, but based his analysis on the four leukaemia cases diagnosed during that period. Had the two additional cases diagnosed during 1983—which were known to Sir Douglas and listed by him in Table 2 of his report—been included in the calculation, Seascale would have been top of the leukaemia league table with an incidence of 24 times the national average. A further cancer case, a 14 year old girl who developed a fatal sarcoma in 1974, was left out of the statistics because of a 'discrepancy'. If she is included, Seascale goes to the top of the all-cancers league table.[41] This point is important because, although Sir Douglas commented that radiation is the only known cause of leukaemia in children,[42] there are observed excesses of cancers of other radio-sensitive tissues as well.

The Black report is more fundamentally flawed when it

159

considers the causes of the cancers that it found, perhaps incorrectly, to be 'unusual but not unparalleled'. Its conclusion that radiation was not the likely cause of the observed cancers was based on information supplied by the National Radiological Protection Board. That board's advice was that, in addition to the 0.6 deaths that would be expected among the Seascale young people in the period under consideration, an extra 0.1 deaths would result from the known Sellafield discharges, planned and unplanned. There were in fact four deaths in that period. Sir Douglas concluded that:[43]

> To attribute these additional deaths from leukaemia to radiation it would require that the total discharges from Sellafield has in fact been 40 times greater than reported, and that monitoring and extrapolation of doses to the public were in error by a similar factor.

This conclusion is unsatisfactory. As has been pointed out by other commentators, its logic is circular; presumably, had he considered the subsequent additional deaths mentioned above, he would have concluded that radiation was even less likely to have been the cause. Secondly, he accepted without question the NRPB advice on cancer induction at low doses, in spite of the criticism that has been levelled at it, some of which is described below. And lastly, perhaps most importantly, it is not at all impossible that some people, especially children, have received 40 times the dose from the known discharges.

This very much higher dose could have arisen in three ways. Firstly, as discussed above, calculations of received doses depend critically at the rate at which radioactivity is diffused in the sea. Solvent discharged from Sellafield has the effect of restricting the dispersion of plutonium and enabling it to return to shore in greater than estimated quantities. The effect of solvent discharges was not taken into account by the NRPB. Secondly, one of the assumptions it made was that the time spent on the beach by local children was 25 hours per year. This seems to be very conservative; in any seaside community there are numbers of children who, as their parents might say, 'live in the sea'. Seascale and the Cumbrian coast were presumably, at least until recently, no different. Thirdly, the mechanism of cancer induction by plutonium is still an area of considerable uncertainty in medical circles. The NRPB calculations assumed that the blood forming cells (which, when damaged by radiation, may result in leukaemia) are evenly distributed through the bone marrow. Plutonium, if ingested, tends to accumulate on the inner bone surfaces, not in the marrow, and the alpha radiation given off, which is intense but can travel only a few millimetres, can therefore only reach a relatively small number of the target cells. But minutes of a recent DHSS meeting held to follow up Sir Douglas Black's study indicated that recent research has established that the blood-forming cells are not distributed evenly through a bone marrow, but concentrated near the inner bone surfaces.[44] If this is so, the leukaemia risk from a given dose of plutonium would be very much greater than that calculated by the NRPB and assumed by the Black report.

Cancer induction at low doses of radiation

The International Commission on Radiological Protection (ICRP) is the organisation responsible for advising governments on the maximum acceptable levels of exposure both for workers in the nuclear industry and for the general public. The Commission arrives at its advice firstly, by deciding what acceptable levels of risk are, and secondly, by deciding what levels of exposure will ensure that those risks are not exceeded. Acceptable risks for nuclear workers were set by observing the risks associated with other occupations having high safety standards, and the figure arrived at was a 1 in 10,000 risk of death per annum.[45] For the general public the ICRP decided that acceptable risks in everyday life could be assumed to be an annual chance of death of between 1 in 100,000 and 1 in a million.[46]

ICRP then worked out maximum permissible exposure levels for both groups. The essence of its calculations of cancer induction at low doses is that it performs a linear extrapolation down from observed cancer induction at high doses using, as a major data base, figures from Hiroshima and Nagasaki. At its simplest, linear extrapolation assumes that if 10 cancers were induced in a 100,000 population by exposure to 10 units of received dose, then 1 in 100,000 will be induced by exposure to 1 unit. The Commission considers that this method is conservative—that it tends to over-estimate the incidence at low doses.

The permitted maximum doses are, and have been since 1977, 5 rem/year for workers and 0.5 rem/year for the general public.[47] Both these maxima are subject to an additional 'as low as reasonably achievable' clause, and authorising departments in Britain have made it clear that doses should not exceed ten per cent of the ICRP limits for the public. (As noted above, this ten per cent target has not, to date, been achieved at Sellafield for the critical groups most at risk.) It should be emphasised that radiological protection does not attempt to eliminate risk, but to keep it to acceptable levels. Sir Edward Pochin, the father of radiological protection in Britain and appearing for the NRPB at the Sizewell inquiry, made it clear that there is no 'safe level' of dose:[48]

The indication from such surveys is that there can be shown to be no threshold for cancer development.

Answering questions about the levels of radiation that can cause chromosome rearrangements, Sir Edward agreed that such rearrangements can be caused by doses much lower than the ICRP limits, and he 'fully accepted the presence of chromosome abnormalities in many or most cancers'. But he did not accept the need to reduce the permitted levels:[49]

I believe that the quantification of risk is determined by the estimation of actual disease in irradiated populations, and not by the histological examination of chromosome breaks. . .

Radiological protection crucially depends on the method of 'the estimation of actual disease' being right. If it were shown that linear extrapolation produces not an over-

162

estimate, but a severe under-estimate of the numbers of cancers induced at low doses, the Sellafield incidence might be more easily understood. Before turning to the work of Dr Alice Stewart and her colleagues in this field, it might be of interest to discuss the excess incidence of leukaemia among the workforce at the Sizewell 'A' power station.

Leukaemia at Sizewell 'A'

The Magnox power station at Sizewell was commissioned in 1966, the sixth on the CEGB's system. Like all the others, it is a twin-reactor station, each reactor being cooled by carbon dioxide, moderated by graphite and fuelled by natural uranium. Power workers number about 450 men.

Very early in the Sizewell inquiry the CEGB witness responsible for radiological protection was asked whether there was any CEGB station where the incidence of leukaemias was significantly[50] in excess of the anticipated incidence. His reply stated that:[51]

> There is no CEGB station where the incidence of leukaemia or other radiation induced diseases are statistically significantly in excess of the anticipated incidence.

This statement directly contradicted that of the Chairman of the CEGB's Epidemiology Advisory Committee, in a letter written soon afterwards:[52]

> The expected incidence of leukaemia among the Sizewell 'A' workforce would be rather less than 1, whereas it has been established that the actual incidence has been significantly in excess of this.

The discrepancy was not resolved for more than a year, when the Board agreed that the incidence of leukaemia among the Sizewell 'A' workforce was significantly in excess of expectation.[53]

Appended to the Chairman of the Advisory Committee's letter is his worked calculation that the expectation, to the end of 1982, was 0.30 cases. Four cases were diagnosed by the same date, resulting in three deaths.[54] Three of the diagnoses were of myeloid leukaemia, which is agreed to be radio-genic, and one was a man who took early retirement at the age of 56, before dying five months later. As Graham Searle, lay advocate for the Stop Sizewell 'B' Association, observed during his closing submissions to the inquiry:[55]

> We do not exclude him, just as we would not exclude all leukaemia victims in the event of all leukaemia victims being, as a matter of CEGB policy, pensioned off before death.

Leukaemia incidence in Leiston, the town nearest the power station, is higher than expectation but not significantly so, although it does have some odd characteristics. To the end of 1982 there were 11 diagnoses in Leiston-cum-Sizewell (including the power station workers) and three more just outside the boundary; compared with the 11, the expectation was 7.9. The ratio of males to females was 9:2, compared with an anticipation of 3.9:4, and of the males the ratio of myeloid to lymphatic was 6:3, against an anticipation of 1.9:2. Dr Michael Bush, the East Suffolk District Medical Officer, undertook a study of leukaemia incidence in his area after public interest and concern had been raised by press reports of the cases at Sizewell 'A'.[56] He was invited by the Inspector to present his report to the Sizewell inquiry, and while being cross-examined agreed that there seemed to be a greater susceptibility, or proneness, to leukaemia among the people of Leiston than is normally found.[57] Dr Bush also made the point that research is going on into the whole question of the levels of radiation that may or may not be leukaemogenic, and he commented that:[58]

> It might be preferable—to put it at its lowest—to have the results of those studies before making a decision to increase the possible radiation levels within a particular locality.

This seemed to those opposed to Sizewell 'B' to be a powerful argument in their favour. A demonstrated proneness to a disease known to be radio-genic would predicate against an additional source of radiation being introduced into the locality, unless and until it can be established that radiation from the existing power station has played no part in the observed incidence.

The CEGB is mystified by the Sizewell 'A' incidence, not surprisingly. There is no similar cluster in or near any of its other nuclear stations, and in fact there was only one other case of leukaemia among its nuclear workforce in the period under study.[59] Power station doses and discharges are very small when compared with those from Sellafield,[60] and because of this the Board has tended to dismiss the possibility that radiation has anything to do with the leukaemia incidence at Sizewell. The Board also considers that useful conclusions cannot be drawn from the incidence found in a group as small as the Sizewell 'A' workforce—although two Fellows of the Institute of Statisticians disputed this view[61]—and prefers to concentrate its studies on all its nuclear workers as a group, rather than on workers at particular stations.[62] Such studies are necessary, but the failure to observe small populations inevitably means that local factors, if they exist, are masked or diluted to the point of non-significance. The danger is that such studies once again become self-fulfilling and, in terms of radiological protection, counter-productive.

A discussion of the mechanisms of cancer induction is beyond the scope of this book. It should be noted, however, that recent studies indicate the possibility that two simultaneous factors may be at work at the genesis of some radiosensitive cancers. These factors are known as the inducing agent and the promoting agent, and research indicates that radiation at low doses may act as the inducer, and the failure of the immune system as the promoter.[63] According to this hypothesis, the chromosome damage that Sir Edward Pochin agreed can be caused by radiation at very low doses would normally be repaired by the immune system. But if that system is inhibited, perhaps by a coincident viral attack, the repair may not take place, or may take place but be faulty, and a cell mutation and then a cancer may occur. Many viral infections are known to be immuno-suppressive,[64] and there is no reason to believe that the immune system is, under normal circumstances, any less effective against cancer than it is against any other

165

disease. Dr Alice Stewart commented that some people believe that:[65]

> cancer is different from other causes of death, but of course it is not. People who have low general rates of mortality also have low rates of cancer mortality, age for age.

Dr Alice Stewart[66]

One of the few witnesses to give evidence at both the Windscale and Sizewell inquiries, Dr Stewart has been involved in the controversy over the health effects of low doses of radiation for several decades, much of that time with her statistician colleague George Kneale. Her Oxford Study of Childhood Cancers was begun in the 1950s as an investigation into the apparent increase of childhood cancers then being diagnosed. Her hypothesis was (and is) that the immune system of children with incipient cancer is impaired, and so they have an increased susceptibility to infectious diseases. In pre-war years such children died of the infection before the cancer became apparent, but the recent use of antibiotics has enabled them to live long enough to die of the cancer. The failing immunological competance thus acted as a mask that hid the real incidence, and the mask was removed by the use of antibiotics.

The data collection required for the Oxford survey also led to the discovery that children whose mothers had received X-rays—even a single X-ray—during pregnancy had a higher incidence of childhood cancers than those whose mothers had not been X-rayed. The dose given by a pelvic X-ray then approached one rad, although the dose now is only one-tenth of that, and Stewart and Kneale found that the risk of childhood cancer was doubled if one rad was given shortly before birth. Their 1970 report[67] has, in spite of considerable resistance, transformed a once-standard practice into an unusual one, and established beyond doubt that the high sensitivity of the foetus to radiation induced cancer.

Very soon after their report was published, Dr Stewart became involved with the data concerning the survivors of Hiroshima and Nagasaki. Her initial interest was aroused

166

because the data in respect of irradiation *in utero* seemed to contradict those of her Oxford study. The Japanese data included information on people who had received a range of doses, from those high enough to be quickly fatal down to very much lower ones. Almost 1,300 children were irradiated before birth at low and intermediate doses, and according to Stewart and Kneale's Oxford calculations, 26 cancer deaths in the children should have resulted. In fact there was only one, which agreed with an expectation from the national average of 0.75, and Dr Stewart began to look for a mask, to see if she could identify a factor that was hiding the effect.

One of the most striking aspects of the A-bomb survivor populations was the speed at which they apparently returned to medical normality. Detailed observation did not begin until 1950, but by that date the people were showing normal, or even lower than normal, incidences of all diseases except radio-sensitive cancers, and, bearing in mind the high doses that some had received, the increased incidence of those was very small.[68] It seemed as though the people of the two cities had completely shrugged off the effects of their experience in less than five years. This has had a profound effect on thinking about the health effects of radiation ever since, and it is the basis of the nuclear industry's confidence that its activities, involving much lower doses, are not detrimental to the health of society.

Dr Stewart found it difficult to believe that people could return to normal so quickly, and became convinced that a 'disaster effect' was operating. Quite apart from the effect of radiation on the populations was the destruction of almost all property, so that those who survived the blast and immediate death through massive irradiation had to live for the first winter in conditions of appalling deprivation. They had, because of and in proportion to their radiation doses, a reduced resistance to infection. They were without shelter and antibiotics. Because the surveys did not begin until 1950 no-one knows how many thousands died during the winter of 1945 from infectious diseases caused by weakness and exposure. Those died, mercifully, before any cancer could manifest itself. Inevitably, those who survived to 1950

167

were unusually healthy, and had a high resistance to all diseases including radio-sensitive cancers. They were a highly selected population.

This Dr Stewart calls the 'healthy survivor effect'. Because of it, she has concluded that it is very wrong to base the system of radiological protection on studies of the A-bomb survivors, because there is a real danger of under-estimating the deaths which would occur in a non-selected population. The ICRP limits, as extrapolated from the Japanese data without correction for the healthy survivor effect, could be understatements of the risk, rather than the conservative estimates that their authors believe them to be.

Dr Stewart's next area of work enabled her to return to the direct observation of cancer incidence at low doses. In 1977 she and Kneale were asked by Dr Mancuso to examine contradictory data concerning Hanford, the huge military nuclear site in Washington State. On the one hand the Hanford workers had a lower than normal rate of premature death—the place seemed to be a health farm. On the other hand, State records indicated that Hanford had a 20 per cent higher incidence of cancer than the rest of the state.

Hanford has been described as a showplace, with levels of doses to its workers lower than those at many power stations, and the very best medical facilities available to them. It also kept very detailed computerised records of the age, work and doses received by more than 31,000 employees. This data was available to Dr Mancuso, at that time retained by the US Department of Energy, and through him to Stewart and Kneale. Their approach was to divide everyone who had died into cancer and non-cancer deaths, and compare the doses received by the two groups. If there was no radiation effect the doses to the groups should have been the same, but on the contrary:[69]

The first observation that as it were hit us, and made us say 'You must go on with this', was that the people who died of cancer had higher doses than the people who died of other causes. . . and that the difference was significant.

Mancuso, Stewart and Kneale's conclusion was that 1–2 per

cent of the population at Hanford had died as a result of occupational exposure to radiation, and this amounted to about 5 per cent of all cancer deaths.

The publication of their 1977 paper[70] caused a furore; as Dr Stewart remarked, it was heresy to say that radiation at levels below the agreed international standards caused anythng. The doors were firmly closed on the team's access to further data, and the only way in which their conclusion could be confirmed or refuted was denied to them, or indeed to any other independent workers in the field. Their subsequent work on the Hanford data[71] has been restricted to a progressive refinement in the analysis of the original material.

But the other original and contradictory observation, that the incidence of premature death among the workforce was lower than average, seemed to indicate that radiation at low doses was good for you. Once again, Dr Stewart set out to look for a mask. It turned out to be a factor whose existence is no longer disputed, but whose effect is sometimes not allowed for—the 'healthy worker effect'. Workers at Hanford, and at all nuclear sites, are a selected population. They are subject to medical screening, and do not include the sick or the retired. They are fitter and healthier than average, and therefore have a lower incidence of all disease than average.[72] In addition they are drawn from the upper social classes, which in any case have a lower incidence of premature death than the lower classes. They are well paid and well looked after. This healthy worker effect runs in the opposite direction to the detrimental effects of radiation and masks it. Like the A-bomb survivors, nuclear workers cannot be regarded as a normal population, and data derived from a study of such populations must be adjusted to compensate before being applied to non-selected populations.[73]

Two criticisms levelled at Mancuso, Stewart and Kneale's conclusions drawn from the Handord data should be noted. The first is that the incidence of individual diseases within the radio-sensitive group was not consistent from year to year. Dr Stewart's approach was to group all such diseases, as classified by the ICRP, together, and she maintained that it is a mistake to look at the year-by-year incidence of individual cancers, rather than at the totality, because

> [Cancer] is like falling off a ladder. It is a random process which bone you break, but falling off the ladder at one time does not reproduce itself the next time.

The other criticism concerned the effect of background radiation. If she was right about the effects of radiation at very low doses, then surely large numbers of cancers would be caused by background radiation? Dr Stewart noted first that it is a constant, that it does not matter how big it is, and what she and her colleagues were concerned with were the additions to it. She then observed that background radiation may well have an important effect:[75]

> We know that something like 90 per cent of cancer deaths are unexplained, and that about 95 per cent of congenital defects are unexplained. So there is plenty of scope for [it] being part of the natural process of life by which we get cancers and get congenital defects. Are we going to add to it?

Alice Stewart's message to the Sizewell inquiry was that conclusions about cancer incidence at low doses based on A-bomb survivor data and other experimental high-dose data were misleading. Her own findings of incidence at high doses agreed well with those of the radiological protection agencies. But those agencies rarely conduct direct observations of low dose populations, prefering to extrapolate down from the high dose data. Dr Stewart's direct observations in the low dose range led her to the conclusion that such an extrapolation leads to a significant under-estimation of risk. She remarked:[76]

> The curious thing is, if you are inside the game, which I am, you will notice that every time they have done an exclusively low dose study someone has come up with a finding that does not fit with this. . . there have been these examples if you go direct to the low dose study you

invariably come up with a higher risk than if you extrapolate it from the high.

If she is right, the incidence at Seascale would be much nearer an explanation. But the accepted wisdom of radiological protection, and of the safety of nuclear installations, would be overturned.

NOTES AND REFERENCES

1. Hansard, 25 April 1984, col. 754.
2. *Investigation of the Possible Increased Incidence of Cancer in West Cumbria.* Report of the Independent Advisory Group, Chairman Sir Douglas Black. HMSO 1984, para. 3.9.
3. Plutonium-238, 239 and 240, and americium-241 account for most of the alpha wastes; caesium-137 dominates the beta.
4. Ref 2, para. 3.11.
5. BNFL/P/1 (ADD 5), p. 1.
6. BNFL/P/1 (ADD 3), p. 9 and (ADD 5), p. 1.
7. BNFL/P/1 (ADD 12), para. 6.
8. BNFL Annual Report 1983/84, p. 10.
9. Hansard, 18 December 1984, col. 93.
10. BNFL's Deputy Managing Director, day 274, p. 68D.
11. H J Dunster, speaking during a discussion following the presentation of his paper *The Disposal of Radioactive Liquid Wastes into Coastal Waters* to the Second UN Confernce on Peaceful Uses of Atomic Energy, Geneva 1958. Volume 12, p. 624 of the Conference proceedings.
12. See Chapter 1, p. 17 and reference 25.
13. *The Guardian,* 2 August 1980.
14. *The Observer,* 3 August 1980.
15. Day 240, p. 12.
16. *An Incident leading to Contamination of the Beaches near to the British Nuclear Fuels Limited Windscale and Calder Works, Sellafield November 1983,* A Report of Investigations into the Circumstances by the Department of the Environment Radiochemical Inspectorate, January 1984, para. 1.2.
17. *Ibid.,* para. 4.2.6.
18. *Ibid.,* para. 4.5.7.
19. *Ibid.,* para. 4.2.8, the annotated document is reproduced at its Annex 6. The RCI report considers it likely that the solvent was not in the event floated off (para. 4.3.2) but the report by the Health and Safety Executive on the incident (*The Contamination of the Beach Incident at British Nuclear Fuels Limited, Sellafield, November 1983*) considers that 'although highly undesirable, the

handwritten addition to the Washout Instructions probably did not contribute to the incident' (para. 23).

20. *Ibid.*, para. 4.4.1.
21. *Ibid.*, para. 5.3.8.
22. *Ibid.*, para. 5.3.7. The HSE/NII report (see note 19 above), para. 28 gives the time of discharge of ST2 as between 00.30 and 05.30 on 11 November—more than 24 hours earlier.
23. *Ibid.*, para. 5.4.11.
24. *Ibid.*, para. 5.4.6.
25. *Ibid.*, para. 9.1.4.
26. Reference 2, recommendation 8, p. 94.
27. Reference 16, para. 9.1.5 (6).
28. See note 19.
29. BNFL Annual Report 1983/84, p. 10.
30. SSBA/S/147.
31. French Supreme Council for Nuclear Safety—Report of the Working Group on Spent Fuel Management (the Castaing Report), appendix 7. (Translations of the Report and parts of the appendices have the inquiry number SSBA/S/76 A and B.)
32. Day 274, p. 72G.
33. SSBA/P/11, para. 20.
34. BNFL/P/1 (ADD 4), para. 12.
35. Day 274, p. 87.
36. *Idem.*
37. See note 9.
38. Reference 2, para. 2.4.
39. *Ibid.*, para. 2.40.
40. *Ibid.*, para. 6.13.
41. *New Scientist*, 18 January 1985, p. 10. See *The Lancet*, 16 February 1985, p. 403, for the discrepancy.
42. Reference 2, para. 2.46.
43. *Ibid.*, para. 4.88.
44. *New Statesman*, 1 February 1985, p. 13.
45. ICRP Publication 26, Pergamon Press, 1976, CEGB/S/40, para. 96.
46. *Ibid.*, paras. 117-118.
47. *Ibid.*, paras. 104, 119. For units see Appendix 1.
48. Day 153, p. 34D. See also day 151, p. 33D.
49. Day 153, p. 40D-41B.
50. Statistical significance here and throughout this section has the precise (and widely accepted) meaning that there is more than a 90 per cent probability that chance would not produce the number observed.
51. Day 32, p. 25F.
52. SSBA/S/54.
53. Day 229, pp. 15-16.
54. The third of these occurred in January 1983.
55. Day 319, p. 40H.

56. His attention was not drawn to the incidence by the CEGB, or the NRPB, or any of the plethora of bodies which share responsibility for health care in the nuclear industry. Day 193, pp. 68–69.

57. Day 193, p. 64G.

58. Day 193, p. 66H.

59. Day 229, p. 18D.

60. The Black Report (ref. 2) contains at p. 9 a block diagram comparing dose commitments from liquid discharges at all the UK nuclear sites in 1978. Sellafield's was 4,750 times greater than the 'worst' civilian power station, Bradwell, and 25,500 times greater than those from Sizewell 'A', the best of the Magnox stations in this regard.

61. Prof R E Blackith, SSBA/P/5, and Dr M Stuart, SSBA/P/6.

62. Day 32, p. 26A; day 222, p. 33D.

63. For example, SSBA/P/5, pp. 13–16.

64. Day 229, p. 28B. It should be noted that Dr Cartwright was discussing the possibility of viruses being the sole cause of leukaemias.

65. Day 298, p. 96F.

66. Dr Stewart gave evidence to the Sizewell inquiry on days 297 and 298.

67. 'Immune system and cancers of foetal origin', Stewart and Kneale, *Cancer Inmunology and Immunotherapy* Vol. 14 (1982), pp. 110–116 (SSBA/S/192) summarises the findings.

68. Figures given in 'Detection of late effects of ionizing radiation: why deaths of A-bomb survivors are so misleading', Alice Stewart, *The International Journal of Epidemiology*, March 1985, p. 5 (SSBA/S/242).

69. Day 298, p. 39D, 64C.

70. 'Radiation exposures of Hanford workers dying from cancer and other causes', Mancuso, Stewart and Kneale, *Health Physics*, November 1977 (CEGB/S/1217).

71. See their papers in the *British Journal of Industrial Medicine*, 1981, pp. 156–166 (CEGB/S/1238), and two papers in 1984, pp. 6–8 (SSBA/S/257) and 9–14 (SSBA/S/258).

72. Dr Stewart noted under cross-examination that 'There is nothing magic about cancer as a probability of dying. It just happens to have a longer latency than others. Therefore, it is more easily obscured by other causes of death'. Day 298, p. 6G.

73. Dr Rosalie Bertell, another witness for SSBA, suggested that a factor of three should be applied (Day 259, pp. 60–61), a figure which BNFL also uses (BNFL/P/1 (ADD 8). The evidence of both Dr Bertell and Dr Stewart on the healthy worker effect is summarised on day 319, pp. 54–65.

74. Day 298, p. 67C.

75. Day 298, p. 51C.

76. Day 298, p. 69D.

CHAPTER 10

RADIOACTIVE WASTE MANAGEMENT

For many, the creation of radioactive wastes is the unacceptable face of nuclear electricity. The imposition of quantities of manufactured poison on scores of future generations, for a modest present benefit easily satisfied by other means, is seen as profoundly immoral, a selfishly expedient action by a thoughtless society. A major factor in the opposition to new nuclear development is a reluctance to condone a significant increase in the volumes of wastes already being produced.

The best known product of the nuclear fuel cycle is plutonium which, as created by the civil power stations, should be regarded as a waste as it has no value. If reprocessing continues, UK reactors operating and under construction will produce 77.5 tonnes of plutonium. A high nuclear programme of PWRs would produce a further 95 tonnes.[1] Plutonium is primarily an alpha-emitter, and toxic in particulate quantities if inhaled or ingested, and it is also a security risk. It is unusual in the unimaginable length of time that it retains these properties. As is well known, its half-life is 24,400 years, about four times longer than recorded history, and as a rule of thumb ten half-lives should elapse before a radioactive substance can be considered to have decayed to natural background levels. It follows that any plans we make for the management of plutonium will have to arrange for its isolation from the environment for a quarter of a million years.

Plutonium, once separated from spent fuel, is stored as a solid (plutonium dioxide), and decays too slowly to generate heat. More difficult to handle is high-level heat generating liquid waste, which also arises solely as a result of reprocessing. It is a mess of decaying radioactive isotopes of a range of middle-order elements, known collectively as fission products (see Appendix 2), and is the most radioactive material in existence. The UK inventory is held in stainless steel tanks at Sellafield, constantly stirred and cooled; the present British nuclear power stations will produce 3,000 cubic meters.[2] BNFL used to comment that the high-level liquid waste so far produced would only be sufficient to fill an average four-bedroomed house—it was meant as a reassurance.

A vitrification plant is due to be completed at Sellafield by 1988, and this will encapsulate the waste into borosilicate glass blocks. This process reduces the volume by between a half and a third, and makes the waste easier to handle and to store, but it cannot, of course, reduce either the radioactivity or the heat produced. After vitrification the current strategy is to store the blocks on the surface for at least 50 years, in dry stores, and to defer a decision as to their ultimate fate until the expiry of that period. The dry stores were mentioned in Chapter 8; two have been in operation at Wylfa since 1970, holding Magnox spent fuel prior to reprocessing, and the CEGB has developed a design for a dry store to hold AGR spent fuel which, because the cladding corrodes slowly under water, cannot be stored wet for more than 10 years. This design can be adapted to hold PWR spent fuel, and NNC is hoping to secure export business with such a store.[3]

The same basic design of dry store can be used to hold vitrified high-level waste or unreprocessed spent fuel from Magnox, AGR or PWR reactors. The main difference is that one used for the glass blocks would appear almost empty because of the much higher heat production by volume. The stores are a remarkable engineering concept because they are designed so that the heat of the material being cooled creates the cooling draught; cooling does not depend on a power supply although loading and handling obviously do. NNC comments that once a store is full, it:[4]

> may be sealed off to form a closed natural-circulation loop, via a heat pipe cooler if necessary. The ability to seal off the vault makes this method of storage very attractive, especially for very long periods.

Dry stores offer a long-term alternative to reprocessing. At a time when the plutonium recovered from civil fuel is an embarrassment, when uranium prices are so low as to render the recovery of unused uranium uneconomic, and when public concern about Sellafield discharges is growing, it seems that only institutional momentum and the foreign contracts can justify continuing with the anachronistic activity of reprocessing.

High-level liquid wastes would not exist without it, and neither would the greater part of intermediate (ILW) and low-level (LLW) wastes. By definition, these (see Appendix 1) are of a toxicity sufficient to require long-term containment, and on scenario C high nuclear background assumptions, 11,000 cu.m. of ILW, and 50,000 cu.m. of LLW will be produced from reactor operation and decommissioning by 2000, and 51,500 cu.m. of ILW, and 380,000 cu.m. of LLW from reprocessing.[5] ILW is stored at Sellafield. Prior to 1983 some was dumped at sea, together with a larger quantity of LLW, but national and international pressure, channelled through the National Union of Seamen, closed that route. Plans to use a disused mine beneath Billingham for the disposal of ILW were stopped by the mine owners (ICI), the elected representatives and the people of the town, and there is currently no disposal route available for ILW.

The most urgent pressure on the authorities is to find a route for solid LLW. Drigg, the BNFL site close to Sellafield, is the only dump in use, as it has been for many years. The Sizewell inquiry was told early in 1983 by a member of the Nuclear Industry Radioactive Waste Executive (NIREX) that the remaining capacity at Drigg was 'estimated to be about 1 million cubic meters',[6] but in October 1984 the Deputy Managing Director of BNFL revealed that the available capacity was only 550,000 cu.m.,[7] a little more than half. The Department of the Environment's National Strategy on Radioactive Waste Management, published in June 1984,[8] indicated that the total amount of LLW estimated to arise between 1984 and 2000 is 500,000 cu.m., one-fifth of which is from industrial and medical sources. Even assuming the extensive use of compaction, and without taking into account the fact that progressive restrictions on pipeline discharges from Sellafield must mean larger quantities for land disposal, the DOE witness to the inquiry agreed that Drigg could be full by 1997.[9]

The virtual halving of the Drigg capacity, of which the authors of the National Strategy were unaware, lends urgency to the search for a successor. The schedule for selecting the sites, possibly holding inquiries for test drilling permission, drilling, evaluating, holding an inquiry for construction, and building the facility was examined during DOE's cross-examination by the Town and Country Planning Association (TCPA).[10] Bearing in mind the traditional slippage in controversial planning applications, and in view of the CEGB's need to know by about 1990 whether it will have to start building on-site storage facilities, the timescale was seen to be tight. Only one site has been named as being under active investigation as an LLW dumpsite, (although NIREX envisages test drilling on three sites) at Elstow in Bedfordshire. The pressure to find that site acceptable must be intense, because there is very little time to find an alternative.

Longer term, the volumes of waste are huge. By 2080 1.2 million cu.m. of compacted LLW will exist if no further stations are built and if reprocessing continues, and up to three times that amount from a PWR programme. 260,000 cu.m. of ILW will arise by that date from the existing stations, and up to 540,000 from a programme. Volumes of vitrified high-level waste could reach 8,200 cu.m. if that from a PWR programme is added to the waste already arising.[11] Two impressions remain. The first is one of a cavalier attitude by government to the whole question of radioactive waste management; the implications in the medium and long term have simply not been thought out. In its closing submissions, TCPA commented that:[12]

It appears to the TCPA that the CEGB's proposal to build a PWR at Sizewell B and its intention that this should form the basis of a series of nuclear power station orders, was formulated (with government backing) without full consideration of its waste management implications on the assumption that the problem, if there is a problem, would simply look after itself.

178

It is extraordinary, and typical of the prevailing attitude, that NIREX, the organisation charged with formulating a policy on ILW and LLW, was not established until July 1982.

The second impression is one of incredulity. All high-level wastes arise from reprocessing. A little less than 80 per cent of the ILW, and a little more than 80 per cent of the LLW, arises from reprocessing. All discharges to the Irish Sea arise from reprocessing, as do large tonnages of a valueless and dangerous metal. The Americans, for political and economic reasons, have never reprocessed civil spent fuel. We have the technology to enable us, with our different types of irradiated fuel, to follow suit.

Discounting and the economics of radioactive waste management

As well as posing unique dangers, nuclear power involves unique difficulties in accounting. This is because the costs of managing the radioactive wastes from a reactor—back end costs—continue to arise long after, even generations after, the reactor has ceased to produce electricity. A conventional industrial activity involves expenditure and then benefit; investment followed by profit. At some stages costs and benefits may be simultaneous, but nuclear power is a highly unusual activity in that it necessarily involves a third stage of a final tranche of costs.[13]

When evaluating and comparing projects for investment appraisal, it is standard practice to apply an annual discount to the costs incurred and benefits that may arise, in order to apply a penalty to projects with benefits arising too far into the future. The system was not designed to test projects with far distant costs, since these are infrequent: 'Almost all expenditure proposals would produce benefits later than costs.'[14] The test discount rate (TDR), set by government and presently 5 per cent, is applied annually to all·costs and benefits of the project under consideration. If a benefit of £100 is expected to arise in 20 years time, 5 per cent (compounded) is deducted for each of the 20 years, and a very much smaller present value arrived at. If, in an alternative project, the £100 is expected to arise in 5 years time, its present value is very much greater.

When used to evaluate nuclear power, or to compare it with other methods of electricity generation, discounting has a small effect on the station's costs during construction and operation, but a profound effect on the uniquely nuclear back end costs, whose present value is reduced to insignificance. A senior CEGB witness agreed to the proposition that:[15]

> By the application of the discount rate of 5%, later costs, and I am thinking about reprocessing or storage of spent nuclear fuel, however large in reality, are effectively minimised to such an extent that they have little if any impact on the net effective cost of Sizewell 'B'.

Thus when the discounting procedure, which was intended to discourage projects with long-delayed benefits, is applied to methods of electricity generation, it has the effect of encouraging the project with long-delayed costs.

Two methods of overcoming this bias towards nuclear were suggested to the Sizewell inquiry.[16] One was that a small negative discount rate, of perhaps –1 per cent, might be applied to long-term costs, with a cut-off at 150 years. The second suggested that all long-term costs should be taken as being incurred during the lifetime of the station, a method which has twice been considered by the US Nuclear Regulatory Commission in respect of decommissioning costs.[17] Either offers a way of providing a more realistic contemporary assessment of the actual levels of back-end costs that will have to be met by future generations.

The test discount rate must make accounting at BNFL a surreal activity. As the company's Deputy Managing Director said:[18]

> In the end, what we do, and the possible variations in the cost of what we do, have such a small effect on the cost of nuclear generation. . . if we reduce the cost of our back-end services by 10%, it is not going to cause people to rush out and buy more electric fires, because the effect is so negligible.

Similarly, if BNFL adds to its costs, the effect on the overall cost of nuclear electricity is negligible. Large sums of money can be spent on, for example, incorporating a carbon-14 removal plant into THORP,[19] without the expenditure having a noticeable effect on present value costs. In the same way, it makes no effective difference to the generating boards whether the management of irradiated fuel involves reprocessing or long-term storage. The additional costs of reprocessing, discounted, are tiny. But it must make a considerable difference to BNFL, which is in business to service an industry to which its activities are economically marginal.

The CEGB assured the inquiry that a 'notional albeit real'[20] sum of money is in fact set aside annually in the accounts, which is intended to appreciate in value at such a rate as to be able to meet back-end costs, the value of which are estimated today but which will actually fall to be met far into the future. This shows an admirable faith in long-term stability, extending over many generations, but does not satisfactorily take into account the unintended result of discounting, which is to give preference to projects with long-delayed costs. In the case of nuclear power, discounting is an incentive to delay, and, as Prof. Jeffery points out (Appendix 5):

> This is clearly an unacceptable result and the practical question is, what method should be used to penalise these uniquely long-term costs. . .? This is not a question of altering the present discounting procedure in general, but of an exceptional procedure for a unique problem, in which positive, direct costs *necessarily* occur long after—in the next and succeeding generations—any benefits have been received.

Reprocessing is the most obvious reminder of the roots of the civil nuclear programme. Although MOD work accounts for less than ten per cent of BNFL's turnover,[21] it is for that work that the Magnox reprocessing line at Sellafield exists. With no short or medium-term use for the recovered plutonium, and raw uranium so abundant that the recycling of the small amounts of unburned uranium is uneconomic, the only way that civil reprocessing can continue is to make its costs appear negligible. This service is performed by applying the test discount rate, so that the present valued costs of reprocessing appear to be as negligible as those of long-term storage, and neither has a noticeable effect on the present price of electricity.

The contribution that we, in this generation, make towards the real costs of irradiated fuel management is tiny. Those costs will fall on future generations, as will the task of looking after the wastes, and guarding against the possibility of their entry into the environment. To produce quantities of radioactive wastes in power reactors, then to increase their quantity and concentration by reprocessing, and then to delegate responsibility for their management to generations to which nuclear power will be a folk memory, is institutional irresponsibility on the grand scale.

NOTES AND REFERENCES

1. BNFL/S/12.
2. BNFL/S/19 and 20.
3. CEGB/P/9 (ADD 8), paras. 7 and 10.
4. 'Dry store for irradiated fuel and active waste', brochure by NNC Special Projects.
5. CEGB/P/21 Tables 1 and 2. These are packaged, i.e. compacted, volumes.
6. CEGB/P/21, para. 46.
7. Day 275, pp. 50–51.
8. DOE/S/12.
9. Day 279, p. 17F.
10. TCPS cross-examination on *ibid.*, pp. 17–30.
11. CEGB/P/21 (ADD 4 REV), Table 8.
12. Day 314, p. 47D.
13. The only other example that came to anyone's mind during the inquiry was the reclamation and reinstatement of land after mining. Day 136, p. 29H.
14. 'Investment Appraisal in the Public Sector', HM Treasury, 1982, para. 3.27.
15. Day 136, p. 30G.
16. SSBA/P/1, pp. 32–34 and SSBA/P/2, pp. 29–32. See also the present Appendix 5.
17. SSBA/P/1 (ADD 7).
18. Day 275, pp. 59B, 60F.
19. BNFL/P/1 (ADD 5), para. 10, and (ADD 9).

20. Day 136, p. 32G.
21. Day 274, p. 32C.

CHAPTER 11

CHOICES

Few industrial activities can have been begun with such high expectations as the development of nuclear power. Those involved in the early days must have worked in an atmosphere of optimism, excitement and scientific creativity, confident that they were beating the sword that they, or their contemporaries, had fashioned, into a ploughshare of great benefit to humanity. It must be a matter of considerable sadness to those scientists and technologists who solved the problems of controlled nuclear fission on an industrial scale, that the main challenge that now faces the industry they created is to find somewhere to put its wastes.

In the first part of this book it was seen how Magnox reactors derived directly from the plutonium piles, and how the fuel cycle services established for military purposes were used by the civil power stations. Through the medium of the Atomic Energy Authority the defence establishment subsidised the genesis of the nuclear electricity programme, and in return the Authority obtained, until 1971, the plutonium that that programme produced.

It has been noted that Magnox reactors in normal operation produce larger quantities of plutonium per unit of electricity generated than either AGR or PWR, and that Magnox plutonium has a higher concentration of the fissile isotope Pu-239.[1] The British civil stockpile is therefore of unusually high quality, but the pre-1969 stockpile had an even higher proportion of Pu-239 due to the characteristic of Magnox reactors that they produce weapons-grade plutonium during their first two years of operation. This is because they are refuelled on-load, and refuelling must take place at a steady pace. Almost as soon as the reactor begins operation lightly-irradiated fuel rods, high in Pu-239, are withdrawn and

185

replaced. If all the fuel rods were permitted the maximum residence in the core a refuelling log-jam would occur three or fours years later.[2] PWRs do not have this property of producing weapons-grade plutonium in their early years, because they are batch refuelled off-load. On-load refuelling at the Hunterston and Hinkley Point AGRs has only recently, and at part load, been made to work so they, too, have been batch refuelled to date.

Ownership of the plutonium produced after 1969 in CEGB and SSEB reactors passed to the generating boards, but the pre-1969 material owned by the UKAEA included the civil weapons-grade plutonium from all the power stations except Wylfa. Parliament was told in 1983 that there was no weapons-grade material in the civil stockpile;[3] therefore it must have been exported, used in the UK, or diluted with lower grade plutonium.

The Magnox stations have never produced economic electricity,[4] nor are they big enough to have made more than a marginal contribution to power requirements on the CEGB system. Leslie Hannah, the Electricity Council historian, has commented:[5]

> At the time they were ordered, every one of the Magnox stations was expected by the CEGB to be uneconomic, and their expectations proved correct, though the losses in the early years were rather greater than even they had expected. The placing of those uneconomic orders could be considered a breach of their statutory duty to provide an economical supply of electricity. . .

To be fair, the early Magnox stations were to a large extent imposed on the CEGB by a government and AEA apparently intent on nuclear at any price, and the CEGB received a sympathetic hearing from the House of Commons Select Committee on Nationalised Industries when, in 1963, it claimed that it should receive compensation from the tax-payer for the higher costs of production necessitated by the nuclear programme.[6] The compensation was in fact paid by the electricity consumer via higher bills, rather than by the taxpayer, although to many people the distinction is academic, but the story illustrates the fact that British nuclear power from its beginnings has been exempt from the normal constraints of commerce and industry.

The AGR was, or rather is, an attempt at a reactor concept that would generate significant amounts of electricity, amounts comparable to those being produced by the latest coal-fired stations. The concept was pushed to the design stage in great haste, at a time when British nuclear confidence was at its height. In the years 1965–1970 the AEA, CEGB and consortia all showed a breathtaking conviction in their own abilities, supported by an unshakeable faith in the inevitability of increasing electricity demand. The failure to build the AGRs has been matched by the failure of the expected demand increases to materialise; had it not been, the Board would have had great difficulty in meeting demand.

The AGR programme has been a financial disaster that few commercial organisations could have survived. A non-nationalised energy supply company could not have had the capital and manpower to spare as the months of delay on the construction sites turned into years and then decades. Certainly American power utilities do not, and in that country the civil nuclear industry, offering different reactors but without an uncancelled order since 1973, is moribund. If the Sizewell 'B' PWR is built, it is quite possible that, by 1988, it will be the only Westinghouse PWR under construction anywhere in the world.[7]

The British nuclear industry, in which research and development, supply and use of nuclear power are all nationalised activities, has avoided the more obvious consequences of financial collapse. We have had no crises on Wall Street or cancellations of almost-complete reactors, and the failure has been less dramatic. Because the industry has never been required or expected to be profitable, the British have been able to keep faith with the dream, in a way that Americans have not been able to for a decade, and financial success is still something promised, something in the future. The merits of both AGR and PWR are argued largely in terms of hoped-for performance, and one of the oddest features of the Sizewell inquiry was that it was about the CEGB wanting to exchange one historic failure for another.

187

As the extent of the AGR failure became apparent, and the Board's preference for the PWR grew, so the power of the AEA waned as that of the CEGB waxed. Sir Walter Marshall has been a proponent of the PWR for many years, even while he was employed by the Authority. The House of Commons Select Committee on Science and Technology noted in 1976 that two years earlier he:[8]

> Was in the Middle East. . . acting almost in a way as an agent, arguing on the one hand nothing for the [UK] steam generating reactor, but doing a hell of a job for the Americans flogging the PWR.

It is a measure of the strength of the PWR lobby that, with the sole exception of the SSEB, not a single government department or institution, neither NNC, nor the National Coal Board, nor even the Department of Trade and Industry, has questioned the CEGB's preference. The CEGB is now the dominant influence in the British nuclear industry.

The two main provisions of the Atomic Energy Act, 1971 transferred the AEA's fuel fabrication and reprocessing business to the newly-created British Nuclear Fuels Ltd (BNFL), and transferred its medical isotope business to The Radiochemical Centre Ltd, later privatised as Amersham International. The Authority's Health and Safety Branch became the National Radiological Protection Board, and in April 1973 the Weapons Group was taken over by the Ministry of Defence. The very extensive research facilities remained to the AEA, as did the prototype reactors at Winfrith (an SGHWR) and Dounreay (the Prototype Fast Reactor) and, perhaps most importantly, it retained its role of providing advice to the government on national nuclear strategy. Although its days of large-scale industrial activity were over, it retained intimate connections throughout the industry. The staff of BNFL and the NRPB were inevitably recruited largely from the AEA, and BNFL, which remains the Authority's biggest contract customer,[9] was initially half-owned by it. The intimacy between the two organisations is reflected in the career of Sir John Hill, who was Chairman of the AEA from 1967 to 1980, and of BNFL from 1971 to 1983.

The AEA still spends large amounts of public money annually and receives by far the largest part of government funds for energy research. Its grant from the Department of Energy, known as the Parliamentary Vote, was £203.8 million in 1983/84. Its business activities brought in another £152 million, and its operating expenditure was £362.7 million.[10] Its largest single project is the development of the fast reactor, or fast breeder reactor, on which it spent £114.8 million in that year. Expenditure also included £16.4 million on AGR development and safety, and £19.4 million on PWR safety research. For the first time, the generating boards contributed towards these costs in 1983/84, to the tune of £10 million.

The fast reactor is the major prestige project remaining to the AEA. Work began in 1954, and the first reactor at Dounreay, the DFR, started up in 1959 at 100 W *(sic)* output.[11] It was closed down in 1977; its successor, the Prototype Fast Reactor (PFR) began operation in 1974 but has yet to achieve full power. Fast reactors are fully described elsewhere[12] —briefly, they differ from conventional (or thermal) reactors in that their fuel contains a high proportion of one of the fissile isotopes, either uranium-235 or plutonium-239. Plutonium derived from the Magnox reactors is suitable, but that derived from AGRs or PWRs would require enrichment. Fast reactors do not have a moderator to slow down the neutrons that cause fission to 'thermal' speeds, and the core is surrounded by a 'blanket' of depleted or natural uranium (i.e. predominantly U-238), and neutrons from the core are absorbed in the blanket to form plutonium-239. Since the mid-1950s thermal reactors have been regarded by committed nuclear scientists as a stop-gap measure until the commercial development of fast reactors, whose theoretical ability to breed more fissile material than they consume offers the possibility of a virtually self-sustaining energy source.

Three characteristics of fast reactors are of particular concern, and make it unlikely that they will ever be licensed for commercial operation in this country. Firstly, the presence of tonnes of plutonium in the core and blanket means that they are potential atomic bombs in the sense that thermal reactors, whose fuel contains low concentrations of fissile isotopes at all stages, are not. Secondly the fast reactor cores are so hot, thermally, that the only coolant able to remove the heat and raise steam for the turbines is sodium under sufficient pressure to keep it liquid. This substance is explosive in contact with air or water. Thirdly, even under optimal conditions, fast reactors only breed a very small percentage of new fissile material. If they are to be self-sustaining in fissile material, the spent fuel and blankets must be extracted and reprocessed quickly, and the plutonium made into new fuel and returned to the reactors. Fast reactor fuel undergoes very much higher levels of irradiation than that of thermal reactors, but reprocessing must be done quickly; there is no leisure to allow the radioactivity to decay. It will have to be handled under very difficult conditions, and it is inevitable that high doses and discharges will result.

The House of Commons Select Committee on Energy reported on the AEA's fast reactor programme in 1984. It noted that £2,400 million (at 1982/83 values) had been spent since 1955, at an annual rate of £85–120 million since 1963, but the Authority saw no immediate prospect of a commercial power station. The Committee's report quotes the then Chairman of the Authority, Sir Peter Hirsch, as saying that another 25 or 30 years work, and another £1,300 million, would be needed before the stage 'where one hopes to obtain a commercial station'. These costs were exclusive of £2,000 million construction costs, and £300 million for a reprocessing plant.[13]

Speaking of the European collaborative agreement to build three commercial demonstration fast reactors, which the UK signed in January 1984, Sir Peter said:[14]

> The one thing that is certain in this new phase of European co-operation in the fast reactor is that Britain's CDFR will be the last of the three demonstration projects to be built.

Despite this, the AEA has made it clear that it would like the reprocessing plant that will be needed to service the three reactors to be built at Dounreay. Not surprisingly, the

Authority's European partners are reported to be 'looking favourably' on the Scottish site.[15]

The AEA has even bigger dreams for Dounreay—that it will become a fast reactor park. In 1985 Dr Marsham, Managing Director of AEA's Northern Division, said:[16]

> To have a strategic plan it is said that you need to have a strategic vision. Here is mine. Before the middle of the next century, preferably well before, our objective should be to establish as one component of our base-load electricity supply, a self-contained nuclear power park of fast reactors and their fuel processing and waste storage facilities. This would have perhaps six to eight fast reactors. . . The only thing coming off site would be 10,000 MW of low cost base load power. . . The park would be self-sufficient in fuel and nuclear plant sites for centuries if required. . . and I see no reason why it should not be regarded as a good neighbour in the locality as is Dounreay now. . . It could set the pattern for base load electricity generation.

Although it is not the AEA's role to concern itself with electricity distribution, it is not clear what it imagines the north of Scotland is going to do with 10 GW of electricity; a figure which is more than double Scotland's present consumption.

The second largest project funded by the AEA is research into fusion power (£22.1 million in 1983/84), and the Select Committee wondered why this money was being spent, if fast reactors are going to provide nuclear electricity for the next 1,000 years. It compared the treatment by the government of research into the renewable sources of energy with that of long-term nuclear projects, in terms of the results and returns demanded of each. The Committee's conclusion was that quite different criteria were applied:[17]

> We perceive (the fusion programme) as being run on a very different basis from that adopted by the Department of Energy in relation to smaller, non-nuclear projects, to which the attitude seems to be one of scepticism rather

than faith.

The Select Committee criticised government-funded energy research as being disproportionate in three ways—
- the ratio of £196.6 million to £47.5 million on nuclear and non-nuclear (including coal) respectively,
- the 'gross imbalance' between spending on generation ('supply side') of £235 million and on conservation and efficiency ('demand side') of £10 million,
- the heavy emphasis on research into electricity (89 per cent of total expenditure) despite the fact that electricity use was only 13.8 per cent of UK energy use in 1983.[18]

It is worth noting (though the Committee did not) that 17 per cent of Britain's electricity was nuclear-generated in 1983.[19] The nuclear component of total energy use in that year was therefore 2.3 per cent, and it received 80.5 per cent of the government energy funding. Conversely, 97.6 per cent of the energy use received 19.5 per cent of the funds.

In this way the government, through the AEA, continues to engineer a bias in favour of nuclear power, a bias that is so strong as to amount to the intentional elimination of all alternatives. Sir Brian Flowers, who was Chairman of the Royal Commission on Environmental Pollution at the time that it published its very influential Sixth Report in 1976, commented two years later:[20]

If nuclear power is inevitable until the end of the century, it is because for the last 25 years we have not invested in anything else.

Sir Brian's words remain accurate, except that he underestimated the timescale of inevitability. By the early 1980s the CEGB was becoming impatient with the failure of the nuclear investment; the Sizewell inquiry marked the beginning of the new drive to transform nuclear power from a relatively minor energy source to the dominant form of electricity production. The Board and the government want nuclear stations to supply the bulk of our electricity by the first decades of the next century. If they succeed, and Britain is predominantly nuclear by the time the next crossroads are reached, in 2020 or so, there is no doubt that the transition from a thermal reactor monopoly to a fast reactor monopoly will be a relatively straightforward business.

That, it seems, is the path down which the united institutional momentum of the country's establishment is pushing us. One of the most striking aspects of nuclear power is the strength of the consensus that supports it. This consensus embraces all the parliamentary parties, all the major unions except the mineworkers', and the entire institutional and power structure. It exists at the heart of our national identity where, with the other central assumptions that dictate our collective self-appraisal, it goes unquestioned and unchallenged. Nuclear power is seen as about to provide the power to fuel our imminent industrial regeneration, and its subsequent expansion; it will play a key role in maintaining and increasing our national wealth. Moreover it is itself the epitomy of the hoped-for new industrial activity in that it is highly technical, amenable to central control, and above all employing a maximum of capital and a minimum of labour.

It is now possible to identify the third, and present, stage in the progress of our national fascination with nuclear technology. First was the belief that our international status required the possession of an independent bomb; we built the bomb but could not maintain our status. Then, closely derived, came pride in our atomic science and in the early lead in power generation technology that it gave us; but that inevitably slipped away because of a limited market and technical haste. Now there is the hope that nuclear power will provide energy that is reliable, controllable, plentiful and immune from disruption, to enable us to reverse the slow decline in our economic and industrial activity that has been taking place since 1945. In this hope we have invested enormous resources.

Those three stages, all of which still appeal to a greater or lesser extent in different quarters, account for the universality of the nuclear consensus. There can be few people who are not affected by an appeal to national prestige, or to technical pride, or to the hope of future prosperity. Indeed it is impossible to oppose nuclear power without implicitly or explicitly rejecting both the patriotism and, more importantly, the ethics of our society which measure progress and success by the rate at which production and consumption increases—to a large degree the universal measure of our age.

It is not difficult to understand why both the state and monopoly capitalism invest so little in conservation and efficiency, and in small decentralised energy systems. They see their job as persuading us to use more, not less, and they are reflecting and sustaining the prevailing ethics in doing so. What is certain is that those ethics are changing. Both the assumption that production and consumption should be maximised, and that the labour content in production should be minimised, are being widely questioned at a time when the objective of an indefinately sustained industrial expansion is being recognised as an obvious absurdity.

European countries, whether by necessity or preference or both, are slowly becoming less profligate and more efficient. Energy use is increasingly monitored and controlled, and even if industrial output were comparable, which it is not, it is difficult to see ways in which society could now use more energy than it did in the late 1970s. On the other hand, it is simple to see many ways in which it can and does use less. Whatever the characteristics—and ethics—of society in the coming decades prove to be, it is at least possible that a power supply system based on large, inflexible and costly units, which pose health hazards for centuries if their detritus is mishandled, will not be appropriate or acceptable. But the nuclear momentum seems to be bent on attempting to secure its own future—and that of the kind of society that engendered it—by allocating inadequate resources to non-nuclear technologies, and thereby creating and maintaining a nuclear monopoly. At best this is characteristically self-confident and irresponsibly short-sighted, if only in terms of the possibility of a nuclear failure, for which there are precedents. At worst it is a cynical restriction of future options. If a long-term nuclear monopoly is estalished, the rest of society will be restricted in its freedom to choose not only its future energy supplies, but also its future structure, attitudes, priorities and liberties.

194

NOTES AND REFERENCES

1. See Chapter 8, note 7.
2. Similarly, when Magnox reactors are finally shut down, fuel rods with a range of irradiations will be in the core, and they will once again yield weapons-grade plutonium.
3. Hansard, 27 July 1983, col. 439.
4. See Chapter 1, note 41.
5. Hannah, *op. cit.*, pp. 243–244.
6. See Chapter 1, note 22.
7. WANA/P/2, para. 5.20.
8. House of Commons Select Committee on Science and Technology Session 1975/76, Q. 283.
9. UKAEA Annual Report 1982/83, para. 14: 'The biggest [contract] customer is BNFL.' Annual Report 1983/84, para. 15 gives: 'BNFL are a major customer.'
10. UKAEA Annual Report 1983/84, p. 60.
11. *Atom* no. 74, p. 308.
12. See for example Walter Patterson's *The Plutonium Business* (Paladin 1984).
13. House of Commons Select Committee on Energy, Session 1983/84, Ninth Report, para. 22.
14. *Nuclear Engineering International,* June 1984.
15. *The Guardian,* 20 September 1984.
16. *Atom* no 341, p. 16.
17. Reference 13, para. 29.
18. *Ibid.,* para. 11.
19. *Atom* no. 334, p. 36.
20. *Bulletin of the Atomic Scientists,* March 1978, p. 22. Sir Brian is now Lord Flowers, and Rector of Imperial College, London. He was a member of the AEA from 1971 to 1981.

APPENDIX 1

GLOSSARY OF INITIALS, ACRONYMS AND ABBREVIATIONS, RADIATION UNITS AND TERMS

Based to a large extent on the Sizewell inquiry Secretariat's document SB24, which was in turn derived from Appendix F to the CEGB's Statement of Case to that inquiry.

A. Initials, acronyms and abbreviations

ACS	Average cold spell
AEA	(UK) Atomic Energy Authority
AGR	Advanced gas-cooled reactor
ALARA	As low as reasonably achievable
APC	Atomic Power Constructions Ltd (no longer in being)
BEA	British Electricity Authority (1948–1955)
BNFL	British Nuclear Fuels Ltd
BWR	Boiling water reactor
CANDU	A Canadian reactor which uses natural (un-enriched) uranium as fuel and heavy water as moderator
CEA	Central Electricity Authority (1955–1957)
CEGB	Central Electricity Generating Board (established 1957)
CHP	Combined heat and power
COGEMA	Compagnie Générale des Matières Nucléaires
DEn	(UK) Department of Energy
DNC	Declared net capability
DOE	(UK) Department of the Environment, or (US) Department of Energy
ECC	Electricity Consumers Council
ECCS	Emergency core cooling system
EdF	Electricité de France
GDP	Gross domestic product
GW	Gigawatt (= 1,000 MW, or 1 million kW)

GWe	Gigawatt electrical
GWh	Gigawatt hour
GWth	Gigawatt thermal
HLW	High level wastes
HSE	Health and Safety Executive
HTR	High temperature reactor
IAEA	International Atomic Energy Authority
ICRP	International Commission on Radiological Protection
IDC	Interest during construction
ILW	Intermediate level wastes
kW	Kilowatt
kWh	Kilowatt hour (the 'unit' of electricity consumption)
LLW	Low level wastes
LOCA	Loss of coolant accident
LWR	Light water reactor (generic term for BWR and PWR)
MAFF	Ministry of Agriculture, Fisheries and Food
mtce	Million tonnes of coal equivalent
MUF	Material unaccounted for
MW	Megawatt (= 1,000 kW)
MW(e)	Megawatt electrical
MWso	Megawatt sent out (the usual unit of power station capacity)
MW(th)	Megawatt thermal
NCB	National Coal Board
NEC	Net effective cost
NII	HM Nuclear Installations Inspectorate
NIREX	Nuclear Industry Radioactive Waste Executive
NNC	National Nuclear Corporation
NPC	Nuclear Power Company (the operating arm of NNC)
NRPB	National Radiological Protection Board
NRC	(US) Nuclear Regulatory Commission
pa	per annum
PCSR	Pre-construction safety report
p/kWh	Pence per kilowatt hour, or pence per unit
PWR	Pressurised water reactor
RCI	Radiochemical Inspectorate (of DOE)

RWMAC	Radioactive Waste Management Advisory Committee
SGHWR	Steam generating heavy water reactor
SNUPPS	Standardised nuclear unit power plant system
SSEB	South of Scotland Electricity Board
TDR	Test discount rate
THORP	Thermal oxide reprocessing plant
UKAEA	United Kingdom Atomic Energy Authority
URENCO	Dutch/West German/UK uranium enrichment company
USDOE	United States Department of Energy

B. Radiation units

The traditional units are being superceded, at least in Europe: the new units are not finding favour in the United States.

Quantity	Old unit	Symbol	New unit	Symbol	Relationship
Activity	curie	Ci	becquerel	Bq	$1 \text{ Ci} = 3.7 \times 10^{10} \text{ Bq}$
Absorbed dose	rad	rad	gray	Gy	$1 \text{ rad} = 0.01 \text{ Gy}$
Dose equivalent	rem	rem	sievert	Sv	$1 \text{ rem} = 0.01 \text{ Sv}$

One Bq represents one disintegration per second. Activities quotes in this unit thus have to be multiplied up with prefixes, eg $\text{TBq} = 10^{12}$ Bq. Units of absorbed dose allow for the fact that different radiations dissipate energy to a different extent in body tissue. Dose equivalent is equal to absorbed dose multiplied by a quality factor. This expresses the biological effectiveness of different types of radiation.

C. *Glossary of Terms*

ACTIVITY (RADIOACTIVITY)
In a given quantity of material, the number of spontaneous nuclear transformations occurring per unit time.

ADVANCED GAS COOLED REACTOR (AGR)
A development of the Calder Hall and early CEGB reactors which operates at higher temperatures and gives greater fuel burn-up. It is being used for the current generation of reactor: the latest design is being built at Heysham II and Torness. The AGR is a reactor having a graphite moderator and carbon dioxide gas as the coolant which uses slightly enriched uranium oxide fuel in stainless steel cans.

ALPHA PARTICLE
A positively charged particle emitted during the decay of some radioactive nuclei; it is composed of two protons and two neutrons and is identical with the nucleus of the helium-4 atom. Alpha particles are positively charged and are relatively heavy and slow moving. They are able to penetrate only a few tens of millimeters of air and are easily stopped by a sheet of paper. They leave a short dense trail of ionisation in the matter through which they pass and they therefore cause more damage in living tissue than other more penetrative radiation. Nuclei emitting only alpha particles have little biological effect unless they are taken into the body by inhalation or ingestion.

AVAILABILITY
The extent to which in any specified period an item of plant is in a state to provide the service for which it was designed.

AVERAGE COLD SPELL DEMAND (ACS DEMAND)
The demand which it is estimated will occur during a spell of cold weather of average severity.

BACKGROUND RADIATION
Also known as natural radiation, its chief sources are

cosmic rays and radioactivity in rocks and soil. Its absorbed dose averages about $\frac{1}{1000}$ gy. per year in the UK. It may be increased by activities such as mining, flying at high altitudes, and the use of slightly radioactive building materials. Medical exposures are usually treated separately in the literature. It should be noted that a major difference between background and man-made radiation is that the latter contains a proportion of alpha radiation.

BASE LOAD
The lowest load continuously supplied by an electrical system over a period of time, normally a year.

BASE LOAD OPERATION
A plant or power station is said to be operating on base load when it is brought into operation at full output for as long as it is available in the year.

BETA PARTICLE
See Electron.

BOILING WATER REACTOR (BWR)
A reactor using water as the moderator and coolant. The water is allowed to boil under pressure in the pressure vessel and may be used to drive a turbine. The steam, however, is radioactive and the turbine must be shielded if the steam is used directly.

CHAIN REACTION
A nuclear reaction that initiates its own repetition. In nuclear fission, a neutron induces a nucleus to fission as the result of which neutrons are released which cause another nucleus to fission and so on.

COMBINED HEAT AND POWER (CHP)
Due to thermodynamic limitations on converting heat into work, about two thirds of the heat produced by fuel in a power station is discharged as low grade heat in the cooling water. A power station which is designed or converted so

that a reasonable quantity of this heat is upgraded for use in industry or for district heating, is known as a CHP power station.

COMMISSIONING

The process during which plant components and system, having been constructed, are made operational and are confirmed by e.g. specific acceptance tests to be in accordance with design assumptions and to have met the performance criteria. Commissioning covers both nuclear and non-nuclear plant. The CEGB has two definitions of commissioning, either of which may represent a unit's final state. Full commissioning is considered to have been achieved when a unit has run at full power for 72 consecutive hours. Interim rating commissioning has been achieved when a plant has run at at least 60 per cent of its design rating for 72 hours.

COOLANT

Of a reactor, any gas or liquid which is passed through its core to remove the heat liberated in the fission process. The coolant may be referred to as reactor coolant or primary coolant.

CORE

That portion of a nuclear reactor containing the fissile material. Sometimes used also to include moderator and support structures.

CRITICAL

Of a nuclear reactor, the condition when it is just capable of sustaining a chain reaction. A reactor is said to be sub-critical when it can no longer sustain such a reaction and super-critical when it is more than capable of just sustaining such a reaction.

CRITICAL MASS

The minimum mass of fissile material needed to make a particular system critical.

DECAY HEAT

The heat produced by the decay of radioactive nuclides, for example, in a shutdown reactor or in fuel removed from a reactor.

DECLARED NET CAPABILITY

The maximum sent-out output of a power station or system taking into account any operational restrictions which would permanently change the output from that originally designed.

DESIGN RATING

The output which a plant is designed to produce.

DISCOUNTING

A method of comparing the economic benefits of different investment proposals, whereby future costs and benefits are given a Present Value by means of the application of the Test Discount Rate.

EFFICIENCY

The ratio between the thermal energy produced in the reactor or boiler of a power station, and the electrical energy produced by the turbine generators.

ELECTRICITY SUPPLY INDUSTRY

Shorthand for the nationalised industry producing and supplying electricity within England and Wales. It consists of the Electricity Council, the CEGB and the 12 Area Boards. It excludes such organisations in Scotland and Northern Ireland, the manufacturers, and those who generate their own electricity.

ELECTRON (BETA PARTICLE)

An elementary particle carrying one unit of negative electric charge. Electrons determine the chemical behaviour of elements and their flow through a conductor constitutes electricity. Electrons emitted from radioactive substances can be stopped by a few millimetres of plastic but are of particular danger if taken into or onto the surface of the body.

ENRICHED FUEL

Nuclear fuel containing more than the natural abundance of fissile atoms. In natural uranium 0.7 per cent normally consists of the fissile atom U-235.

ENRICHMENT

The process of increasing the number of fissile atoms in nuclear fuel above that occurring in the natural material. It is also the term used to denote the fraction of fissile isotope to the total isotopes present in the material, e.g. a material having an enrichment of 3 per cent contains 3 per cent U-235, 97 per cent U-238. Natural uranium contains 0.711 per cent U-235.

FAST REACTOR/FAST BREEDER REACTOR

A nuclear reactor in which no moderator is used to slow down the neutrons. A high concentration of fissile material (usually plutonium) is required. Fast reactors are theoretically capable of breeding more fissile material than they consume.

FERTILE

A non-fissile nuclide from which fissile material can be produced by neutron capture, e.g. U-238.

FISSILE

Of a nuclide, capable of undergoing fission by neutrons, e.g. U-235.

FISSION

The splitting of a heavy nucleus into two parts accompanied by the release of energy and further neutrons. It may occur spontaneously or be induced by the capture of bombarding particles, particularly neutrons.

FISSION PRODUCTS
The nuclides produced in fission, either directly or by the radioactive decay of the fission fragments. Over 300 mainly radioactive fission products have been identified. They represent isotopes of some 35 different chemical elements ranging from arsenic-85 to gadolinium-160.

FUEL CYCLE
The sequence of steps, such as enrichment, fabrication, utilisation, and reprocessing through which nuclear fuel may pass. In some contexts, Fuel Cycle includes all steps from mining of the uranium to the disposal of wastes removed from spent fuel during reprocessing.

FUEL STORAGE POND
A large container, usually made of concrete lined with steel, filled with water in which irradiated fuel is stored after its removal from the reactor. Fuel is stored in this way until its activity has decayed to the desired level and it can be removed from the site. The water acts as a coolant and a radiation shield.

GAMMA RAYS
Electromagnetic radiation, similar to X-rays but usually of shorter wavelength, emitted by a nucleus. Gamma-rays are usually exceedingly penetrating.

HALF LIFE
The time taken for the activity of a radionuclide to lose half its value by decay.

HEAVY WATER
Water consisting of molecules in which the chemical hydrogen is in the form of deuterium (heavy hydrogen) which is present in ordinary water as about 1 part in 5,000. It is used as a moderator in some reactors.

HIGH LEVEL WASTE (HLW)

Wastes in which the temperature may rise significantly as a result of their radioactivity, so that this factor has to be taken into account in designing storage or disposal facilities. In practice only the fission product stream from a reprocessing plant, and unreprocessed spent fuel (if a policy of no reprocessing were to be adopted) qualify as high level wastes.

INTERMEDIATE LEVEL WASTE (ILW)

Solid wastes exceeding the boundaries for low level wastes but which do not require the heat of radioactive decay to be taken into account in the design of storage or disposal facilities.

IRRADIATED FUEL

Nuclear fuel which has been or is being used in a fission process. (Synonymous with spent fuel.)

ISOTOPES

Species of an atom with the same number of protons in their nuclei, hence have the same atomic number and belong to the same element, but they differ in the number of neutrons and thus have different mass numbers. Such atoms have identical chemical properties but their nuclear characteristics, e.g. neutron absorption or fissile properties may be vastly different; as, for example, in the cases of hydrogen (H-1) and deuterium or heavy hydrogen (H-2) and the isotopes of uranium, U-235 and U-238.

LIGHT WATER

Ordinary water, used as a moderator and coolant in the PWR.

LOAD FACTOR

The load factor of a generating plant or the supply system is the ratio of the power (kilowatt-hours) actually generated over a period of time, to that which would have been generated if the plant had worked continuously at full output for the period.

LOW LEVEL WASTE (LLW)

Solid wastes of radioactivity above the 'non-active' category and unsuitable for dustbin disposal, but not exceeding 100 mCi per tonne alpha or 300 mCi per tonne beta.

MERIT ORDER

Each generating unit on an interconnected electricity supply system such as CEGB's will have different avoidable costs of generation. The merit order is a list of all such units on the system in order of increasing avoidable costs, mainly fuel. Not all generating units are needed all the time so those lower in the merit order (i.e. those with higher avoidable costs) are only brought into use at times of high demand while those higher in the merit order (i.e. those with the cheaper generating costs) will be used continuously i.e. they will be run on base load operation. This method of running the system is known as merit order operation.

MODERATOR

A material used in a thermal reactor to reduce the energies of the neutrons from the high value with which they are released in the fission process in order to increase the chances of further fission. The neutrons are slowed-down by means of scattering collisions with the nuclei of the moderator. Typical moderator materials are water and graphite.

NATURAL URANIUM

Uranium as it occurs in nature, containing the fertile isotope U-238 and the fissile isotope U-235 in the proportions 139:1 or 0.7 per cent by weight of U-235.

NUCLEAR REACTOR

A device in which nuclear fission can be sustained as a controlled self-supporting chain reaction. It includes fissile material, such as uranium or plutonium, moderator (unless it is a fast reactor), a control system and, unless its power output is very small, provision for the removal of heat by means of a coolant.

NUCLEAR STEAM SUPPLY SYSTEM (NSSS)

That part of a nuclear power station which produces steam for driving the turbine-generators. In a PWR, the nuclear steam supply system consists of the reactor, the reactor pressure vessel, the reactor coolant circuit and pumps, the steam generators, and the associated auxiliary systems.

PLUTONIUM

A heavy radioactive metallic element with an atomic number of 94 whose principal isotope Pu-239 is an important fissile material. It is produced artificially in reactors through neutron absorption of uranium-238. Military plutonium is defined by CEGB as that having been produced in a military reactor, i.e. at Calder Hall or Chapelcross, but by BNFL as that having an intended military end-use. Civil plutonium is defined by CEGB as deriving from a civilian reactor, but by BNFL as having a civilian end-use.

PRESSURISED WATER REACTOR (PWR)

A power reactor cooled and moderated by light water contained in a pressure vessel which surrounds the core. The water is pressurized to prevent boiling and is circulated through a heat exchanger in which steam is generated in a secondary loop which is connected to a turbine.

PRIMARY CIRCUIT

The main cooling circuit of the reactor which removes heat from the core.

RADIOACTIVITY

The property, possessed by some atoms, of disintegrating spontaneously with the emission of radiation.

REACTOR PRESSURE VESSEL

The vessel containing the fuel assemblies, moderator and coolant of a reactor. Its purpose is to enable the reactor to be operated at pressures above atmospheric. In the case of the PWR it is made of steel.

REFUELLING

In a nuclear reactor, the removal of spent fuel and the introduction of new nuclear fuel. Refuelling is known as ON-LOAD REFUELLING when this process is accomplished while the reactor is operationally supplying heat and the power station generating electricity; and as OFF-LOAD REFUELLING when the reactor has to be shut down before refuelling can take place as is the case with the PWR.

REPROCESSING

The chemical treatment of spent or irradiated fuel to separate the contained uranium, plutonium and fission products.

SPENT FUEL

Nuclear fuel whose period of irradiation in a reactor is complete (synonymous with irradiated fuel).

THERMAL REACTOR

A reactor in which the chain reaction is sustained primarily by fission brought about by thermal neutrons. Such a reactor uses a moderator to slow down the neutrons produced in fission. Magnox, AGR and PWR are all types of thermal reactor.

THORP

The facility BNFL is to build at Sellafield to reprocess uranium oxide fuels, and which was the subject of the 1977 Windscale inquiry.

URANIUM (U)

A heavy, slightly radioactive metallic element with an atomic number of 92. As found in nature, it is a mixture of isotopes U-235 (0.7 per cent) and U-238 (99.3 per cent). The artificially produced U-233 and the naturally-occurring U-235 are fissile. U-238 is capable of undergoing fission with high-energy neutrons and is fertile.

URANIUM DIOXIDE (UO$_2$)
Used as fuel in AGRs and PWRs because of its chemical and radiation stability, good gaseous fission product retention and high melting point. Frequently abbreviated to uranium oxide.

VITRIFICATION
The embodiment of radioactive wastes into a form of glass.

APPENDIX 2

A TECHNICAL NOTE

Reprinted from Prof. Margaret Gowing *Independence and Deterrence: Britain and Atomic Energy 1945-1952,* Vol. 1, pp. 458-464, by kind permission of the copyright holder, the United Kingdom Atomic Energy Authority.

Fission and Fissile Material

The most effective particle for inducing nuclear changes is the neutron. It is heavy and, being uncharged, is extremely penetrating, as it can move freely, unchecked by forces of electrostatic attraction or repulsion, until it collides with an atomic nucleus. If atoms of a heavy unstable element such as uranium[1] are bombarded by neutrons, some of these atoms may split into roughly equal fragments, creating new atoms of ligher elements. Because lighter elements have a lower proportion of neutrons some neutrons will become surplus,[2] and will be emitted. Some of these free neutrons may go on to collide with other uranium nuclei and cause further fissions, and in this way a 'chain reaction' is created. At each fission a large amount of energy is released, mainly in the form of kinetic energy of the neutrons and the fragments. As they are slowed down by interaction with surrounding material, heat is generated. If every fission results in exactly one new fission, a chain reaction will be maintained at a steady rate; to achieve this, each neutron causing a fission must liberate enough neutrons to replace itself and also to compensate for neutrons which will be unproductive for some of the reasons explained below. In a steady reaction of this kind the multiplication factor (known as k) is 1; if the multiplication factor is less than 1 the reaction will die out. However, if each fission yields enough neutrons to cause more than one new fission, the multiplication factor is more than 1, and therefore the neutron population and the number of fissions will increase exponetially in a 'divergent chain reaction'. The system is then said to have excess k. The rate of exponential growth will depend on this excess k: if each fission leads on average to 1.5 new fissions, the multiplication factor is 1.5 and the excess k is 0.5. The excess k can obviously be increased by minimising neutron loss as well as by increasing neutron yield.

Atoms consist largely of empty space, and if an atom were magnified to the size of a house the nucleus would still appear to be smaller than a pinhead; the wonder is that neutrons ever hit nuclei. Some nuclei present better targets than others and the likelihood that a nucleus will be effectively hit is measured by what is called its nuclear cross-section. Cross-sections vary from element to element, between isotopes of the same element, and also according to neutron energy; boron-10, for instance, is 100,000 times likelier to absorb low neutrons than is boron-11, and 10 million times likelier than dueterium (hydrogen-2). Each nucleus has several different cross-sections: for protons, neutrons or other particles; for particles moving at different speeds; and for elastic collision, absorption or fission. A chain reaction is only possible with material in which free neutrons are most likely to collide with nuclei and to split them. Neutrons are ejected in the fission process at very high speed—10,000 miles a second—but they can be slowed down by 'elastic collisions', i.e. by the sort of collision that takes place between billiard balls. Very slow neutrons moving at a mile a second are called 'thermal neutrons'[3] and these are the ones most likely to cause fissions in uranium-235.

Of unproductive neutrons, which fail to cause fissions, some may be lost by escaping entirely from the system and some may be captured in non-fissionable nuclei. Neutron escape, like loss of heat, is a surface effect which depends on size and shape, so that loss is greater from a flat plate than a sphere of the same weight, and relatively greater from a small sphere than a big one. The larger the system, the smaller is its surface in relation to its volume, and the less likely is it that sufficient neutrons will escape to cause the chain reaction to die out. The size at which the production of free neutrons by fission is just able to maintain the neutron population at a constant level, after having provided for neutron loss by escape and non-fission capture, is called the critical size of the system. Below this critical size no chain reaction is possible.

One isotope of natural uranium—uranium 235—is fissile. But natural uranium consists mostly of uranium-238, and uranium-235 constitutes only 0.7 per cent, or one part in 140. It is however, only the presence of this small proportion of uranium-235 which makes a fission chain reaction possible in natural uranium. Uranium-238 is not fissionable, but it will absorb free neutrons by non-fission capture.

In order to sustain a chain reaction in natural uranium, a supercritical quantity of very pure metal is needed. This metal is usually disposed in a lattice arrangement in a material which will slow down the emitted neutrons to thermal velocities. At these velocities they are more likely to be captured by a uranium-235 nucleus and bring about fission, and less likely to be captured and absorbed by an atom of uranium-238. Materials called 'moderators', which have low atomic weights and a low propensity for capturing neutrons, are used to slow the neutrons down. The two best moderators are heavy water[4] and very pure graphite. The spacing in the lattice is carefully calculated to slow the neutrons sufficiently without wastage, and both uranium and moderator must be pure and free from contaminants that would capture neutrons. Next, some means of control is needed so that the reactor can be started up and shut down at will, and its reactivity varied during operation. This control is usually provided by rods, containing a neutron-absorbing material such as boron, which can be progressively inserted or withdrawn to give a very precise degree of control. Finally, arrangements must be made to remove the heat of fission by means of a liquid or gaseous coolant.

Fissile material: isotopic separation
Since uranium-235 and uranium-238 are chemically identical they cannot be separated by any chemical means, but only by a process which exploits the slight difference in atomic mass. Four methods of isotopic separation were tried by the

Manhattan Project (the United States atomic bomb programme) during the war. Of these, electromagnetic separation is no longer used industrially; thermal diffusion is used for separating isotopes of carbon; the centrifuge method is only now becoming successful; gaseous diffusion plants are operating on a large scale.

In the diffusion process a gaseous compound of uranium (uranium hexafluoride) is made to diffuse through a series of very finely porous barriers. The molecules containing the lighter uranium-235 nuclei tend to pass through the membrane a little more readily. The enrichment at each stage is extremely slight and a 'cascade' of many successive stages is needed. The end-product contains a higher proportion of fissile uranium-235 atoms than the feedstock, the degree of enrichment depending on the number of stages used in the cascade.

In a high-speed centrifuge the forces acting on the two isotopes are slightly different because of their different atomic weights, so that the heavy nuclei tend to go to the periphery. Again, many stages are necessary.

By using slightly enriched uranium in the sort of nuclear reactor which has been described, the critical size of the reactor can be reduced.

Fissile Material: plutonium production

If a slow-neutron controlled chain reaction is sustained in a uranium reactor, plutonium is produced in the following way. Many of the neutrons liberated by the fission of uranium-235 nuclei are captured by uranium-238 to form uranium-239. This has a half-life of 23 minutes, and decays[5] to form neptunium (93 protons). In its turn, the neptunium—with a half-life of 2.3 days—decays to form plutonium-239 (94 protons). This plutonium, which has a half-life of 24,000 years, is fissile (or fissionable). A material like uranium-238 from which fissile material can be produced is called 'fertile'.

Besides plutonium, fission products are also formed in the reactor. These are mostly radioactive isotopes of elements in the middle of the periodic table, and some of these fission products may decay to form radioactive daughter products. Fission products include strontium-90, caesium-137 and iodine-131.

Irradiated fuel elements taken from the reactor will therefore contain uranium (depleted in its fissionable uranium-235 isotope), plutonium and various fission products. These can be separated from one another by a complex chemical process (reprocessing) to obtain plutonium; the depleted uranium can then be restored by enrichment in a diffusion plant[6] and can be recycled through the reactor.

Bombs

A fast-neutron, uncontrolled chain reaction in almost pure fissile material can be used as a super-explosive. Assembling either uranium-235 or plutonium-239 in a more than critical mass can initiate a divergent chain reaction which releases tremendous quantities of energy in a period of time measured in millionths of a second. A few kilograms of uranium-235 in the bomb dropped on Hiroshima had an effect equal to some 20,000 tons of TNT; in that bomb, two sub-critical pieces of uranium-235 in a gun-like assembly were shot together so that they suddenly became one supercritical mass. In the plutonium atomic bomb a different device was used. A hollow sphere of plutonium was placed in the centre of a much larger sphere made up of TNT and other conventional explosives; when these conventional explosives were detonated they compressed the ball of plutonium so that it became supercritical, and an atomic explosion resulted.

Nuclear Reactors

As we saw, a controlled chain reaction in a natural or enriched uranium reactor can be used to produce plutonium. The fission of nuclei in such a reactor releases a vast amount of energy, and the heat energy liberated has to be removed from the reactor to permit safe operation. A gaseous or a liquid coolant, with a low-capture cross-section for neutrons —air, light or heavy water, carbon dioxide, helium or liquid sodium—can be used. If the hot coolant leaving the reactor is then passed through a heat exchanger, it can boil ordinary water and so raise steam to drive a turbine. An atomic reactor can thus be used simply as a new way of boiling water, replacing the coal or oil furnace of a conventional electrical power station. Reactors can be designed with different characteristics, as either plutonium producers or power producers—or indeed as dual-purpose plants, though they cannot be optimised for both purposes at the same time.

A considerable range of nuclear reactors is theoretically possible using various combinations and permutations of coolant and moderator, various forms of fuel element, and various degrees of fuel enrichment. Within the core of a reactor all the materials used—for moderating, cooling, fuel canning or structural purposes—must be chosen with an eye to their low absorption of neutrons, so that k is not wasted. For example, if ordinary water is employed as a coolant instead of heavy water, its greater appetite for free neutrons has to be compensated for by using enriched uranium as the fuel. The highest standards of purity are necessary to avoid the absorption of neutrons by impurities and particular care must be taken to exclude impurities that, like boron, have high neutron capture cross-sections.

The only reason that a moderator is needed in reactors which use natural or slightly enriched uranium as a fuel is to minimise the probability that too many neutrons will be absorbed in uranium-238, and too few will be available to cause further fissions in uranium-235. This problem is avoided if uranium-238 is not used in the core. Thus, with pure (or nearly pure) uranium-235 or plutonium as the fuel, the chain reaction can be maintained by fast neutrons and a moderator is not required. Such a reactor is called a fast reactor because the neutrons are not slowed down to thermal velocities. Neutrons in excess of those needed to sustain the reaction may be absorbed in a 'blanket' of natural or depleted uranium surrounding the core, and so may be used to form more plutonium. It is possible in this way to breed more fissile atoms than are used up in the core; hence the name 'fast breeder reactor'.

NOTES

1. Both thorium and protactinium also undergo fission when bombarded by fast neutrons. The advantage of uranium is its abundance (compared with protactinium) and its susceptibility to fission by slow neutrons.

216

2. The number of neutrons per fission in uranium-235 averages 2.5.
3. The velocity of movement of molecules is related to temperature, and thermal neutrons are moving at speeds appropriate to their ambient temperature.
4. Heavy water is a better moderator than ordinary 'light' water which has a greater tendency to absorb neutrons. In heavy water, which is present in ordinary water as about one part in 5,000, the hydrogen atom is replaced by deuterium or heavy hydrogen (hydrogen with one neutron).
5. By the loss of an electron; it gains one positive charge by losing a negative one, thus changing from atomic number 92 to 93.
6. It is uneconomical to enrich uranium by adding uranium-235. In practice uranium-238 is removed in the plant.

APPENDIX 3

ORGANISATIONS PARTICIPATING IN THE SIZEWELL INQUIRY, AND THE CLASSIFICATION OF INQUIRY DOCUMENTS

1. Organisations

The initials shown are those used to identify the organisation within the document classification system.

Proponents and supporters
- CEGB—Central Electricity Generating Board
- BNFL—British Nuclear Fuels plc
- NNC—National Nuclear Corporation
- APG—A Power for Good
- PNPP—Pro Nuclear Power People

Neutral organisations
- DEn—Department of Energy
- DOE—Department of the Environment
- DTP—Department of Transport
- ES—Ergonomics Society
- LPA—Local Planning Authorities, being Suffolk County and Suffolk Coastal District Councils
- MAFF—Ministry of Agriculture, Fisheries and Food
- NCB—National Coal Board
- NII—HM Nuclear Installations Inspectorate
- NRPB—National Radiological Protection Board

Objectors
- BAND—Billingham against Nuclear Dumping
- CES—Centre for Energy Studies, South Bank Polytechnic
- CND—Campaign for Nuclear Disarmament
- CP(EADC)—Communist Party (East Anglian District Committee)
- CPRE—Council for the Preservation of Rural England

ECC—Electricity Consumers Council
FOE—Friends of the Earth
GLC—Greater London Council
IFOE—Ipswich Friends of the Earth
JEP—English, Welsh and Scottish Ecology Parties
JPC—Parish Councils of Middleton-cum-Fordley, Theberton & Eastbridge, and Yoxford
LTC—Leiston Town Council
NCLP—Norfolk County Labour Party
NCC—Northumberland County Council
N&N SOC—Northumberland and Newcastle Society
NUM—National Union of Mineworkers
PAG—Portskewett Action Group
RIBA-ER—Royal Institute of British Architects—Eastern Region
SPS—Suffolk Preservation Society
SSBA—Stop Sizewell B Association/Ecoropa
TCPA—Town and Country Planning Association
TULA—Consortium of Trade Unions and Local Authorities
WANA—Welsh Anti-Nuclear Alliance
WBC—Wansbeck Borough Council
YND—Yorkshire, Nottinghamshire and Derbyshire County Councils

Invited witnesses/organisations
The following were invited to give evidence by the Inspector:
    Dr Michael Bush (District Medical Officer)
    Sir Alaistair Frame (on project management)
    D.C. Ion (on fossil fuel prices)
    T.A. Kletz (on risk assessment)
    Nature Conservancy Council
    SSEB (on the economic merits of the AGR)
    J. Williamson (on exchange rates)
Apart from the invitees, parties to the inquiry who appeared in their own names are not included on this list.

The Inspector
Sir Frank Layfield QC was appointed by the Secretary of State for Energy. Counsel to the Inquiry was Henry Brooke QC, and the Inspector was assisted by four Assessors:
> Prof. J.M. Alexander
> Prof. C.D. Foster
> Prof. W.B. Hall
> Dr. J. Vennart.

2. Inquiry documents

The inquiry amassed an unparalleled corpus of literature about every aspect of the case for and against the PWR. This is available for study, and the librarian at the Department of Energy, Millbank, London SW1 should be contacted in the first instance.

Classification.
1. Statements of Case: these outlined the case being presented by any party, and were classified for example CEGB 01.
2. Proofs of evidence: these contained the detailed evidence on which the case rested, and their authors were available for cross-examination, e.g. CEGB/P/21.
3. Addenda: these were additions to proofs whose contents formed part of the evidence, e.g. CEGB/P/4 (ADD 6).
4. Supporting documents: either complete documents or extracts cited in support of a proof. Between 2,000 and 3,000 were submitted to the inquiry, e.g. CEGB/S/1283.
5. Written submissions: the authors were not available for cross-examination, e.g. WS/45.
6. Others: for example, the Inspector, e.g. INQ/64; Counsel to the Inquiry, e.g. CI/44; the Inquiry Secretariat, e.g. SB/24.
7. Transcript: daily transcripts were referred to by day number and page, e.g. day 150, p. 121C. They were produced on paper with the letters A–H pre-printed in the left hand margin, to facilitate the identification of a passage within a page. Daily transcripts frequently exceeded 100 pages, or about 40,000 words.

8. Closing submissions: all the major participants presented these, and they are important statements as they were designed to draw the Inspector's attention to the most important parts of the respective cases. They are therefore useful summaries. Their texts were not circulated separately, but are recorded on the transcripts. With the exception of the Electricity Consumers Council, which presented its closing submissions on day 200, these were read to the inquiry from day 305 until its close. That of the CEGB, which was the last, took 4 weeks to read.
9. Transcript indexes: these were produced on a weekly basis and consolidated from time to time using a computer. They were prepared by the Secretariat and intended for its use, but were available to others.

APPENDIX 4

CABINET MINUTES 23 OCTOBER 1979 (DR/S/13)

A meeting of the Cabinet Ministerial Committee on Economic Strategy was convened on Tuesday 23 October 1979 at 10 Downing Street. The meeting discussed four subjects, the first of which was 'Nuclear Power Policy and the Nuclear Industry'. The following members of the Cabinet were present for the nuclear power debate:

> Margaret Thatcher (Chair)
> Geoffrey Howe
> Keith Joseph
> Lord Soames
> James Prior
> Peter Walker
> Michael Heseltine
> John Nott
> David Howell
> John Biffen

It should be noted that the meeting took place immediately prior to David Howell's announcement to the House of Commons on 18 December 1979 (see Chapter 2). The minutes of the meeting are reproduced below: in the original the text is marked 'Confidential' on each page.

NUCLEAR POWER POLICY AND THE NUCLEAR INDUSTRY
CONFIDENTIAL

The Committee had before them a memorandum by the Secretary of State for Energy (E(79) 54) discussing his proposals for a future policy with regard to thermal nuclear power, and for the structure of the nuclear industry.

THE SECRETARY OF STATE FOR ENERGY said that a

substantial nuclear programme of thermal reactors was essential to the nation's long term energy needs. In addition, as his paper showed, the cost of nuclear power was likely to be significantly below that of the alternative fuels with the calculations robust against significant adverse movements in the assumptions. If progress was to be made it was important to have a vigorous nuclear construction industry capable of meeting the requirement. And for this, it was important that the industry should have faith in the Government's commitment to nuclear power. To this end he proposed a programme of constructing 15 GW of nuclear power over the period from 1982 as a basis for the industry's planning. Nuclear power elsewhere in the world was based on the Pressurised Water Reactor (PWR) which was generally thought to have cost advantages over other reactor types. Provided the necessary United Kingdom safety clearances could be obtained, this system should also be considered for United Kingdom stations. He therefore proposed that the licensing agreement which the National Nuclear Corporation (NNC) had with Westinghouse should be activated, so that detailed designs could be prepared for a United Kingdom PWR reactor. The construction of such a reactor would be made conditional only on safety clearances from the Nuclear Inspectorate and planning approval for the site. He also proposed that the industry should be reorganised, to strengthen the role of the National Nuclear Corporation relative to the Central Electricity Generating Board (CEGB). His aim would be that by the time the first PWR could be constructed, the NNC would be in a position to assume full responsibility for the station, and not merely for the 'nuclear island'. He proposed that NNC should end their supervisory management agreement with GEC, but that GEC involvement in NNC should remain close: stemming as it would from their shareholding and the rights this gave them to appoint directors to the company. The aim should be the creation of a strong company and management team capable of standing alone.

In discussion there was general support for the concept of a substantial nuclear programme, and for the inclusion in that programme of PWRs, provided always that they could be designed to satisfy the stringent safety requirements of the

223

Nuclear Inspectorate. It was noted that such a programme would not reduce the long term requirement for coal, because of the likely decline in world oil supplies towards the end of the century. But a nuclear programme would have the advantage of removing a substantial portion of electricity production from the dangers of disruption by industrial action by coal miners or transport workers.

On the other hand, it was also noted that there were substantial problems in achieving a nuclear programme. Opposition to nuclear power might well provide a focus for protest groups over the next decade, and the Government might make more rapid progress towards its objective by a low profile approach, which avoided putting the Government into a position of confrontation with the protesters. The existing production of nuclear electricity in Britain using MAGNOX stations had a long record of safe operation, and local people near the various nuclear sites were generally content with them. It was important to build public confidence from that experience. A low profile by Government was not necessarily incompatible with giving a firm lead to the industry, since the industry involved only a few firms. But there would be a problem in maintaining a low profile once a decision was made to proceed with a PWR. Although the Three-Mile Island Reactor in the USA was not a Westinghouse design, it would be associated in the public mind with the PWR system. It would therefore be desirable to avoid any firm commitment until the report of the inquiry into that accident was available.

In further discussion the Committee noted that if the Westinghouse agreement was activated soon, a public inquiry into the siting of the first PWR could not take place before 1981 because the Nuclear Inspectorate would need the intervening period to carry out their safety assessment. On the one hand it was arguable that the first such inquiry should be wide-ranging, so as to establish the broad facts of the system. But on the other, there was a danger that a broad ranging inquiry would arouse prolonged technical debate between representatives of different facets of scientific opinion. In considering tactics for inquiries, it would be important to bear in mind that, in parallel with the development of a thermal reactor programme, there was also a programme in hand for identifying sites for the disposal of nuclear waste, and the UKAEA would be bringing forward proposals for a Fast Reactor. Both of these would also involve inquiries.

Finally it was suggested that in view of the substantial lawsuit between Westinghouse and Rio Tinto Zinc, on which an appeal court hearing would be taking place in Chicago early in November, it might be desirable to defer any commitment on the Westinghouse licensing agreement for a few weeks.

THE PRIME MINISTER, summing up the discussion, said that the Committee were agreed that the Government should aim to achieve a sizeable nuclear programme, and that this should include the prospect of PWRs, subject to satisfactory safety clearances being obtained. A decision on the balance between PWRs and other reactors in the programme would fall to be made at a later date. The Committee were also agreed on the proposals for restructuring the industry, and for enhancing the role of the NNC, as proposed in the paper from the Secretary for Energy. They recognised the great importance of appropriate presentation for achieving the Government's objective, and generally favoured a low profile approach. They were agreed that no commitment should be made towards a PWR, until the report of the Three Mile Island accident was available, although if this were to be delayed beyond the end of the year, this decision might need to be reconsidered. The Secretary of State for Energy should consult with the Secretary of State for the Environment in preparing his proposals for handling the presentation of the nuclear programme, and should consult the Secretary of State for Trade before any approach was made to Westinghouse, so that the applications for the Rio Tinto Zinc lawsuit could be considered.

The Committee—

Took note, with approval, of the summing up of their discussion by the Prime Minister, and invited the Secretary of State for Energy, the Secretary of State for the Environment and the Secretary of State for Trade to be guided accordingly.

THE TEST DISCOUNT RATE (TDR)
(from *An Economic Critique of the CEGB's Case for a PWR at Sizewell*, by J.W. Jeffery (SSBA/P/1), pp. 71–75)

The latest (1982) edition of the Treasury booklet 'Investment Appraisal in the Public Sector' (DEN/S/15, referenced below as IA) gives in its bibliography of official publications; first the White Paper on the Nationalised Industries (Cmnd. 7131: CEGB/S/59) and second, 'The Test Discount Rate and the Required Rate of Return on Investment', Government Economic Services Working Paper No. 22, HM Treasury, 1979: SSBA/S/31. (The Treasury paper, by G.P. Smith, is referenced below as GPS.)

The first point that emerges from a study of these documents is that the TDR is essentially testing benefits. This is because costs are assumed to occur early (usually before benefits start) and therefore will be little affected by discounting. IA, 3.27 says, 'For example, almost all expenditure proposals would produce benefits later than costs'; GPS, 1.2, 'a high discount rate discourages investment in that the costs, *which occur early* (added emphasis), have a high present value relative to the benefits which are typically spread out over a long period'; GPS, 2.3, 'a high discount rate practically annihilates the present value of very distant benefits'. There is no mention of anihilating costs because these are assumed not to be distant.

The second point is the extreme difficulty and subjectivity of deciding what the rate should be, and of finding any satisfactory theoretical basis for the decision. The TDR seems initially to be a means of comparison; GPS, 1.1, 'Some method is needed of comparing, for example, a benefit of £100 next year with a benefit of, say, £150 in five years' time'. It becomes (GPS, 1.3) 'a means of promoting efficient resource use. . . (by) nationalised industries. . . the discount rate used in the public sector should be similar to the return which private firms would consider acceptable on new investment'. There was no attempt at justification: this was 'The view taken'. GPS, 2.4 has 'An alternative approach', i.e. 'a rate which reflects explicitly society's valuation of present versus future *consumption* (added emphasis), the Social Time Preference (STP) rate'. Unfortunately (GPS, 3.15), 'The STP rate cannot be discovered by direct inquiry nor inferred'. 'It would, therefore, have to be a "planners' rate".' The General Conclusion (GPS, 4.1) is that 'economic theory provides useful insights but no clear prescription for a magic number'. The best description of the practical meaning of the TDR is given in GPS, 3.2, 'We would like such a simple criterion to lead to optimal investment decisions, taking into account the institutional, political and economic constraints within which decisions have to be made. This is a lot to expect of a single number. A more practical aim is to consider how the TDR can best help to nudge decisions in the "right" direction'.

TDR as a Penalty for Projects with Long Term Benefits
It would seem that a rather simple idea has attracted a good many accretions. The TDR is primarily an accounting method of testing the suitability of an investment project. It applies penalty to projects which would have benefits too far in the future. The question of costs is not considered because normal projects have their costs early, and certainly not long after the benefits have been received. The discount figure is difficult to fix. An interdepartmental committee sat for a year in 1975/6. GPS, 4.5 says, 'Given that there was no very scientific way of deriving a number, the committee re-commended a rate of 7 per cent (real terms) as striking a reasonable balance between the consideration of profitability, cost of capital and social time preference'. This figure was the mid-point of a 6–8 per cent range 'judged to reflect a reasonable balance between the various pointers available at the time. Later evidence shifted this judgement to a range of 5–7 per cent and in the event 5 per cent was preferred' (GPS, 5.2).

In other words, the rate to be used as a penalty for benefits too far in the future is fixed by the judgement of those who wish to use it to 'nudge decisions in the "right" direction'.

Theoretical Aspects of TDR

The theoretical basis in accountancy for using a common TDR for costs and benefits lies in the Present Value (PV) concept. This was referred to earlier in GPS 1.1, but it runs into difficulties if extended over long periods, especially more than one generation. Professor David Collard[1] lists a number of economists who have discussed the general difficulties associated with ordinary discounting, most of which increase with the length of time involved, but he is particularly concerned with inter-generational problems on very long term projects and quotes Mishan[2] as follows:

> are we justified in valuing 100 in 50 years' time as equivalent to $100 \times (1.10)^{-50}$? Not if the 100 in 50 years' time will accrue to different people. If in 50 years' time the 100 accrues to a person B of a new generation, the enjoyment he derives therefrom might be every bit as great as that derived from it now by a person A of the existing generation. Person A would therefore have no business in evaluating the future worth of 100 by discounting it for 50 years at 10% when he himself is not, in any case going to receive it; when, in fact, person B is going to receive it. Whenever intergenerational comparisons are involved, as they may be in determining the rate of depletion or destruction of a non-renewable asset, it is as well to recognise that there is no satisfactory way of determining social worth at different points of time.

Apart from the intergenerational problem, it is very noticeable in this, as in the other quotations, that it is primarily benefits which are under consideration. But the problem—the unique problem—with nuclear accounting is long term costs, extending over not just two, but many generations. The whole concept of Present Value becomes meaningless over such time scales—who knows what interest rates will be available or relevant in 2100?

If one uses the normal TDR (e.g., +5 per cent pa) in a comparison between two projects with equal benefits occur-

228

ing early, and equal costs, in one case occurring before and along with the benefits and in the other largely long after the benefits finish, then the latter project will get overwhelming preference. If such cases were expected to occur to a significant extent the practical usefulness of discounting all cash flows in the same fashion would have to give way to distinguishing between benefits and costs. It is a tribute to the uniqueness of nuclear power, that it is the only example which comes to mind in which benefits might be received by one generation and costs *necessarily* carried by the next and succeeding generations.

That normal discounting for such long term nuclear costs is inappropriate can be seen from the fact that it makes delay (above any physical necessity) appear profitable. In construction, delay increases IDC and has other penalties. In operation, delay would be penalised by poorer cash flow, reducing PV and increasing NEC. But for the unique long term costs of nuclear power, normal discounting is a powerful incentive to delay. This is clearly an unacceptable result and the practical question is, what method should be used to penalise these uniquely long term costs, similar to the method used for penalising benefits which would occur too far in the future? This is not a question of altering the present discounting procedure in general, but of an exceptional procedure for a unique problem, in which positive, direct costs *necessarily* occur long after—in the next and succeeding generations—any benefits have been received. If the method is to be a form of discounting, then the discount rate for costs must be negative, in order to increase costs with time from commissioning date. If a compound interest rate—an exponential increase in costs with time—is required, there would have to be a cut-off date beyond which the discounting factor remains constant. Alternatively, since investment yielding a real 5 per cent rate of profit is becoming increasingly difficult to find, it might be better to change to simple interest—a linear increase in costs or decrease in benefits—and dispense with a cut off. However, since we are only looking for an ad-hoc method for one unique case, it may be better to leave everything else as in the normal method and use a small negative compound rate (say—1 per cent) for these unique nuclear costs, with a cut off at, say, 150 years. As long as some method along these or other lines is used to prevent necessary long term costs and unnecessary planned delays actually benefiting the case for proceeding with the project containing them, the exact form is not so important.

REFERENCES

1. D. Collard, *Faustian Projects and the Social Rate of Discount*, University of Bath Papers in Political Economy. Working Paper 1179, October 1979, (SSBA/S/30). On general problems; Arrow and Fisher, 1974 (on uncertainty), Scott, 1973 (diminishing marginal utility of incomes), and Sen, 1967 and Lecomber, 1977 (the isolation paradox) are referenced. On the Faustian aspect of discounting, especially the inter-generational problems, Pigou (1924), Ramsey (1928), Eckstein (1958), Nash (1973), Fisher and Krutilla (1975), Mishan (1975), Pearce (1976) and Clark and Fleishman (1979) are discussed.
2. E.J. Mishan, *Cost-Benefit Analysis*, Allen and Unwin, 1975.

APPENDIX 6

THE NON-PROLIFERATION TREATY, AND SAFE-GUARDS THAT APPLY TO THE UK

1. The NPT

The Treaty for the Non-Proliferation of Nuclear Weapons[1] was signed by the US, USSR and UK (the depository signatories) in 1968, and came into force in March 1970. At December 1984 118 other states had signed.

It divides the world into nuclear weapons states (NWS) and non-nuclear weapons states (NNWS)—i.e. those countries which have proliferated into weapons, and those which have not. The treaty is a bargain between them. The former have pledged to undertake negotiations in good faith to end the arms race and to effect complete nuclear disarmament (Article VI). The treaty also encourages the peaceful use of nuclear energy throughout the world (Article IV). In return, the NNWS have agreed to forego the development of nuclear weapons, and to refrain from using their civil facilities for that purpose (Article II). In order to detect and deter such diversion, the civil nuclear facilities of the NNWS are subject to 'full scope' safeguards and inspection by the IAEA (Article III); there is no equivalent system imposed on the NWS to monitor progress towards disarmament. In the context of the failure of Article VI to control the arms race, Dr. H. Blix, the Director-General of the IAEA said:[2]

It is clear to me that a continuing lack of progress on disarmament would eventually undermine the NPT barrier to horizontal proliferation. Perhaps more importantly, it could also undermine. . . the convictions of States that it is in their own security interests not to possess nuclear weapons.

231

Of the five states usually regarded as NWS France and China have not signed the NPT. Notable non-signatories among the NNWS are India, South Africa, Pakistan, Spain, Argentina and Brazil, all countries with known nuclear competance, and with power reactors operational or under construction (Table 8.1). A summary of the provisions of the ten Articles is:

I — NWS agree not to give nuclear weapons to any other states, nor to help any other state manufacture them.

II — NNWS agree not to receive such weapons or assistance, should it be offered.

III — NNWS agree to IAEA safeguards, and all states agree that all materials or equipment transferred to NNWS for peaceful purposes will be subject to IAEA safeguards.

IV — All signatories have an 'inalienable right' to develop nuclear power, and agree to co-operate especially with NNWS in that development.

V — Provides for the sharing of benefits accruing from peaceful nuclear explosions.

VI — 'Each of the Parties to the Treaty undertakes to persue negotiations in good faith on effective measures relating to cessation of the nuclear arms race at an early date and to nuclear disarmament, and on a Treaty on general and complete disarmament under strict and effective international control.'

VII — All states have the right to sign regional non-proliferation treaties.

VIII — Provides for amendment by majority, and for 5-yearly reviews.

IX — Provides for ratification (i.e. the application of safeguards).

X — Any signatory may withdraw on three months notice if 'extraordinary events, related to the subject-matter of this Treaty, have jeopardized its supreme interests'.

2. Safeguards that apply to the UK

a. IAEA

Dr Blix noted that:[3]

Safeguards cannot by themselves physically stop any country from doing anything.

He was referring to the 'full scope' safeguards that are applied to NNWS signatories to the NPT. Britain's safeguards arrangements with the IAEA[4] are voluntary, and were entered into to encourage others to sign the NPT, and to reassure NNWS that they would not be commercially disadvantaged by safeguards.

In the UK, IAEA designates civil facilities for inspection from a list prepared by HMG. Currently the two designated plants are both at Sellafield; the oxide fuel storage ponds and the plutonium store.

b. Euratom

The European Atomic Energy Community (Euratom) applies separate but co-ordinated safeguards to all civil facilities in the Common Market.[5] All are inspected. The UK's refusal to permit Euratom access to the dual-purpose Magnox reprocessing line is discussed in Chapter 8.

NOTES

1. UN Document A/RES/2373.
2. Dr. H. Blix, 'Building Confidence', *IAEA Bulletin*, September 1984, p. 6.
3. *Ibid.*, p. 4.
4. Cmnd. 6730, 1977.
5. Cmnd. 4865, 1973.

INDEX

234